泱泱中华书系·地域文化系列

邯郸成语典故读本
Handan Idioms between English and Chinese
【汉英对照】

刘安平 蔡其伦 高宇征 李玮 ◎ 主编

北京大学出版社
PEKING UNIVERSITY PRESS

内 容 简 介

邯郸是中国春秋战国时期"战国七雄"之一的赵国的首都,有着三千多年的历史。

邯郸是中国著名的成语之乡,据考证,在汉语的万余条成语中,有1584条和邯郸有关,且大部分含有历史典故,是中华文化的瑰宝。

在本书中,我们精选了129条和邯郸相关的成语典故,并将其译成了英文,根据它们的内容和特点,将其归纳成了八大类——贤士篇、谋略篇、励志篇、军事篇、教训篇、和谐篇、改革篇、哲学篇等。海内外读者们可以从本书中了解到邯郸悠久的历史和灿烂的文化,同时有效地提高自己的汉语和英语水平。

图书在版编目(CIP)数据

邯郸成语典故读本(汉英对照)/刘安平,蔡其伦,高宇征,李玮主编.—北京:北京大学出版社,2011.4

(泱泱中华书系·地域文化系列)

ISBN 978-7-301-18425-7

Ⅰ.邯… Ⅱ.①刘…②蔡…③高…④李… Ⅲ.①文化史—邯郸市—通俗读物②汉语—成语—典故 Ⅳ.①K292.23-49②H136.3

中国版本图书馆 CIP 数据核字(2011)第 007519 号

书　　　　名:	邯郸成语典故读本(汉英对照)
著作责任者:	刘安平　蔡其伦　高宇征　李　玮　主编
策划编辑:	李　玥
责任编辑:	李　玥
标准书号:	ISBN 978-7-301-18425-7/H·2744
出　版　者:	北京大学出版社
地　　　址:	北京市海淀区成府路 205 号 100871
电　　　话:	邮购部 62752015　发行部 62750672　编辑部 62765126　出版部 62754962
网　　　址:	http://www.pup.cn
电子信箱:	zyjy@pup.cn
印　刷　者:	北京宏伟双华印刷有限公司
发　行　者:	北京大学出版社
经　销　者:	新华书店
	720 毫米×1020 毫米　16 开本　15.5 印张　272 千字
	2011 年 4 月第 1 版　2011 年 4 月第 1 次印刷
定　　　价:	29.00 元

未经许可,不得以任何方式复制或抄袭本书之部分或全部内容。

版权所有,侵权必究

举报电话:010-62752024;电子信箱:fd@pup.pku.edu.cn

前言

邯郸，位于河北省南端，是晋、冀、鲁、豫四省的交汇点，西依太行山，东临华北平原，是南北交通的重要通道，有"九省通衢"之称，是历代兵家逐鹿中原的必争之地。

邯郸历史悠久，文化灿烂，是中华文明的重要发祥地之一。早在8000年前，这里就有人类繁衍生息，孕育了新石器早期的磁山文化；战国时期，邯郸作为赵国都城达158年之久，是我国北方的政治、经济、文化中心，也是草原游牧文化与中原农耕文化的重要交汇处；秦统一中国后，邯郸为天下三十六郡郡治之一；汉代与长安、洛阳、临淄、成都共享"五都盛名"；东汉末年，曹魏集团在邯郸南部邺城一带建都；北宋时期，邯郸东部的大名成为北宋都城汴梁的"陪都"——大名府。

邯郸是我国历史文化名城。8000年的历史铸造了丰富的邯郸历史文化，它包括磁山文化、赵文化、女娲文化、北齐石窟文化、建安文化、广府太极文化、梦文化、磁州窑文化、成语典故文化等，其历史源远流长，内涵博大精深，风格丰富多彩。

邯郸的成语典故文化，为我们留下了许多脍炙人口的故事，堪称我们中华文化中的一颗璀璨明珠。

当我们走在邯郸市区的学步桥头，看到燕国少年学习邯郸人走路的石像，"邯郸学步"的典故会立刻涌上我们的心头。传说燕国少年就是在这里学邯郸人走路的。这个妇孺皆知的故事时刻教育着我们，让我们明白它在今天的重大启示意义：无论是国家的经济发展，还是人们的事业和生活，如果一味地照抄照搬他人之模式，而忽视了自身的特点，就会跟燕国少年在邯郸学步一样弄得不伦不类,而成为别人的笑柄。

在邯郸老城区的街道里,有一个短小但却十分著名的巷子——回车巷。相传这里就是赵国的贤臣蔺相如回避大将廉颇的窄巷。巷口立着一块石碑,它不断向经过这里的人们叙述着"负荆请罪"的故事。

出了邯郸城区向北走,我们就来到了家喻户晓的黄粱梦,它以成语"黄粱一梦"或"黄粱美梦"而闻名。在这里我们可以看到远近闻名的吕仙祠,里面有一个横卧在地的石像,他就是这个成语中的主人公——卢生。

看到邯郸西南的插箭岭、火车站广场上的雕像和市中心那巍峨的丛台城楼,我们会不由自主地想到当年赵武灵王"胡服骑射"、气吞万里如虎的英雄气概。这位赵国的一代雄主,自继位之后,奋发图强,锐意改革,终使赵国成为战国七雄之一。

在邯郸市的主干道人民路与滏西大街的交叉口,我们可以看到一个伟人的雕像,他手持书卷,若有所思。他就是战国时期重要的思想家、文学家、政治家——荀子。由于他知识渊博,学问精深,曾被赵国拜为上卿。他对华夏文明的影响和贡献之大,令燕赵堪比齐鲁,令后人高山仰止。

荀子不但继承了儒家思想,还对其有所发展,是儒家继孔子和孟子之后的另一位儒学大家。他提倡的"性恶论",常被人们与孟子的"性善论"相比较。他还是诸子百家中法家的代表人物之一,他的弟子韩非、李斯师从他的思想和帝王之术,对秦始皇统一中国起到了极大的帮助作用。他的学问涉及哲学思想、政治问题、治学方法、立身处世之道、学术论辩等方面。他的名言"非我而当者,吾师也;是我而当者,吾友也;谄谀我者,吾贼也。""学不可以已"、"天行有常,不为尧存,不为桀亡。""锲而舍之,

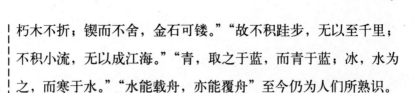

前　言

朽木不折；锲而不舍，金石可镂。""故不积跬步，无以至千里；不积小流，无以成江海。""青，取之于蓝，而青于蓝；冰，水为之，而寒于水。""水能载舟，亦能覆舟"至今仍为人们所熟识。

作为中国著名的成语之乡，邯郸给我们提供了丰富的成语与典故资源，据统计有1584条之多。为了弘扬中华民族的传统文化，培养我们的民族自尊心和自豪感，挖掘、展示、发扬和传播我们的地方特色文化，我们精选了故事发生在邯郸或者与邯郸相关的部分成语，将它们翻译成了英文，以飨读者。我们衷心希望能够通过此途径，将我们邯郸的文化瑰宝更加广泛地进行传播。由于我们编写组人员水平有限，翻译中难免有各种错误发生，在此希望读者不吝赐教。

刘安平

2011 年 1 月 10 日

目 录

贤士篇

1 不可多得 2
Hard to Come By 2
2 大公无私 4
Just and Selfless 4
3 独步一时 6
To Have No Equal in One's Time 6
4 击缶秦公 7
King of Qin Playing the Fou 7
5 布衣之交 8
Friends in Days of Simple Life 8
6 毛遂自荐 9
To Volunteer One's Services 10
7 一言九鼎 11
A Word Carrying the Weight of Nine Tripods 12
8 脱颖而出 12
Talent Showing Itself 13
9 因人成事，三寸之舌 14
To Rely on Others to Succeed in Work; a Silver Tongue 15
10 漆身吞炭 17
Lacquering One's Body and Swallowing Charcoals 18
11 众人国士 19
A Mediocre Man and a State Talent 20
12 赵衰举贤 21
Zhao Shuai Recommending the Wise Man 21
13 排难解纷 22
Pouring Oil on Troubled Waters 23
14 图穷匕见 24
When the Map Was Unrolled, the Dagger Was Revealed ... 24
15 坐怀不乱 25
Keeping His Mind Undisturbed with a Woman in His Bosom ... 26
16 程婴杵臼 27
As Sincere as Cheng Ying and Chujiu 27
17 汉思李牧 28
The Emperor Wen of Han Dynasty Missing Li Mu 28

18 简子谦卑	29
Jianzi's Humility	30
19 天经地义	30
The Principles of Heaven and Earth	31
20 天下无双	32
Unparalleled in the World	33
21 三千剑客	34
Three Thousand Swordsmen	34
22 董狐之笔	35
Dong Hu's Brush Pen	35
23 一狐之腋	37
The Armpit Underfur of a Fox	37
24 一日千里	39
A Thousand Li a Day	40
25 一字千金	41
One Word Worth a Thousand Taels of Gold	41
26 坚守一心	42
Serving the Country Wholeheartedly	43
27 季子裘敝	43
Jizi in Poor Clothing	44
28 赤心陈事	44
To Give an Account Genuinely	45
29 疾风劲草	46
Only High Wind Knows the Sturdy Grass	46
30 乐此不疲	47
Always Enjoying It	48
31 鸱衔腐鼠	49
An Owl Picking Up a Dead Mouse	49
32 代笔捉刀	50
Taking a Knife on Behalf of Others	50

谋略篇

1 按兵不动	53
Immobilizing the Troops and Not Throwing Them into Battle	53
2 百发百中	55
A Hundred Shots, a Hundred Bull's-Eyes	55
3 抱薪救火	56
Carrying Firewood to Put Out a Fire	57

目 录

4 不可同日而语 58
No Comparison between the Two 59
5 出奇制胜 60
To Defeat the Opponent with a Surprising Action 61
6 推心置腹 62
To Repose Full Confidence in People 63
7 价值连城 64
A Jade Worth Cities 65
8 完璧归赵 66
Returning the Jade Intact to Zhao State 67
9 窃符救赵 68
Stealing the Military Tally to Save Zhao State 69
10 围魏救赵 70
Besieging Wei to Rescue Zhao 71
11 两鼠斗穴 72
Two Rats Fighting in the Hole 73
12 生报死仇 73
To Take Revenge after One's Death 74
13 唇亡齿寒 75
If the Lips Are Gone, the Teeth Will Be Cold 75
14 退避三舍 76
To Give Way to Avoid a Conflict 77
15 前事不忘，后事之师 78
Past Experience Is a Guide for the Future 79
16 丛台置酒 81
Giving a Feast on Congtai 81
17 独智之虑 82
Consideration from a Person with Unique Wisdom 82
18 不翼而飞 83
Disappearing Without Trace 83
19 唱筹量沙 84
To Count Aloud the Chips of Meting Out the Sand 85
20 奇货可居 86
Hoard as a Rare Commodity 87
21 嫁祸于人 89
Shifting Calamity to Others 89
22 金城汤池 90
Being Secure Against Assault 91

23 挥汗如雨	92
To Drip with Sweat	92
24 不绝若绳	93
As Precarious as a String Which Is Going to Break	94
25 食不甘味	94
To Have No Appetite for Food	95
26 鸡口牛后	96
Fowl's Beak and Ox Buttocks	96
27 以卵投石	97
Knocking an Egg Against a Stone	98
28 自陈功过	99
To Manifest One's Merits and Demerits	99
29 山鸡舞镜	101
The Pheasant Dancing in Front of the Mirror	101
30 包藏祸心	102
To Conceal the Evil Intention	102
31 反侧自安	103
From Tossing about in Bed to Obtaining a Peaceful Mind	104
32 四分五裂	104
To Be Split	105

励志篇

1 志在四方	108
Having a Great Ambition	108
2 取而代之	109
To Supersede Somebody	110
3 鹿死谁手	111
In Whose Hands Will the Deer Die?	111
4 不让肉食	112
Not Being Allowed to Eat Meat	112
5 争先恐后	113
To Rush on to Be the First	114
6 青出于蓝,而胜于蓝	115
Indigo Blue Is Extracted from the Indigo Plant But Bluer than the Plant	115
7 破釜沉舟	116
To Break the Cauldrons and Sink the Boats	117

目 录

军事篇

1 背水一战 119
To Fight with One's Back to the River 120

2 拔旗易帜 122
To Pull the Enemy's Flags and Let One's Own Flags Fly 123

3 秋风落叶 124
Autumn Wind Sweeping the Fallen Leaves 125

4 旷日持久 125
A Long-Drawn-Out Situation 126

5 攻难守易 127
It Is Difficult to Attack but Easy to Defend 128

6 不遗余力 128
Sparing No Efforts 129

7 扬兵戏马 131
Displaying One's Strength 131

8 作壁上观 132
To Stay Behind the Breastworks and Watch Others Fight 133

9 犹豫不决 134
To Be in Two Minds 135

10 乘胜追击 136
To Pursue Enemy Troops in Retreat 136

11 釜底抽薪 137
To Take Away the Firewood from under the Cauldron 137

教训篇

1 大儒纵盗 140
Great Scholar Conniving the Robbers 140

2 邯郸学步 141
Learning to Walk in Handan 142

3 纸上谈兵 143
An Armchair Strategist 143

4 铸成大错 145
To Make a Gross Error 145

5 割地求和 146
Ceding Territory for Peace 147

6 郭开之金 147
The Bribe Received by Guo Kai 148

7 中饱私囊	148
To Line One's Pockets with Public Funds or Other People's Money	149
8 步履蹒跚	150
Walking Staggeringly	150
9 人人自危	152
Everyone Finds Himself in Danger	153
10 贪得无厌	154
To Have an Unlimited Desire for More	155
11 利令智昏	156
To Bend One's Principles to One's Interest	157
12 市道之交	158
The Fellowship of Opportunists	158
13 胶柱鼓瑟	159
Stubbornly Sticking to Old Ways in the Face of Changed Circumstances	160
14 前倨后恭	161
Haughty Before and Reverent Afterwards	162
15 兵破士北	163
The Defeated Army	163
16 人心难测	164
The Human Heart Is a Mystery	164

和谐篇

1 路不拾遗	167
No One Picks Up and Pockets Anything Lost on the Road	167
2 奉公守法	168
To Be Law-Abiding	169
3 不教而诛	170
To Punish Without Prior Warning	170
4 蔡女没胡	171
Cai Wenji Fell into the Huns	171
5 同甘共苦	172
To Share Pleasures and Pains	173
6 简子筑台	174
Jianzi Building a Platform	174
7 负荆请罪	175
To Proffer a Birch and Ask for a Flogging	176
8 梅开二度	177
The Plums Booming Twice	178

目　录　XI

9 津女棹歌 179
Ferry Girl's Oaring Songs 179

改革篇

1 河伯娶妻 182
Hebo Getting Married 183
2 胡服骑射 184
The Policy of Adopting Hu Tribe's Clothing and Learning Their Cavalry Archery 185
3 腹心之患 186
Diseases in One's Vital Organs 186
4 主父入秦 187
Zhu Fu Visiting Qin State 188

哲学篇

1 得心应手 190
The Hands Respond to the Heart 190
2 利害唯己，谁贵谁贱 191
What Is Advantageous and What Is Hurtful, Who Is Noble and Who Is Humble, All Depend on Yourself 192
3 穷通自乐 193
Enjoyment Outside the Dust and Dirt 194
4 死亦可乐 195
Even Death Can Be Happy 196
5 乐极生悲 197
Extreme Joy Begets Sorrow 198
6 一枕黄粱 199
A Golden Millet Dream 200
7 兼听则明 201
Listening to All Sides 201
8 南辕北辙 203
Diametrically Opposed to Each Other 203
9 智者千虑，必有一失 204
Even the Wise Are Not Always Free from Error 205
10 豚蹄穰田 206
To Expect Tremendous Return from Meager Investment .. 206
11 鹬蚌相争 208
When the Snipe and the Clam Grapple, the Fisherman Profits .. 208

12 舍本逐末 210
To Neglect the Root and Attend to the Tip 211
13 掩耳盗铃 212
To Plug One's Ears While Stealing a Bell 213
14 惊弓之鸟 214
A Bird Startled by the Mere Twang of a Bow-String 215
15 望洋兴叹 216
To Lament One's Littleness Before the Vast Ocean 217
16 三人成虎 218
A Repeated Slander Makes Others Believe 219
17 覆巢毁卵 220
The Nest Being Overturned, No Eggs Staying Undestroyed .. 221
18 赵王之爵 221
The King of Zhao State's Wine Vessel 222
19 交浅言深 223
To Have a Hearty Talk with a Slight Acquaintance 223
20 一言兴邦 224
A Timely Warning May Avert a National Crisis 225
21 前功尽弃 228
All One's Previous Efforts Wasted 228
22 危于累卵 229
Hazardous Like a Pile of Eggs 229
23 败军之将 230
A Defeated General Cannot Claim to Be Brave 230
24 强而后可 231
Promising after Importuning 232
25 罚不当罪 233
Punishment Does Not Fit the Crime 233

贤士篇

不可多得

东汉末年，有个叫祢衡的著名文学家，博学多才，善于论辩，文章写得又快又好，但是非常自傲，好与人争斗。

名士孔融非常欣赏祢衡的才学，于是向汉献帝推荐祢衡，称祢衡是不可多得的人才。

汉献帝被曹操挟制，无法做主，就把荐表给曹操，由他来决定。

曹操召祢衡来见，但祢衡却看不起曹操，称病不去。后来虽然去了，但是言辞中却得罪了曹操。

曹操心中冒火，就叫祢衡当鼓吏，在自己大宴宾客时让他击鼓，借以当众羞辱，不料却被祢衡击鼓时大骂了一顿。曹操本想杀了祢衡，但怕留下害贤的名声，就叫他去劝说刘表来降，好借刘表之手杀掉他。

不料刘表非常器重祢衡，奉为上宾。但是刘表无法忍受祢衡的傲慢，就派他到江夏太守黄祖那里去做书记。

祢衡起草文书时，总是一挥而就，黄祖非常佩服。黄祖的儿子黄射对祢衡过目不忘的本事更是赞不绝口。祢衡的代表作《鹦鹉赋》赢得了众人的称赞，众人都夸他是不可多得的人才。

但是他的狂妄自傲没有任何收敛，一次黄祖在船上宴客，祢衡口出不逊并大骂黄祖，被黄祖所杀，时年仅 25 岁。

这则成语形容非常稀少的人才，非常难得。

我们不仅要掌握专业技能，而且要学会与人相处，德才兼备才能被社会认可和接纳。

Hard to Come By

In late East Han Dynasty, Mi Heng, a well-known litterateur who was learned, versatile and good at debate, and could write articles quickly and wonderfully. However, he was very proud and often had strife with others.

Kong Rong, another famous scholar, greatly appreciated Mi Heng's talent and learning. So he recommended Mi Heng to Emperor Xian of East Han Dynasty and called Mi Heng a talented man who was hard to come by.

At that time, Emperor Xian was coerced by Cao Cao, the prime minister, and had no right to decide, so he had the recommendation memorial sent to Cao Cao and let him decide it.

Cao Cao summoned Mi Heng, but Mi Heng looked down upon him and refused to go by pleading sick. Finally Mi Heng went, but offended him with proud words. Greatly angry, Cao Cao appointed him a drummer and ordered Mi Heng to play the drum for his guests in a banquet so as to insult him, but Mi Heng scolded Cao Cao badly when drumming. Cao Cao intended to kill Mi Heng, but fearing that others would blame him for killing a virtuous man, he ordered Mi Heng to persuade Liu Biao to surrender and wanted to kill Mi Heng by Liu Biao's hand.

Unexpectedly, Liu Biao valued Mi Heng very highly as an honorable guest. But Liu Biao could not endure Mi Heng's pride, so sent him to Huang Zu, a governor of Jiangxia, as a secretary.

When drafting a document, Mi Heng always finished it without a stop. So Huang Zu admired him greatly. Huang She, Huang Zu's son, spoke highly for Mi Heng's ability to recite after reading only once. Mi Heng's masterpiece, *The Ode on Parrot*, won people's admiration and they described Mi Heng as a talent who was hard to come by.

But Mi Heng's pride was never restrained. Once when Huang Zu held a banquet for his guests on a ship, Mi Heng scolded Huang Zu with humiliating words. And Huang Zu killed him when he was only 25 years old.

This idiom describes a person who is a scarce talent and hard to come by.

We students should not only be skillful in our majors, but also should learn how to communicate with others. Only in this way can we be accepted by the society.

大公无私

春秋时期，晋平公在位时，一次，南阳县缺一名县令。于是平公问大夫祁黄羊，谁适合担任这个职务？

祁黄羊毫不犹豫地回答说："解狐可以。"

平公听了，感到很惊讶，说："解狐不是你的仇人吗？你为什么要推荐你的仇人呢？"

祁黄羊答道："您是问我谁适合担任县令这一职务，而没有问谁是我的仇人。"

于是平公派解狐前去任职。解狐任职后，为民众做了许多好事和实事，受到了南阳民众的称赞。

又有一次，朝廷需要一位军中尉。平公又请祁黄羊推荐，祁黄羊回答说祁午合适。

平公又问："祁午是你的儿子，难道你就不怕别人说闲话吗？"

祁黄羊坦然作答："您是要我推荐适合做军中尉的人选，而没有问我的儿子是谁。"

平公接受了这个建议，派祁午担任了军中尉的职务。

结果，祁午不负众望，干得非常出色。

孔子听到这两件事情，感慨地说："祁黄羊推荐人完全是拿才能做标准，不因为他是自己的仇人还是自己的儿子，也不怕别人议论。像祁黄羊这样的人才是大公无私！"

这则成语比喻一个人一心为公，毫无私心。

我们应该学习祁黄羊的这种精神，实事求是，不因私人恩怨而影响工作。

Just and Selfless

During the Spring and Autumn Period, Jin Pinggong, the ruler of Jin State, once asked Qi Huangyang who was best qualified for the position when Nanyang county needed a magistrate.

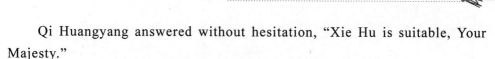

Qi Huangyang answered without hesitation, "Xie Hu is suitable, Your Majesty."

Hearing this, the ruler was greatly surprised, and asked, "But isn't he your personal enemy? How come you recommend him?"

Qi Huangyang smiled and said, "Your majesty, you are not asking me who my personal enemy is. You are asking who is best qualified for the magistrate's position."

The ruler therefore appointed Xie Hu magistrate. After Xie Hu started his new job, his achievements won acclaim from both his colleagues and the local people.

Later, the court needed a personnel official. The ruler called in Qi Huangyang again to recommend a qualified person. Qi Huangyang answered that Qi Wu should be equal to this task.

The ruler was surprised, and said, "Isn't Qi Wu your son? Aren't you afraid of what other people will say?"

Qi Huangyang answered frankly, "Your majesty, you asked me to recommend who is best qualified for the position, but did not ask me who my son is."

The ruler followed the advice and appointed Qi Wu the personnel official.

Finally, Qi Wu didn't miss others' trust and did a well job.

When Confucius heard these two events, he praised Qi Huangyang highly and sighed with emotion, "Qi Huangyang recommends only those who are best qualified, no matter whether they are his enemy or his son. He is not afraid of what other people might say about him. We can only say that man like him is really just and selfless."

This idiom is used as a metaphor for a person who is very just and selfless.

We should learn the spirit from Qi Huangyang which means people should be down to the earth and do not let personal affairs affect work.

3 独步一时

蔺相如奉赵惠文王之命，带着和氏璧出使秦国，凭借自己超凡的勇气和过人的智慧，保住了和氏璧。既扫了秦王的脸面，保住了赵国的尊严，又得以安全归来，一时间在赵国名声大震。

一次他面对自己的朋友慎子，颇为得意地说，"人人都说秦王像老虎一样凶残，绝对碰不得。但是这一次，我不但摸过了他的头，还拍过了他的肩。"

慎子非常敬佩蔺相如的勇气和智慧，因而称赞说："太好了！先生真是天下独步一时的人啊！"

现在我们用这个典故表示独一无二，一时无双。每个人都应该有过人的一面，青年人更应该具备这样的个人素质，这样在今后的社会竞争中才不会被淘汰。

To Have No Equal in One's Time

Ordered by King Huiwen of Zhao State, Lin Xiangru escorted the Jade of He Shi to Qin State. With super courage and wisdom, Lin Xiangru returned the jade intact to Zhao State. Because Lin Xiangru not only made the King of Qin State lose face and kept the dignity of Zhao State, but also returned safely, he earned a great reputation in Zhao State.

Once talking with his friend Shen Zi, Lin Xiangru said proudly, "Everyone says that the King of Qin State is as ferocious as a tiger and no one dare to touch him. But this time, I have not only touched his head, but also patted his shoulder."

Shen Zi admired Lin's courage and wisdom greatly, so he praised highly and said, "Great! You are really a person who has no equal in the time."

Now we use this idiom to indicate having no equal in one's time. Everybody has his extraordinary aspect. Young people are definitely supposed to obtain this kind of personal ability, so that they will not be knocked out in competition.

击缶秦公

这个典故发生在战国时期，赵惠文王和秦王在渑池相会。

秦王在宴席上酒喝多了，就说："我听说赵王喜欢音乐，请奏瑟以助兴。"

赵王奏瑟一曲，秦国的史官上前写到"某年某月，秦王与赵王喝酒，秦王命令赵王鼓瑟。"

蔺相如走上前说："赵王听说秦王善于唱秦腔，请把缶交给秦王演奏，互相高兴高兴。"秦王生气，不答应。

蔺相如说："五步以内，我可以把我的血溅到大王身上。"

秦王手下想杀蔺相如，蔺相如大怒，呵斥左右都退下。

秦王无奈地敲了一下缶。蔺相如同样派赵国的史官记载下来"秦王为赵王击缶"。蔺相如最终维护了赵国的尊严。

青年人应该学习蔺相如的机智勇敢，这样才能在社会中立足。

King of Qin Playing the Fou

The event of this idiom took place during the Warring States Period, King Huiwen of Zhao State and the King of Qin met in Mianchi.

At the banquet, the King of Qin had been drunken, so he said, "I heard the King of Zhao likes music very much, please play the Se for fun."

The King of Zhao played the Se and the historian of Qin approached them and wrote down "in a certain month of a certain year, the King of Qin drank with the King of Zhao, and the King of Qin ordered the King of Zhao to play the Se."

Lin Xiangru walked forward and said, "The King of Zhao heard the King of Qin is good at Shaanxi opera, please give the Fou to the King of Qin to play, so they can amuse each other." The King of Qin was not glad and he did not agree.

Lin Xiangru said, "In five steps, I can splash my blood over Your Majesty's body."

The underlings of the King of Qin wanted to kill Lin Xiangru. Xiangru glared at them and scolded loudly. Those underlings drew back.

The King of Qin had no choice but to play the Fou once. Lin Xiangru asked the Historian of Zhao to write down, "The King of Qin played the Fou for the King of Zhao." Eventually, Lin Xiangru defended the dignity of Zhao State.

Young people should learn the intelligence and bravery from Lin Xiangru, so that they can base themselves on the society.

5 布衣之交

战国时期，秦王贪图赵惠文王的和氏璧，遂派使者传言愿意用十五座城池来换取。赵国便派蔺相如持和氏璧前往秦国。

但是秦王拿到和氏璧后，不再提交割城池之事。蔺相如用计骗回宝物，然后怒斥秦王说："大王您想要这块和氏璧，让人给赵王送信，赵王召集群臣商议，大家都认为秦国贪婪，凭借其国家的强大，用空话来换取和氏璧，想用城池来交换恐怕是做不到的。大家商议认为不应该把和氏璧给你。但我认为布衣之交尚且不相欺骗，况且是国家之间呢？"

"布衣之交"亦作"贫贱之交"，指老百姓之间的交往，亦指显贵者与没有官职的人相交往。

这则典故告诉人们做人要诚信，做一个普通老百姓要如此，一旦成为国家的官员，更应该以诚为本。

Friends in Days of Simple Life

During the Warring States Period, the King of Qin State coveted the Jade of Heshi, owned by King Huiwen of Zhao State. Therefore, he sent an envoy to pass on a message that he would like to exchange fifteen cities for it.

Hearing that, the King of Zhao State sent the retainer Lin Xiangru hold the jade and headed for Qin State.

But after the King of Qin State took Jade of Heshi, he did not mention anything about ceding the fifteen cities as he previously pledged. So Lin Xiangru got back the jade by artifice. Then he rebuked the King of Qin angrily, "Your majesty, you want to get this jade and therefore you sent an envoy to convey this message to our king. Our king called the ministers together to discuss it. They all said that Qin is greedy. You attempt to barter empty words for the jade by right of your power. They are afraid that the fifteen cities will not be ceded to us. So they thought the jade should not be given to you. However, in my opinion, even friends in days of simple life don't deceive each other, let alone two countries."

This idiom is also called "friends in days of poverty", meaning the friendship between the common people. It also refers to the friendship between an official and a commoner.

It tells us that people should be honest. A common citizen is supposed to be honest, so are the officials.

毛遂自荐

战国时期，有一个叫毛遂的人，他是赵国平原君门下的食客。毛遂在平原君家里已经住了三年，一直没有表现出什么才能，因此没有引起别人的注意。公元前257年，秦国侵略赵国，包围了赵国的都城邯郸，平原君奉命到楚国去讨救兵。他选了19位文武双全的门客，一同前往楚国。就在出发那天，毛遂突然站在平原君面前，自己推荐自己，要求同平原君一起去楚国。

平原君对毛遂自荐的举动，感到很惊奇，便阻止他道："一个具有才能与贤德的人，好比一把锥子藏在口袋里，锥子的尖立时就能看见。可是您在我这里都三年了，还从未听到过您有什么值得称道的事情，足见您没有什么才能了。"毛遂反驳道："如果您要是早一点允许我帮您谋划，那我的才能早就显露出来了。"他坚决要去楚国，平原君只好带他同行。

他们到达楚国，就与楚王商谈联合抗秦的事，可是从早晨谈到中午，还没有谈出结果。毛遂等得不耐烦了，看看机会已到，便冲到楚王面前，一手提剑，一手拉住楚王衣服，慷慨激昂地陈述共同抗秦的利害关系。毛遂的行为使楚王既害怕，又佩服，立刻答应签订盟约，并派出兵将前往赵国解围。

平原君亲自领略了毛遂的才干，心里非常敬服。他拉着毛遂的手，赞许地说："毛先生的三寸长的舌头，真是胜过百万大军啊！"

从此以后，毛遂就成了平原君的尊贵的门客了。

我们现在用它比喻自告奋勇，自我推荐。

我们应该学习毛遂的自信和勇敢，敢于在众人面前展露自己的才华。

To Volunteer One's Services

In the Warring States Period, there was a man named Mao Sui, a hanger-on in Lord Pingyuan's house in Zhao State. Mao Sui had been living there for three years without showing his talents. So he attracted nobody's attention. In 257 B.C., the troops of Qin State invaded Zhao State and besieged its capital Handan. Lord Pingyuan was ordered to go to Chu State to ask for reinforcements. He chose nineteen hangers-on who were well versed in both civil and military arts to go to Chu State with him. At the day they were just about to start off, Mao Sui suddenly appeared before Lord Pingyuan and recommended himself to go to Chu State with them.

Lord Pingyuan was surprised at Mao Sui's behavior. He dissuaded him and said, "A person with virtue and talent is just like an awl hidden in the bag, which can be spotted immediately. However, you have been in my house for three years, I have never heard anything laudable about you. So it serves to show that you have no talent." Mao Sui refuted him, "If you had allowed me to scheme for you, my talent would have demonstrated earlier." At the insistence of Mao Sui, Lord Pingyuan had to take him to go with them.

As soon as they arrived in Chu State, they began to negotiate over the alliance to resist Qin State. From morning to noon, the matter was not settled yet. Mao Sui became impatient, and he took a chance to dash to the King of Chu, with a sword in one hand and the clothes of the king in the other. At the same time, Mao Sui stated the advantages and disadvantages of the union to resist Qin vehemently. The king was not only frightened by Mao Sui's behavior, but also admired his courage. He immediately agreed to sign the oath of alliance, and sent his troops to help Zhao State.

Lord Pingyuan realized Mao Sui's talent this time, so he admired him greatly. Holding Mao Sui's hands, he praised, "Your convincing eloquence is more useful than a million troops."

From then on, Mao Sui became a respected hanger-on of Lord Pingyuan.

Now, we use this idiom to indicate that someone volunteers to do something or recommends himself to do something.

We should learn the self-confidence and courage from Mao Sui and dare to expose our special talent in public.

7 一言九鼎

战国时，秦国的军队团团包围了赵国的都城邯郸，形势十分危急，赵国国君孝成王派平原君到楚国去求援。

平原打算带领20名门客前往，已挑了19名，尚少一个定不下来。这时，毛遂自告奋勇提出要去，平原君半信半疑，勉强带着他一起前往楚国。

平原君到了楚国后，立即与楚王谈及"援赵"之事，谈了半天也毫无结果。这时，毛遂对楚王说："我们今天来请您派援兵，您一言不发，可您别忘了，楚国虽然兵多地大，却连连吃败仗，连国都也丢掉了，依我看，楚国比赵国更需要联合起来抗秦呀！"毛遂的一席话说得楚王口服心服，立即答应出兵援赵。

平原君回到赵国后感慨地说："毛先生一至楚，而使赵重于九鼎大吕。"（九鼎大吕：钟名，与鼎同为古代国家的宝器。）

成语"一言九鼎"由这个故事而来，比喻说话力量大，能起很大作用。形容人说话信誉极高，一言半语就起决定性作用。

我们应该培养自己的威信，在今后的人生道路中，让自己的一言一行都能起到举足轻重的作用。

A Word Carrying the Weight of Nine Tripods

During the Warring States Period, Qin troops besieged Handan, the capital of Zhao State. The situation was quite critical, so King Xiaocheng of Zhao State sent Lord Pingyuan to go to Chu State to ask for help.

Lord Pingyuan intended to take 20 hangers-on with him, and he had already chose 19. Only one person hadn't been decided. Then Mao Sui volunteered to go to Chu State. Lord Pingyuan was dubious about him, but he still took Mao Sui together reluctantly.

When they arrived in Chu State, Lord Pingyuan began to negotiate over the reinforcements from Chu for quite a long time, but reached nothings. Then Mao Sui said to the King of Chu, "We come to ask for an ally, but you never say a word. Don't forget that although Chu State is large and strong, you still suffered defeat by defeat so as to make the capital be occupied. In my opinion, Chu needs the union even more urgently than Zhao!" The King of Chu was convinced by Mao Sui, and sent his troops to help Zhao.

When Lord Pingyuan returned to Zhao, he sighed with emotion, "When Mr. Mao arrived in Chu, he made our Zhao State value more than nine tripods."

The idiom "A Word Carrying the Weight of Nine Tripods" originates from this story. It is used to indicate the importance of one's words or the authority of the speaker whose few words count.

We should develop our own prestige from now on. Only in this way shall we play a very important part in the society in the future.

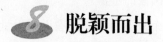

脱颖而出

战国时期，秦国围攻赵国首都，形势危急，赵王派平原君去楚国求救。平原君决定带20名文武双全的食客做随从，但只挑得19人，这时一个叫毛遂的人自我推荐，主动要求跟他去。

平原君看不出他有什么才能，问道："先生在我这多长时间了？"

毛遂答道："三年。"

平原君就说："如果一个人真的有才能，就像放在口袋里的锥尖，总有一天会刺穿口袋露出来了的。而你呆在我这儿这么久了，并没有显出什么本领啊。"

毛遂答道；"我今天就是要请您把我放进口袋里。假如您早一点把我放进去，不光是锥尖刺破口袋，连锥子上的环都早露出来了。"

平原君见他说得有道理，就同意他一同前去。后来，在劝说楚王发兵救赵国的关键时刻，毛遂挺身而出，表现了过人的才能，协助平原君完成了使命。

该成语故事比喻有才能的人本领显露出来。

我们不能埋没自己的才能，应该学习毛遂在适当的时候展露自己的才华。

Talent Showing Itself

During the Warring States Period, Qin State besieged the capital of Zhao State. The situation was very critical. The King of Zhao State sent Lord of Pingyuan to Chu State for help. Lord of Pingyuan decided to take twenty disciples who are both versed in literary and military arts as his attendants. However, he has only chosen nineteen of them. One man named Mao Sui took the initiative and recommended himself. Lord of Pingyuan could not perceive his ability, so he asked, "How long have you been here?" Mao Sui answered, "Three years." Lord of Pingyuan continued, "A real talented man is like an awl in a bag, the point of which would pierce through the bag and reveal itself some day. You've been here for such a long time, but you didn't show any outstanding ability." Mao Sui explained, "This is the reason why I plea you to put me into the pocket. If you did it earlier, not only the point of the awl had pierced through the bag, but also the ring of which had revealed itself outside of the bag." Lord of Pingyuan felt his words reasonable and approved of his request. Later on, at the critical moment of persuading the King of Chu State to send armies to rescue Zhao State, Mao Sui came out boldly, demonstrated his exceptional talent and helped Lord of Pingyuan to complete the mission successfully.

We use this idiom to mean the talented man's ability showing itself.

We should not neglect our own ability and learn from Mao Sui to expose our talent at an appropriate moment.

因人成事，三寸之舌

"因人成事"，是毛遂讥讽不顶用的同伴的话；"三寸之舌"则是平原君称赞毛遂的话。

平原君一行到楚国要求楚王迅速派出援军，和赵国联合抗秦。可是楚王惧怕秦国，不肯答允。两个人从清早谈判到中午，也没谈出结果。

毛遂等20人，在殿前阶下，等得焦急起来。那19人就对毛遂开玩笑说："毛先生，上殿去露露锥尖吧！"

毛遂二话不说，提剑登阶，从容上殿，对平原君说："赵楚联合抗秦的利害关系，两句话就可以说清楚，为什么说了这么半天还决定不下来呢？"

楚王问平原君："这是什么人？"

平原君说："是我的家臣，也是我的随员。"

楚王便转向毛遂呵斥道："还不快给我下去！我正在同你们君主谈话，你算个什么？"

毛遂按剑而前，对楚王说："你仗着楚国是个大国，就这样随意呵斥人？你要知道，眼前在这十步之内，你的性命全在我的手里，即使是大国也没有用。你叫嚷什么！"楚王不做声了。

毛遂接着说："现在楚国土地方圆五千里，雄兵百万，这是称霸天下的本钱。象楚国这样强盛，天下各国都不能对抗。白起带了几万兵来和楚国打仗，一战就夺去了你们的鄢、郢等地；再战就烧掉了夷陵的楚先王墓；三战干脆俘虏了大王你的先人，这是百辈的仇恨啊，连赵国都感到羞耻，而大王却不知道好歹！军事联盟是为了楚国，不是为赵国。在我主人面前，你叫嚷什么？"

楚王又害怕又惭愧，连连称是，满口应承说，"确实像先生说的，我愿意用全国的兵力参加同盟。"

毛遂又逼问:"联合抗秦的事定了吧?"

楚王忙说:"定了。"

定盟仪式结束后,毛遂对殿外的19个人说:"你们这些老爷碌碌无能,就像人们所说的依靠别人成事的!"

这件大事,就这样靠着毛遂的口才而终于取得了成功。平原君因此很称赞毛遂,其余19人也更信服他了。

平原君回到邯郸,感慨地说:"我不敢再鉴别人才了!毛先生到了楚国一次,就使赵国的声望提高了百倍。毛先生的三寸长的舌头,比百万雄兵还强啊!"后把毛遂奉为上等门客。

以后,人们就把自己没本事,而靠别人的力量办成事的叫做"因人成事"。用"三寸之舌"来形容人的能说会道、善于辩论。

青年人应该锻炼自己的口才,不仅要能言善辩,而且要以理服人。

To Rely on Others to Succeed in Work; a Silver Tongue

"To Rely on Others to Succeed in Work" is the word that Mao Sui used to criticize his peers. "A Silver Tongue" is the word that Lord Pingyuan used to compliment Mao Sui.

After arriving in Chu State, Lord Pingyuan immediately inquired for the King of Chu to talk about the military alliance with Chu to fight against Qin State, and also asked that the Chu sent a reinforce army to help Zhao in no time. But the King of Chu was fear of Qin, so he couldn't agree. The talk between them lasted from early morning to mid-noon, but nothing turned out.

The twenty members, including Mao Sui, of Lord Pingyuan's delegation were waiting outside the palace, worrying about the negotiation. The other 19 members made fun of Mao Sui and said, "Mr. Mao, how about entering the palace to show you off."

Without any reply, Mao Sui went upstairs to the palace with a sword in hand. He took it easy and asked Lord Pingyuan, "it is easy to express the advantages and disadvantages of the military alliance of Chu and Zhao to fight against Qin. How could it take so long a time?"

The King of Chu turned to Lord Pingyuan and asked, "Who is this man?"

Lord Pingyuan replied, "He is one of my retainers, my servant."

"Get out! I am talking with your lord, how dare you be so rude?" The King of Chu turned to Mao Sui and scolded.

Mao Sui put his hand on the sword and went forward towards the King of Chu and said, "How can you scold people like that only because Chu State is a powerful big state? You see! I can kill you easily in this short distance no matter how powerful your state is. Shut up!" The King of Chu said nothing and fell into silence.

Mao Sui continued, "At present, Chu has acreage of more than 5,000 li and more than a million soldiers, which are the base of building a new empire of Chu State. No states can withstand your army. But General Bai Qi of Qin has fought against your state for three times only with tens of thousands of soldiers. The first time, they got your cities like Yan and Ying; the second time, they burnt down your ancestor's tomb in Yiling; the third time, they captured your forefathers. Qin is your deadly enemy. Zhao State feels ashamed of this, how can you feel noting? The military alliance between our two states is at your advantage. How dare you shout in the face of my lord?"

The King of Chu felt scared and ashamed and nodded to say, "What you have said is true, and I will ally with Zhao State with all my soldiers."

Mao Sui asked forcefully, "Is that military alliance against Qin settled?"

The King of Chu answered immediately, "Yes, it is a deal."

After the ceremony, Mao Sui said to the other 19 outside companions, "You all are those who need to rely on others to succeed in work."

This great event was completely succeeded due to Mao Sui's eloquence. Lord Pingyuan said high of Mao Sui on this event and the other 19 companions admired him more.

Coming back to Handan, Lord Pingyuan sighed with emotion and said, "I dare not to appreciate person with ability any more. The reputation of

贤 士 篇

Zhao State was enhanced by 100 times because of Mao Sui's visit to Chu. His three-inch long tongue is more powerful than one million soldiers." Since then Mao Sui was treated as senior consultant.

Since then, people use the idiom "To Rely on Others to Succeed in Work" to describe those who are unable to do their own work and rely on others, and the idiom Silver Tongue to describe those who have the gift of gab and are good at debating.

Young people should practice their eloquence. They should not only have a silver tongue, but also should convince people by reasoning.

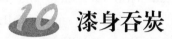

漆身吞炭

春秋末期，晋国被智、赵、韩、魏、范、中行六家大臣所把持。公元前458年，智伯联同韩、赵、魏三家共灭范氏、中行氏并分掉了这两家的土地。公元前455年，智伯又要韩、赵、魏三家割地给他。赵襄子不给，并说服韩、魏与赵联合，于公元前453年灭掉了智氏。

晋国有个人，名叫豫让，原先在范氏、中行氏手下办事，默默无闻。后来投到智伯门下，智伯对他十分赏识。智伯死后，他发誓要为智伯报仇，杀掉赵襄子。他改名换姓，到赵襄子宫中的厕所里干以泥抹墙的杂活，身边暗藏匕首。不料赵襄子为人十分警觉，上厕所时，心生怀疑，叫人把正在涂墙的豫让抓了起来，并搜出了暗器。豫让直截了当地对赵襄子说，他要为智伯报仇。手下想把豫让杀了，赵襄子却说："他是有义气的人，我谨慎地避开他就是了。"命手下放豫让走了。

过了一段时间，豫让把漆涂抹在脸上身上，使人看上去像是患有严重皮肤病，又吞下炭去，使声音变得嘶哑。他沿街乞讨，他的妻子迎面走过，也没认出他来。一位最知心的朋友认出了他，流着眼泪对他说："以你的才干，去给赵襄子办事，一定会得到他的尊宠和亲近，那时你要报仇还不容易吗？何苦一定要把自己作践成这副模样！"豫让说："在人手下为臣，心里却想着杀他，这是怀二心以服侍其君。我之所以要漆身吞炭，就是要让天下以及后世怀二心服侍其君的人感到羞愧！"

豫让躲在赵襄子必定要经过的一座桥下。赵襄子来到桥头，马忽然受惊。赵襄子说："这一定是豫让！"手下立即把躲在桥下的豫让揪了出来。

豫让要求赵襄子脱下衣服，让他用剑斩衣，以表示已经为智伯报仇。赵襄子答应了。豫让达到目的后拔剑自杀。后用"漆身吞炭"这个典故来比喻舍身酬知己或雪耻复仇。

Lacquering One's Body and Swallowing Charcoals

During the late Spring and Autumn Period, Jin State was actually governed by six ministers: Zhi, Zhao, Han, Wei, Fan and Zhonghang families. In 458 B.C., Zhi Bo united with Han, Zhao and Wei to eliminate Fan and Zhonghang, and divided up their land successfully. In 455 B.C., Zhi Bo forced the families of Han, Zhao and Wei to cede territory to him. Zhao Xiangzi refused the demand and destroyed the family of Zhi in alliance with Han and Wei in 453 B.C..

There was a man called Yu Rang in Jin State who once served the families of Fan and Zhonghang and remained in obscurity. However, he was greatly appreciated after he became the family-minister of Zhi Bo. After Zhi Bo was killed, Yu Rang swore to take revenge and assassinate Zhao Xiangzi. Therefore, he concealed his identity and his name, plastering the toilet walls with a hidden dagger in Zhao Xiangzi's palace. Yet Zhao Xiangzi was very alert, and when he went to the toilet, he suddenly had doubt and ordered his guards to capture Yu Rang who was plastering the wall. When Yu Rang's hidden weapon was found, he declared frankly that he was seeking revenge for Zhi Bo. The guards intended to execute Yu Rang, but Zhao Xiangzi said, "He is a loyal man. I will be more cautious to keep away from him later on." Then he released Yu Rang.

After some time, Yu Rang began to lacquer all over his face and body as if he had suffered from some kind of serious skin disease. He also made his voice hoarse by swallowing charcoals. He made himself a beggar in the streets, and even his wife didn't recognize him face to face. One of his intimate friends recognized him and told him with tears, "You can easily get favor and trust from Zhao Xiangzi by means of your abilities if you serve Zhao family. Wouldn't it be easier to kill him when he was off guard? There is no need to hurt yourself in this way." Yu Rang said, "If I am the family-minister of Zhao and conceive the idea of killing him, I am not a faithful person. I lacquered myself and swallowed charcoals only to shame those people and the later generations who are unfaithful to their masters."

One day Yu Rang lurked under a bridge which Zhao Xiangzi was certain to cross. When Zhao came to the bridge, his horses were suddenly shied. Xiangzi said, "Yu Rang must be here." His guards searched and hauled out Yu Rang from under the bridge.

Yu Rang asked Zhao Xiangzi to take off his dress and allow him to cut it with his sword, indicating that he had revenged. Zhao agreed. Having realized his wish, Yu Rang committed suicide with his sword. This idiom indicates the determination to sacrifice oneself to requite one's intimate friend or to seek revenge.

11 众人国士

豫让在赤水桥下，等待行刺赵襄子，但是，襄子的马突然受惊，豫让被卫士们所抓获。

赵襄子问他说："你不是曾经跟随范氏和中行氏吗，智伯消灭了他们，你没有替他们复仇，反而成为智伯的家臣，为什么智伯死后，你如此坚决地为他复仇呢？"

豫让说："我奉范氏、中行氏时，他们把我当普通人看待，所以我就像普通人一样报答他们；智伯把我当作国士看待，我当然要像国士那样来报答他。"

襄子长叹："豫让，你为智伯竭忠尽义，已经做到了；而我也已经宽恕过你一次，也算仁至义尽，为成全你的大名，你是应该死在这里的，为你考虑，我也不忍心再放你；何去何从，是生是死，现在由你自己选择。"

豫让说："我听说贤明的主人不掩盖他人的美德，但是忠臣有为名而死的气节。您以前宽恕过我，天下人都夸您贤明。今天，我情愿死在这里。但是我希望您把衣服给我，让我刺几剑，就算让我报仇了，这样我就死而无憾了。"

赵简子认为此人真是义士,便让随从把自己的衣服交给豫让。豫让拔剑,跳起三次击刺这件衣服,然后自刎而死。当天,赵国所有的有志之士都为他哭泣。

我们要学会信任别人,与人坦诚相待,这样才能赢得别人的信赖。

A Mediocre Man and a State Talent

Yu Rang hid under the bridge over Chishui River to assassinate Zhao Xiangzi when Zhao's horses got suddenly frightened as they came to the bridge and Yu Rang was caught by the guards.

Zhao Xiangzi interrogated him, "You once served the families of Fan and Zhonghang. Zhi Bo eliminated both of them. You didn't revenge for them and became the family-minister of Zhi Bo. But why are you so resolved to revenge for him after Zhi Bo had died?"

Yu Rang said, "When I was in the family of Fan and Zhonghang, they regarded and treated me as a mediocre man, so I rewarded them as a mediocre man. But Zhi Bo regarded and treated me as a state talent, so I must requite him as a state talent."

ZhaoXiangzi sighed and said, "Yu Rang! You have shown your faithfulness to Zhi Bo. And I have forgiven enough because I have released you once. To be worthy of your faithful reputation, you are supposed to sacrifice yourself and I can't bear to release you any more in behalf of you. To live or to die, it's up to you."

Yu Rang said, "I heard a wise master wouldn't cover others' virtue, but a faithful minister didn't fear death for righteousness. You once released me, and all the people would praise your virtue. Today I am ready to die, but I have a final request for allowing me to thrust your dress to show my mind of revenge. Then I will die without any regret."

Zhao Xiangzi was deeply touched by his faithfulness and let the guards hold the dress for him. Yu Rang leapt and cut the dress three times with his sword before committing suicide. Hearing this, all the persons of fidelity and integrity in Zhao wept for the death of Yu Rang.

We should be frank and candid with others. Only by this way can we win other people's trust.

赵衰举贤

春秋时期，晋文公问大臣赵衰，谁可做元帅、上卿、将军。赵衰虽然才能过人，但出于公心，每次都向晋文公推举贤能之人，如为人忠诚谨慎的栾枝，广有谋略的先轸，见多识广的胥臣等人。自己则多次退让。

晋文公说："赵衰多次推让，都没有失去礼仪。谦让是为了推荐贤哲，礼仪是推广道德，推广道德，贤哲就来了。他自己多次退让，是有德的行为。但是如果我不用他，就是废弃了道德的标准。"

于是将军队分成五支，让赵衰统领新上军。

后来，大将子犯亡故，蒲城伯接任他的职务，请求晋文公给他派一员副将。

晋文公说："赵衰三次让贤，不失礼义。此人既有才又有德，我还有什么可担心的呢？请让赵衰给你做副将。"于是，使任命赵衰做上军的副将。

我们现在通常用这个典故来比喻礼让贤哲。

Zhao Shuai Recommending the Wise Man

During the Spring and Autumn Period, Wengong, the ruler of Jin State asked his minister Zhao Shuai, "Who can be the marshal, the minister, and the general?" Although Zhao Shuai was very talented, he was selfless, and recommended some talented people to Wengong, such as Luan Zhi who was very cautious and loyal, Xian Zhen who knew tactics, Xu Chen who was very knowledgeable and so on. However, he was always stepping aside himself.

Wengong said, "Zhao Shuai has declined many times without losing the etiquette. His modesty is for recommending the wise men, his etiquette is for spreading morality, and if morality is popularized, the wise men will come. Therefore, his stepping aside for many times a virtuous behavior. If I don't appoint him, moral standards will be abandoned."

Then Wengong divided the army into five branches, and appointed Zhao Shuai the commander of the New Upper Army.

Later, General Zi Fan died, and General Pu Chengbo replaced his position and asked Wengong to dispatch an assistant general for him.

Wengong said, "Zhao Shuai has declined and recommended the other wise men for three times, and without losing the etiquette. I thought that he was not only talented, but also virtuous. I am no worried to let him be your assistant." Therefore, Wengong appointed Zhao Shuai the assistant general of the Upper Army.

Now we usually use this idiom to indicate the courtliness for the wise men.

13 排难解纷

战国时代，秦国侵略赵国，兵临赵都邯郸。赵王求魏国援助，魏国派大将辛垣衍劝说赵国尊秦王为帝，以换取秦国退兵。对此赵国大臣意见不一。

这时齐国人鲁仲连正访问邯郸。他听说赵国要向秦国屈服，就去求见赵相平原君赵胜，请他引见辛垣衍，平原君应允。

鲁仲连见辛垣衍后，列举历史事实，分析当时形势，严厉斥责他"尊秦为帝"的谬论，并指出如果屈服了秦国，将对赵国、魏国都有极大的祸害。

辛垣衍听罢，十分钦佩，就撤回了原来的劝说，并表示立即返国回报魏王。秦军得了这个消息，不免大吃一惊，为防止意外，立刻退兵五十里。

后来魏公子无忌窃符救赵，大败秦军，解除了这次秦国对赵国的入侵。

平原君对鲁仲连又钦佩又感激，准备封地给他，他不肯受，送他千金为酬，他也不要。鲁仲连说："以天下为己任的仁人志士，为人排忧解难是绝对不会收取任何报酬的。"

原指为人排除危难，解决纠纷。今指调停双方争执。

"排难解纷"告诉我们要学会协调解决纷争，帮助别人解决一些实际困难，从而赢得别人的尊重和钦佩。

Pouring Oil on Troubled Waters

During the Warring States Period, Qin troops invaded Zhao State, and laid siege to its capital Handan. The King of Zhao pled for Wei's help, but Wei sent senior general Xin Yuanyan to try to talk Zhao into serving the King of Qin as their emperor in order to get the withdrawal of the Qin troops in return. The ministers of Zhao had different opinions about it.

At that time Lu Zhonglian from Qi State was paying a visit in Handan. Hearing that Zhao would submit, he requested an interview with Zhao Sheng, Lord Pingyuan, the prime minister of Zhao, who agreed to recommend him to Xin Yuanyan.

Having met Xin Yuanyan, Lu analyzed the present situation by citing the historical events and rebuked sharply the absurd idea of "serving the King of Qin as emperor". Lu also pointed that if Zhao had submitted, it might have been an awful disaster to both Zhao and Wei.

Hearing this, Xin Yuanyan admired Lu deeply. So he took back his words and promised to return to report it to the King of Wei immediately. Qin troops were greatly surprised at the news and retreated 50 li so as to avoid a thunderbolt.

Later prince Wuji, the younger son of the King of Wei, stole the military tally to rescue Zhao, and Qin troops were defeated.

Lord Pingyuan had a tremendous admiration and gratitude for Lu Zhonglian and wanted to offer fief to him, but Lu refused. Then the Lord wished to reward him with one thousand pieces of gold, which Lu didn't accept either. Lu Zhonglian said, "A real sage regards benefiting the world as his own duty. So I will take nothing while I am trying to help them to pour oil on troubled waters."

The original meaning of this idiom is to help one to get rid of danger or to settle quarrels. Today it indicates mediating a dispute.

It tells us that we should learn to mediate the disputes and help others to solve some practical problems, and then we may win the admiration and respect from others.

图穷匕见

秦国是战国七雄中的最强大的国家，它不断蚕食其他六国的领土，以图最终能够一统天下。公元前228年，秦国的大军向北进犯，包围了赵国都城邯郸。由于赵王错杀了大将李牧，秦军终于攻下邯郸、灭掉赵国并俘虏了赵王。

赵国灭亡，北方的燕国顿时危在旦夕。燕国的太子丹决定派遣荆轲为刺客，到秦国都城咸阳杀死秦王嬴政，以解除亡国之威胁。

荆轲出发前，太子丹做了三项周密准备：由勇士秦舞阳陪同荆轲前往咸阳行刺；带上嬴政一直想杀死的秦国叛将樊於期的人头作为礼物；再拿上燕国打算要献给嬴政的最肥沃的燕地督亢地区的地图。这后两项准备，是为了取信于秦王的安排，那卷地图更有特别功用，里面藏着刺杀秦王嬴政用的一把锋利的匕首，刀锋上还淬过了烈性毒药。

秦王接见荆轲时，见到仇人被斩的人头，又听说燕国欲献上大片土地，遂兴奋不已地打开地图。地图全部展开时匕首出现了，荆轲一个箭步跑过去，拿起匕首，同时又拉住了秦王的袍袖，但秦王挣脱而逃，衣袖都撕断了。荆轲和秦王绕着巨大的铜柱追逐一番之后，秦王才得到机会，抽出佩戴的长剑砍伤了荆轲，众大臣侍卫随后用乱刀将荆轲杀死了。

"图穷匕见"现在常常用来比喻真相显露出来的意思。

害人之心不可有，防人之心不可无。我们应该注意，任何阴谋诡计终有败露的时候，我们为人处世时应该光明磊落。

When the Map Was Unrolled, the Dagger Was Revealed

Qin State was the most powerful among the seven states during the Warring States Period and never ceased to nibble the territories of the other six in order to unify. Qin troops marched north and besieged Handan, the capital of Zhao State, in 228 BC. Since the King of Zhao killed the famous general Li Mu wrongfully, at last the Qin troops occupied Handan, captured the King, and extinguished Zhao State.

The destruction of Zhao State put its north neighbor, Yan State, in imminent danger. To avoid the threat, Prince Dan of Yan State decided to send Jing Ke to Xianyang, the capital of Qin State, to assassinate Yingzheng, the King of Qin State.

Prince Dan made three careful preparations before Jing Ke, the assassinator's starting. First, he found a brave and strong man named Qin Wuyang to accompany him to Xianyang to help him. Moreover, he took with him the head of Fan Wuju, a betrayed Qin general, whom the King of Qin had been expecting to kill. Finally, he took the map of Dukang, the most fertile area of Yan, to present to Yingzheng. The last two arrangements would help Jing Ke win the trust of the king. The map had a special use, for rolled in it was a sharp dagger with its blade being soaked in virulent poison, which would be used to stab the king.

The King of Qin State was greatly pleased and began to open the map after he saw the head of his enemy and heard that Yan State would cede vast territories. As the map was unfolded, the dagger emerged. Jing Ke leapt up with a big stride, grabbed the dagger, and caught the king by his sleeve. Yingzheng struggled to escape with the sleeve torn up. Jing Ke pursued him around the big bronze columns for several rounds before the king obtained a chance to draw out his sword and hurt Jing Ke. Then the ministers and guards swarmed to kill Jing Ke with their weapons.

This idiom indicates that hidden intentions will be revealed in the end.

We should not harbor ill intentions against others, but never relax vigilance against evil-doers. Plots and tricks may not be disclosed until the last minute. In life we should be always honest with others.

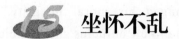

15 坐怀不乱

关于"坐怀不乱"的典故最早出现在《荀子》中:"柳下惠与后门者同衣,而不见疑,非一日之闻也。"这个故事自汉代以来已经广为传颂,可谓家喻户晓。相

传在一个寒冷的夜晚，柳下惠宿于郭门，有一个没有住处的妇人来投宿，柳下惠恐她冻死，叫她坐在怀里，解开外衣把她裹紧，同坐了一夜，并没发生非礼行为。于是柳下惠就被誉为"坐怀不乱"的正人君子。此外，他为人刚正不阿，得罪权贵，多次遭到贬谪，但不离开父母之邦，所谓"虽遭三黜，不去故国；虽荣三公，不易其介"。柳下惠得到了孔子、孟子等人的高度评价。

后来人们用"坐怀不乱"来形容男子在两性关系方面作风正派。

我们也许会面临各种诱惑，这时一定要坚定自己的信念，摒除杂念。只有抵制住各种诱惑才能有光明的前途。

Keeping His Mind Undisturbed with a Woman in His Bosom

This idiom is from the book Xunzi. "No sexual relations happened between Liu Xiahui and a woman although they were covered by the same clothing for a whole night. It is not the first time for me to hear this kind of things that happened on him." Since Han Dynasty, this story had been eulogized broadly and could be called a household one.

It is said that in a cold night, Liu Xiahui lodged in Guo's house. Later, a woman also came to this house for shelter. For fear that she would be frozen to death; Liu Xiahui let her sit in his bosom and untied his overclothes to wrap her up. They sat together for a whole night, but no sexual relations happened between them. As a result, Liu Xiahui was praised as a perfect gentleman who kept his mind undisturbed with a woman in his bosom. Furthermore, he was upright and never stooped to flattery, and consequently he offended the dignitaries and was demoted many times. Despite all these, he never left his country. That's what is called "Although he was demoted three times, he never left his country; although he became the highest-rank officials, he never changed his moral integrity." Liu Xiahui got high appraisement from people like Confucius and Mencius.

We often use this idiom to describe a man who is decent in the sexual relations.

We may be faced with various temptations in the society. What we should do is to strengthen our beliefs and remove the evil thoughts. Only when a person could resist the temptations can he have a bright future.

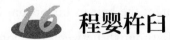

程婴杵臼

晋国大夫屠案贾擅自率兵屠杀了晋国大臣赵朔、赵同、赵括、赵婴齐满门。

赵朔之妻由于是公主，得以藏在宫中，后来生下遗腹子一名，但宫外的兵马追索甚急。赵朔的朋友程婴与门客公孙杵臼为救赵氏孤儿，设下计谋，用其他的婴儿的性命和公孙杵臼的性命救下了这个孩子。

最终赵氏遗孤赵武在晋国大臣韩厥的帮助下，由晋景公为赵氏恢复了封邑，并诛杀屠氏以报家仇。

现在我们用这条典故泛指危难之际足可信赖托孤的人；为知己者竭尽赤诚保全后嗣的人。

我们要学会分辨是非，在危难的时候坚持自己的信念，敢作敢为。

As Sincere as Cheng Ying and Chujiu

One day Tu Angu, the minister of Jin State, led his army and massacred the whole family of Zhao without the King's authorization, including the ministers Zhao Shuo, Zhao Tong, Zhao Kuo and Zhao Yingqi.

Zhao Shuo's wife, the daughter of the king, hid in the palace to survive the massacre, and later gave birth to a posthumous child. But the military forces outside the palace were eager to track down the child. In order to save the orphan of Zhao, Cheng Ying, Zhao Shuo's friend, devised a stratagem with Zhao Shuo's retainer Gongsun Chujiu. They found a baby to pretend to be the child of Zhao Shuo. Later on Gongsun Chujiu and the sham orphan were killed, but the true orphan was safe.

Eventually, with the help of the minister Han Jue, the orphan of Zhao who was called Zhao Wu regained the vavasory which used to belong to the family of Zhao. Moreover, under the order of Duke Jing of Jin, he avenged his family's blood by killing the whole family of Tu.

Today, the idiom refers to the man who is so reliable that you can entrust an orphan to his care in time of danger. It also refers to the man who exerts all his power to protect the heir of his bosom friend.

We should learn to distinguish between the good and the bad. When in danger, we should stick to our beliefs, have the courage to act and dare to take the responsibility.

汉思李牧

李牧，战国末期赵国将领，善于用兵。惠文王时，李牧率兵驻守北疆，打败匈奴军队，积有战功，深得军心。

公元前233年，秦国派兵攻打赤丽、宜安，他率军奋起反击，大败秦军，因功封武安君。

第二年，秦军越太行山，攻打番吾，又被他击败。

秦国为统一天下，发动战争，灭韩以后，转而攻赵。李牧和司马尚率兵堵击，相持一年。秦收买赵国佞臣郭开，诬陷他造反，被杀身亡。

汉文帝困于匈奴的侵扰，曾说若得廉颇、李牧为将，匈奴的忧患即可解除。

我们要努力做一个对社会有用的人。对社会做出突出贡献的人都会被世人所记住所缅怀。

The Emperor Wen of Han Dynasty Missing Li Mu

Li Mu, a general of Zhao in late Warring States Period, was an expert in tactics. During the reign of King Huiwen, Li Mu led the troops to guard the northern border. He defeated the Hun troops, gained many victories, and won the respect of the troops.

In 233 B.C., the King of Qin dispatched troops to attack Chili and Yi'an.

Li Mu commanded the army, launched a counterattack and achieved great triumph. Because of the victories, he got the title as Lord of Wu'an.

The next year, Qin troops went across Taihang Mountain to invade Fanwu and were defeated by him once more.

In order to unify the world, Qin State waged wars. After extinguishing Han State, Qin started to attack Zhao. Li Mu and Sima Shang led the troops to intercept the enemies and were locked in a stalemate for one year. Qin bribed a treacherous Minister Guo Kai of Zhao State and made a false charge again him of rebellion. Then, Li Mu was killed.

When Emperor Wen of Han Dynasty was trapped in Xiongnu's invasion, he once said if he could get Lian Po and Li Mu as generals, the miseries of Xiongnu would be relieved.

We should try our best to do some useful work to the society. A person who once made great contribution to the society will be cherished and remembered by people.

18 简子谦卑

战国时期，晋国上卿赵简子（赵国君主的先人）总是乘破车，御瘦马，穿着黑公羊皮长袍。

他的管家说："车子新了才会安全，马肥了速度才会快，狐白的皮袍才温暖而且轻薄。"

简子回答说："我不是不知道啊。但是我听说，君子衣服好了就会变得更加谦恭，见识短浅的人衣服好了，就会变得越发傲慢。我这是小心提防，害怕有见识短浅的人那样的心思啊。"

我们现在用这个典故来比喻要时常保持谦卑之心。

我们在做人做事方面应该保持低调。丰富的内涵是一个人立足于社会的最重要的条件之一。

Jianzi's Humility

During the Warring States Period, Zhao Jianzi (the ancestor of the kings of Zhao State), was a senior minister of Jin State. However, he was always riding an old carriage, driving thin horses, and wearing a robe of black ram's skin.

One day, his house manager said, "A new carriage will be safer, a strong horse will be faster and a robe of white fox skin warmer, lighter and thinner."

Jianzi answered, "I also know that. However, I have heard that good clothing can make a man of honor more humble, but a short-sighted person more arrogant. So what I do now is just to avoid having a short-sighted mind."

Now we use this idiom to indicate that a person should always keep a humble heart.

We should be low-pitched when conducting ourselves and handle affaires. The rich virtue of self-control is one of the most important qualities when we want to establish themselves in the society.

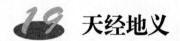

天经地义

公元前 520 年周景王姬贵死后,按习俗由他正夫人所生的世子姬敬继位。但是,景王生前曾与大夫宾孟商议过,打算立非正夫人所生的长子姬朝为世子。这样,姬朝也有资格继位。于是,周王室发生了激烈的王位之争。

在这种情况下,晋顷公召集各诸侯国的代表在黑壤盟商讨如何使周王室安宁。参加商讨的有晋国的赵鞅、郑国的游吉、宋国的乐大心等。

会上,晋国的赵鞅向郑国的游吉请教什么叫"礼"。

游吉回答说:"我国的子产大夫在世时曾经说过,礼就是天之经,地之义,也就是老天规定的原则,大地施行的正理。它是百姓行动的依据,不能改变,也不容怀疑。"

贤 士 篇

赵鞅对游吉的回答很满意，表示一定要牢记这个道理。其他诸侯国的代表听了，也大都表示有理。

接着，赵鞅提出各诸侯国应全力支持敬王，为他提供兵卒、粮草，并且帮助他把王室迁回王城。

后来，晋国的大夫率领各诸侯国的军队，帮助敬王恢复王位，结束了周王室的王位之争。

我们要遵循社会当中的道德规则。如果大家都按规则行事，很多不必要的纷争就可以避免。

The Principles of Heaven and Earth

After Ji Gui, King Jing of Zhou Dynasty, died in 520 BC, the prince Ji Jing who was born by the Queen should succeed the throne according to the custom. However, when King Jing was alive, he once discussed with a senior official named Bin Meng that he was about to make Ji Chao who was not born by the Queen the prince in order that Ji Chao was also qualified to succeed the throne. A fierce fight for the throne broke out in the court of Zhou.

Under such circumstance, Duke Qing of Jin State called on all the representatives of the feudal States, including Zhao Yang from Jin State, You Ji from Zheng State, Le Daxin from Song State, etc., to deliberate how to quiet down the fight in Heirangmeng.

During the deliberation, Zhao Yang from Jin State asked You Ji from Zheng State how to explain the word "Rite".

You Ji answered "When a senior official in our country named Zi Chan was alive, he once said that Rite was the natural development of things. It was the principles of heaven and earth that all the people should follow. Nobody could change it, nor could they doubt it."

Zhao Yang was quite satisfied with You Ji's answer. He said he would remember it by heart. Other representatives from the feudal countries also agreed with the principle.

Then Zhao Yang suggested that all the representatives of the feudal states should support King Jing and that they should supply him with soldiers and provisions to help him move the court back to the capital.

Later on, the senior official of Jin State was followed by the armies of the feudal states to help King Jing regain the throne. The fight for the throne was over.

We should follow the moral rules of the society. If everyone does so, many conflicts can be avoided.

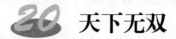

20 天下无双

信陵君魏无忌窃符救赵后,怕哥哥魏王追究,避居赵国。

他听说毛公和薛公很有才能,便去邀请,但两人不肯来见。

他打听到毛公藏在赌徒中,薛公藏在卖酒人家,便去寻访,终于结识了两人。

平原君知道后,说:"以前听说信陵君为人天下无双,今天看来他行为荒唐,徒有虚名!"

信陵君说:"既然平原君耻笑我,那我该离开这儿了。"

平原君知道说错了话,向信陵君谢罪。信陵君名望更大了。

这时秦国出兵攻魏。魏王派人请信陵君回国。

信陵君怕魏王追究他的窃符之罪,不肯回国,并告诫下人:"谁为魏王使者通报,处死!"

只有毛、薛两人冒死进言:"秦灭了魏,公子国破家亡,怎么见天下人?"信陵君立即省悟。

信陵君回到魏国,魏王把上将军的印信授给他。

信陵君率齐、魏等六国兵将,大破秦军,威震天下,被誉"天下无双"。

后人就用"天下无双"做成语,形容出类拔萃,独一无二。

青年人要学习信陵君,做一个出类拔萃,善于听取意见的人。

Unparalleled in the World

After sealing the tally to save Zhao State, Wei Wuji, Lord of Xinling, feared that his elder brother, the King of Wei State, would look into his crime, so he hid himself and stayed in Zhao State.

He heard that the reverend Mr. Mao and Mr. Xue were very capable, and sent his men to invite them to his place, but they two refused.

He inquired about the two men and got news that Mr. Mao hid himself among the gamblers, and Mr. Xue hid in an alcohol shop. So he went to look for them and at last he got to know them.

Lord Pingyuan was told the news and he commented, "I have heard before that Lord Xinling's behaviour is unparalleled in the world, but now I consider that his behaviour is stupid enough, and he has all his goods in the window."

Lord Xinling said, "Now that Lord Pingyuan looks down upon and sneers at me, I think it is time for me to leave."

Lord Pingyuan knew that he had said wrong words, so he apologized to Lord Xinling, and Lord Xinling had a greater reputation.

At that time, the King of Qin State dispatched troops to attack Wei State, so the King of Wei State sent a messenger to invite Lord Xinling to return.

But Lord Xinling was afraid that the King of Wei State would look into his crime of stealing the tally, so he refused to return and warned his understrappers, "Those who report to me the request of an interview for the messenger of Wei State, will be killed right away."

Only two men, the reverend Mr. Mao and Mr. Xue, took the risk of death and advised him, "If the Qin troops destroyed Wei State, you would lose both your home and your motherland. How could you face the people under the sun?" Lord of Xinling became aware immediately.

When Lord Xinling returned to Wei State, the king conferred him the general commander's official seal.

Lord Xinling commanded the allied army of six states, such as Qi, Wei, etc, and defeated the Qin troops seriously. And he became well-known, and praised as "Unparalleled in the World".

Later people began to use "Unparalleled in the World" as an idiom to indicate that a person is outstanding and supereminent, in a class by oneself.

Young people should learn from Lord Xinling and behave as an outstanding person who is good at listening to different opinions.

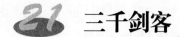

三千剑客

战国时期，赵国的赵惠文王喜爱剑术，所以门下养有善剑术的门客三千多人。他们日夜在宫中互相搏击不休，每年死伤的有一百多人，但是赵惠文王仍然乐此不疲。赵国人都去练剑，没有人从事生产，国力受到了影响。

直到有一天，太子派人请庄子来到宫中劝说，赵惠文王才戒掉了这个癖好。

现在我们通常用这个典故来比喻手下兵将多或者是门客多。

我们可以有自己的业余爱好，但不能沉溺其中，玩得不能自控有害无益。

Three Thousand Swordsmen

During the Warring States Period, King Huiwen of Zhao State was very fond of fencing, and supported more than three thousand swordsmen who were good at fencing. They fought with each other in the palace day and night, with a result of more than a hundred killed and injured every year. But King Huiwen was still keen on it. Because of that, many people of Zhao State were busy practicing fencing skills, and few cared for farming and production; therefore, the nation's power was influenced.

It was not until one day when the prince dispatched someone to invite Zhuangzi to the palace to persuade the king that he gave up such a hobby.

Now, we usually use this idiom to indicate that one has a large number of soldiers or the retainers.

We can keep our own hobbies, but should not indulge in them. If we can't control ourselves, these hobbies will bring us more harm than benefit.

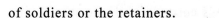 董狐之笔

晋灵公继位后，十分荒淫而骄横，他常站在楼上，用弹弓射路上的行人，让身边的美人取乐。有一次厨师煮熊掌不合口味，晋灵公便把厨师杀了，并命人分尸八块，用竹篓装了抛尸荒野。

相国赵盾（赵国君王的先人）对这些肆无法纪的行为非常愤慨，屡次向晋灵公苦苦进谏。晋灵公不但不听，还怀恨在心，要秘密除掉赵盾。

赵盾闻讯，逃亡避难。赵盾的侄儿赵穿早已看清了晋灵公的腐败本质，趁他酒醉时将他杀死。之后，赵穿立晋成公为国君，赵盾复任相国。由于赵盾精明强干，得到朝野的普遍赞誉。

史官董狐却持有不同意见，他毫不隐瞒地在史简中写道："赵盾杀其君。"

赵盾见后极为震惊，去找董狐解释自己并无杀君之罪。董狐坚持说："你身居相位，国君被杀时虽然离开了都城，但并未走出国境；国君被杀后，你也没有查办凶手，杀君罪名国相不负，当属何人？"

后来，孔子听到了这件事，他评论道："'董狐，古之良史也，书法不隐。'应受到称赞；赵盾也是'古之良大夫也，为法受恶，'实属冤枉。"

从此，后人便把"董狐之笔"这个典故作为史家秉公直书的典范加以颂扬。

青年人应该做一个正直的人，对社会上的一些不正之风要敢于揭露和批判。

Dong Hu's Brush Pen

After Linggong of Jin State succeeded to the throne, he became very incontinent and overbearing. He often stood on the building and shot the passersby with a slingshot for his beauties' pleasure. Once the bear's paws cooked was not to his taste. As a result, he gave orders to kill the cook.

What's more, under his command, the cook's corpse was dismembered into eight pieces and afterwards it was put in a bamboo basket and abandoned in the wilderness.

The Prime Minister, Zhao Dun (the forefather of the kings of the Zhao State), was very indignant at his unscrupulous behaviour. He frequently admonished Linggong, but the king didn't follow his advice, instead, he accumulated resentment in his mind and planed to get rid of Zhao Dun secretly.

Hearing that, Zhao Dun fled. Zhao Dun's nephew, Zhao Chuan had already seen through Linggong's corrupt nature, and one day killed Linggong when he was drunk. Later on, Zhao Chuan enthroned King Chenggong of Jin State, and Zhao Dun became the Prime Minister again. Because Zhao Dun was intelligent and capable, he won praises from the government to the public. However, Dong Hu, the historiographer, held a different idea. He wrote openly in the historical record, "Zhao Dun murdered his king."

Reading that, Zhao Dun was astounded. He hastened to Dong Hu and explained he didn't commit the crime of regicide. Dong Hu persisted, "As the Prime Minister, although you left the capital, at the moment the King was murdered, you were still within the border. After the King was killed, you didn't investigate into the case and penalize the murderer. Except you, who should bear the accusation of regicide?"

Subsequently, learning of this event, Confucius commented, "Dong Hu, an excellent historiographer in ancient times, recorded events truly in historical record, deserved praise. Zhao Dun was also an outstanding minister in old days, but took the blame for the fault of others because of the law. He was wronged really."

Ever since then, people set Dong Hu's characters of being true to facts as a model to praise.

Young people are supposed to be upright. They should reveal and struggle against the immoral and dishonest ways and customs in the society.

贤士篇

23 一狐之腋

战国时期，周舍是赵简子的臣子。有一次，他在赵简子的门口站了三天三夜，等候接见。赵简子派人问周舍："你这样坚决地要见我，到底是为了何事？"

周舍回答说："我很想做一个行事正直、敢于直谏的人，能够经常拿着笔墨和木牍跟随在您的左右，看到您犯了过错就把它记下来。如果每天记录下来并且时刻提醒您改正，那么，一月下来就有所收获，一年下来成效就更大了。"

赵简子听了很高兴，他立刻答应了周舍的请求。从此以后，赵简子就和周舍住在一起，出门也把他带在身边，以便有了过错后，周舍能够及时提醒他改正。

哪知没过多久，周舍死了，赵简子十分悲痛。一次，赵简子和诸位大夫在洪波台饮酒。赵简子喝得酩酊大醉，流下了眼泪。

大夫们都吓得离开座位走过去，他们说："我们不知犯了何罪？"

赵简子说："你们都没有犯什么罪过，只是我记起了我的朋友周舍从前说过的话，他说：'一千只羊的皮加起来，抵不上一只狐狸腋下的皮毛价值高；许多人俯首帖耳、唯唯诺诺，抵不上一个正直之人的直言相谏的益处大。从前商纣王因昏聩无能而灭亡，周武王却因光明正大而昌盛起来。'自从周舍死后，我就再也没有听到过有人当面指出我的过错，并提醒我改正，看来我的灭亡日子不太远了，因此我才伤心而流泪啊。"

"一狐之腋"这个典故原意是指一只狐狸腋下的皮毛，现多用来比喻珍贵的事物。

忠言逆耳，那些能够当面指出你的过错的人往往是最值得结交的朋友。

The Armpit Underfur of a Fox

During the Warring States Period，Zhou She was an official under the ruler Zhao Jianzi. He once stood at the doorway of Zhao Jianzi's mansion for three days and nights in order to be given an interview. Hearing that, Zhao Jianzi sent a servant to ask Zhou She, "What on earth is the reason that you insist on calling on me?"

Zhou She answered, "I am eager to be a righteous and outspoken man, who will frequently follow you with a pen, ink and wooden tablet in hand, and who will write it down when you make a mistake. If the man persists in writing down the mistakes every day and remind you to correct them at any moment, then after a month, you will make gains. After a year, the effect will be more remarkable."

Hearing that, Zhao Jianzi was delighted. He agreed to Zhou She's request immediately. Ever since then, they lived under the same eaves. When Zhao Jianzi went on a journey, Zhou She was accompanied so as to remind him to correct mistakes in time in case he made any.

Beyond expectation, before long, Zhou She died. Zhao Jianzi was as sad as he lost his son. One day, Zhao Jianzi drank with his ministers on Hongbo Platform. Zhao Jianzi was on the fuddle and shed tears.

The ministers were frightened by this scene. They left their seats, walked forward and asked, "Your majesty, did we commit any kind of crime?"

"No, you didn't." Zhao Jianzi replied, "I just thought of the words said by my friend Zhou She. He said, 'The value of a thousand goat skins is inferior to that of a fox's armpit underfur; the benefit of numerous people's obsequiousness is inferior to that of a righteous man's plainspokenness. Formerly, due to the fatuousness of King Zhou, the Shang Dynasty perished; in contrast, owing to the fairness of King Wu, the Zhou Dynasty came to prosper.' Since Zhou She passed away, I have never heard anyone who pointed out my mistakes to my face and reminded me to correct them. It seems that my perdition day will not be long. That's the reason why I am so sad and shed tears."

The original meaning of the idiom "The Armpit Underfur of a Fox" is the skin under the fox's armpit. Today, this is a metaphor for something very precious.

Good advice may sound harsh to ears. People who dare to point out your faults face to face are true friends.

24. 一日千里

战国时期，燕国太子丹在赵国做人质时，与同在赵国、尚未做秦王的嬴政相处良好。

后来，嬴政回国做了秦王，太子丹又在秦国做人质，嬴政不但没有顾念旧情、加以特别照顾，反而处处冷待、刁难他，太子丹见此状况，便找了个机会，逃回了燕国。

回国后，太子丹一直耿耿于怀，想报复嬴政。但由于国小力薄，难以实现自己的复仇愿望。

不久，秦国出兵攻打齐、楚、韩、魏、赵等国家，渐渐逼近了燕国。

燕国国君害怕极了，太子丹也忧愁万分，就向他的老师鞠武求教能够阻挡秦国侵吞的好办法。鞠武说："我有一个好朋友，名叫田光，他很机智，有谋略，你可跟他商讨一下。"

田光被请来了，太子丹非常恭敬地招待了他，并说："希望先生能替我们想个办法，抵挡秦国的侵吞。"

田光听了，一言不发，拉着太子丹的手走到门外，指着拴在大树旁的马说："这是一匹良种马。在壮年时，一天可以跑千里以上，等到它衰老时，劣马都可以跑在它的前面。您说这是为什么呢？"

太子丹说："那是因为它精力不行了。"

"对呀！现在您听说的关于我的情况，都还是我壮年的事，您不知道我已年老了，精力不行了。"

田光停了停又接着说："虽然有关国家的大事我已无能为力，但我愿向您推荐一个人，我的好朋友荆轲，他能够承担这个重任。"

后来，太子丹结交了荆轲，派去行刺秦王，但最后行刺以失败告终。

"一日千里"这个典故指马跑得很快，一天能跑一千里，现在形容人进步很快或事业发展极其迅速。

一日千里只是美好的愿望，做人做事还是要脚踏实地。只有一步一个脚印，才能水到渠成。

A Thousand Li a Day

During the Warring States Period, Prince Dan of Yan State was a hostage in Zhao State, who got along well with Prince Ying Zheng, another hostage before becoming the King of Qin State.

Later, Ying Zheng went back to his state and was made the king while Prince Dan became a hostage in Qin State. Ying Zheng did not keep their old friendship in mind and look after him, but disfavored and created difficulties for him regularly. Owing to this, Prince Dan sought a chance and fled to Yan State.

After he returned, Dan brooded on the hatred and always wished to revenge on Ying Zheng, but his dream could not come true because Yan State was not large and powerful enough.

Soon Ying Zheng dispatched troops to attack Qi State, Chu State, Han State, Wei State and Zhao State, and then Qin troops came nearer and nearer to the borders of Yan State.

The King of Yan was scared. Prince Dan was also deeply worried, so he went to his teacher Ju Wu for an idea to prevent Qin's annexation. Ju Wu told him, "I have a good friend named Tian Guang who was intelligent and full of strategies. You may consult him."

Tian Guang was invited into the palace. Prince Dan entertained him politely and said, "I hope you can consider an idea for us to prevent Qin's annexation."

Tian Guang listened and kept silent, then he held Dan's hand and walked outdoors, pointed at a horse tied to a tree and said, "This is an excellent steed. When it is in the prime of its life, it can run over a thousand li in a day; but when it goes old, even bad horses could run ahead of it. Can you tell me why?"

Dan said, "Because its energy declined."

"Right. What you have heard of me happened when I was in my prime. But now I am too old and my energy has declined."

贤士篇

Tian Guang paused and then went on, "I cannot help you much with the national affairs, but I am willing to recommend to you my good friend Jing Ke who can take on the important tasks."

Later Prince Dan consorted with Jing Ke and dispatched him to assassinate Ying Zheng, the King of Qin State, but failed at last.

The idiom "A Thousand Li a Day" means that a horse runs very fast and can run a thousand li a day. Now we use it to mean that a person makes progress at a tremendous pace or his enterprise develops rapidly.

A thousand li a day is only a tempting expectation. People should be practical and do things step by step. Success will come when conditions are ripe.

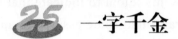

25 一字千金

战国末年，在阳翟有个大商人，名叫吕不韦。有一次他在赵国的都城邯郸，遇见了作为人质关在赵国的秦国公子子楚。他认为这是一个升官发财的好机会，便施展计谋，把子楚救出赵国，送回秦国。后来子楚作了国王，就封吕不韦作丞相，以报答他的恩情。

吕不韦权大势大，光是封地就有蓝田十二县、洛阳十万户。他为了树立自己的威信，命令门下的儒生、宾客，编写《吕氏春秋》，这部书有二十六卷，一百六十篇文章。这部书编写完毕，吕不韦下令把它贴在咸阳城门上，并且发出布告：如果有谁能够把它增加一个字，或者减去一个字，就赏他一千金。

我们后来使用这个成语来形容文字价值极高，赞扬别人的文章写得好，文辞精彩、奇妙。

我们无论学习或工作都应该有一种认真的态度，鼓励别人随时纠正自己的错误。

One Word Worth a Thousand Taels of Gold

At the end of the Warring States Period, there was a rich merchant named LuBuwei living in Yangzhai. He once happened to meet Zi Chu, the prince of Qin State who was held as a hostage in the capital of Zhao State,

Handan. He considered it a good chance to grab power and wealth, so he used some stratagems to help Zi Chu escape from Zhao and return to Qin. Later on, Zi Chu became the King of Qin State. He conferred the title of prime minister to Lu Buwei so as to reward his favor.

Lu Buwei was very puissant and powerful. He had the fiefdom of twelve counties in Lantian and one hundred thousand families in Luoyang. In order to establish his prestige, he organized scholars and guests in his house to compile a book "Spring and Autumn by Lushi" which contained twenty-six volumes, one hundred and sixty essays. When the book was finished, Lu Buwei ordered his men to stick it on the gates of Xianyang, the capital of Qin. He also announced that if anyone could add or delete a word, he would award him a thousand pieces of gold.

Later on, people use this idiom to indicate that the language of an essay is very valuable, or to praise that some essays are appropriate and wonderful with beautiful diction.

We should be serious and encourage others to correct our mistakes no matter in work or study.

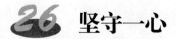

坚守一心

赵国大臣李兑预感到赵惠文王的两个儿子要为王位而同室操戈、刀枪相对。公子赵章与手下田不礼,兵力强壮而骄横,有可能会不顾利害。

他因此劝宰相肥义称病不出,把政事交给公子成。

肥义不同意,说:"我的话已说在前头了,我要保全我的诺言,哪能保全我的身体!况且坚贞之臣,灾难临头才操节显现,忠诚之臣,大祸来到才德行彰明。"

我们通常用这个典故来比喻对国家、民族忠贞不渝的气节。

这个典故给我们的启示是:在国家最需要我们的时候,我们要勇于为祖国和人民的事业贡献自己的一切。

Serving the Country Wholeheartedly

Li Dui, the minister of Zhao State, had a premonition that the two princes of King Huiwen of Zhao would start an internal strife for the throne. Prince Zhao Zhang and his subordinate Tian Buli were arrogant and had strong military strength. They might fight regardless of the benefit and the calamity.

He therefore advised the Prime Minister Fei Yi to ask a sickness leave and let Prince Chen to conduct the public affairs.

Fei Yi did not agree and said, "I have promised earlier and I must remain true to my commitment. How could I only consider preserving my body? Faithful officials will unfold their good conducts in face of disaster and loyal officials will show their virtues in face of catastrophes."

We often use this idiom to indicate people's faith and loyalty toward their country and nation.

It tells us that we must be ready to contribute ourselves to our motherland and its people whenever we are needed.

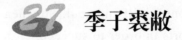
27 季子裘敝

战国时期，说客苏秦将入秦，他想劝说秦惠王实施"连横"之策略对付其他的诸侯国。

在赵国的时候，赵国奉阳君李兑曾经送与他"明月之珠、和氏之璧、黑貂之裘、黄金百镒。"

到秦国后，苏秦游说秦王的奏章上了十次，游说还是没有成功。李兑送给他的黑貂皮衣服也穿破了，百斤的黄金也用光了，一切费用都没有了，只好垂头丧气地离开了秦国。

我们用这个成语来比喻破衣烂衫，表示奔波劳碌、贫穷疲惫之态。后来多以此表示怀才不遇。

这个典故给我们的启示是：每一个人在自己的一生中，都会遇到困难和艰辛，而这个时候也正是考验自己的灵魂和意志的时候。所以我们在遇到困难或陷入困境之时，一定要继续努力，顽强拼搏，才能取得最后的成功。

Jizi in Poor Clothing

During the Warring States Period, Su Qin, a persuasive speaker, planned to enter Qin State. He wanted to persuade King Hui of Qin to implement the strategy of "Horizontal Alliance" to deal with other countries.

In Zhao State, Li Dui, Lord of Feng Yang, presented to him "pearl of the bright moonlight, Jade of Heshi, garment of sable fur, and gold of a hundred Yi."

When he arrived in Qin State, he failed to persuade the King after ten times of offering the memorial to the throne for support. He had worn out the garment of sable fur and used up all the gold, so he had to leave Qin dejectedly.

We often use this idiom to indicate the state of being ragged, tired, poor and exhausted. Later, we employ it to indicate the condition of having genius unrecognized.

It tells us that everyone will meet difficulties or hardships in our life and it is a good test to one's will and soul. So when falling into trouble, we should make greater efforts in order to succeed.

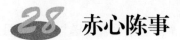

赤心陈事

王莽的新朝灭亡后，刘秀奉命领兵平定河北的豪强势力。平定了在河北南部称天子的王郎后，刘秀住在邯郸，白天在温名殿休息。

大将耿弇得空求见，他说，"如今更始政治败坏，君臣淫乱。听说更始皇帝的使者从西边来了，想要您交出兵权，千万不可以服从。我愿意回幽州，多发精兵，从长计议。"

刘秀坐起来说:"你要说话不算数,我杀了你。"

耿弇说:"大王你待我就像父亲对待儿子一样,所以我才把自己的心剖开,真心实意为大王运筹谋划。"

刘秀说:"刚才我是对你开玩笑。"

我们用这个典故比喻非常真诚地述说。

这个典故给我们的启示是:我们如果想在事业或工作上有所建树,与他人相处时应该做到和谐、真诚、互信、互敬、互爱。

To Give an Account Genuinely

After the destruction of Xin Dynasty of the regent Wang Mang, Liu Xiu led the troops under orders to suppress the despots in Hebei. After defeating Wang Lang who called himself the King in the south of Hebei, Liu Xiu lived in Handan. In the daytime, he had a rest in the Wenming Hall.

One day, the general Geng Yan paid a visit to him, and said, "Nowadays, under the rule of King Gengshi, the politics was very corrupted and both the emperor and the ministers were loose in morals. It was said that the envoy of King Gengshi came from the west to ask you to hand over the military power. You mustn't obey him. I would like to return to Youzhou and recruit more picked men. We can give the matter further thought and discuss it later."

Liu Xiu sat up and said, "If you go back on your word, I will kill you."

Geng Yan said, "Your Majesty, the way you treat me is just like a father to his son. So I opened up my heart and gave an account of the plans genuinely and sincerely to you."

Liu Xiu said, "Just now I was just kidding."

This idiom means narrating something genuinely and sincerely.

It tells us that if we want to make success in our career or study, we should a relationship of harmony, honesty, mutual trust, respect and love with others.

疾风劲草

王霸是西汉末年颍阳人。刘秀起兵路过颍阳时,王霸和一帮朋友前去投奔。

入伍后王霸忠心耿耿,多次打胜仗。因为在昆阳大破王莽军队的战役中,立了大功,王霸受到刘秀的信任。

刘秀的部队渡过黄河,在河北邯郸和王郎作战时,遭到了重大挫折。

王郎重金悬赏捉拿刘秀,形势很危急。

这时王霸的朋友们都悄悄溜走了,只剩下王霸。刘秀对王霸说:"在颍阳投奔我的人现在都走了,只剩下你一人留下来了,真是疾风知劲草啊!"

后来刘秀得了天下,封王霸为偏将军,始终都很器重他。

"疾风劲草"比喻在重大考验面前不变心。

这个典故给我们的启示是:我们要忠于祖国、忠于人民,在祖国需要时要勇于成为疾风劲草。

Only High Wind Knows the Sturdy Grass

Wang Ba was from Yingyang Prefecture in the end of the West Han Dynasty. When Liu Xiu rose up and rebelled against the government, his troops passed Yingyang Prefecture and Wang Ba joined in the troops with a group of his friends.

In the army, Wang Ba was loyal and devoted, and he won many battles. In the famous Kunyang Campaign, Liu Xiu led his troops against Emperor Wang Mang's main army and defeated it completely. And Wang Ba made great achievements in the campaign and he won Liu Xiu's trust from then on.

Later Liu Xiu led his army across the Yellow River and fought Wang Lang in Handan, Hebei Province, but he met with tremendous setback and failures in his military operations.

Wang Lang offered a great reward for catching or killing Liu Xiu, and the situation was terribly dangerous.

At that time, all of Wang Ba's friends escaped from Liu Xiu's army silently, but only Wang Ba stayed there. So Liu Xiu said to him, "All those who followed me and joined my army in Yingyang Prefecture have left me except you. It is indeed that 'Only the High Wind Knows the Sturdy Grass'!"

Later when Liu Xiu conquered the whole country and became the emperor, he made Wang Ba a side general and always regarded him highly.

Now we use "Only High Wind Knows the Sturdy Grass" to indicate that one person never changes his belief in the face of important trials.

It tells us that we must be loyal to our motherland and people. And we must become the "sturdy grass in high wind" when we are needed.

 乐此不疲

西汉末年，王莽废除刘氏皇帝，建立了新朝，引起天下大乱。各地农民纷纷举行起义，共同讨伐王莽。刘秀在与王莽的政府军的多次战役中，屡立战功，因功勋卓著而被刘玄封为"萧王"。

后来，刘秀被派往河北去平定各地的豪强势力。刘秀与另一草莽英雄邯郸人王郎曾在今河北省中南部的滹沱河、滏阳河流域交战多年，最终艰难取胜，平定了河北，有了自己的根据地，后来扫荡群雄，登上皇位。

刘秀看到，经过多年的兵灾和战乱，百姓迫切需要休养生息。于是他废除苛法，精简官吏，兴修水利，发展生产，使天下逐渐兴盛起来。

刘秀六十多岁时还勤于政事，天不亮就坐朝，到日落才回宫。

皇太子劝他注意身体，不要过度劳累。他摇摇头，答道："我乐于这样，不感到疲倦。"

这个典故形容对某一事物特别爱好，沉浸其中，不知疲倦。

这个典故给我们的启示是：青年人如果在学习和工作上能够做到乐此不疲，那么你的成功就指日可待了。

Always Enjoying It

In the late period of West Han Dynasty, Wang Mang dethroned the emperor of the Liu family and established New Dynasty. It caused a chaos in the country. The peasants from every part of the country rebelled and fought against Wang Mang. Liu Xiu performed meritorious deeds repeatedly in the campaigns against Wang Mang's troops. For his outstanding performance, Liu Xuan entitled him Lord Xiao.

Later, Liu Xiu was dispatched to crush the regional powers in Hebei. In the drainage area of Hutuo River and Fuyang river of Hebei, Liu Xiu fought for several years with Wang Lang, another uprising hero from Handan. Finally, Liu Xiu won the victory with great difficulty. He occupied Hebei as his own base area. Then Liu Xiu overwhelmed the rest of the warlords and became the emperor of East Han Dynasty.

Liu Xiu found that after many years of war and the chaos caused by it, the common people were eager to rehabilitate and live a peaceful life. Therefore he abolished the cruel laws, reduced the number of officials, built irrigation projects and developed production. Gradually he made the country prosperous.

In his sixties, Liu Xiu was still always busy with state affairs. He started working in court before dawn and returned after sunset.

The prince advised him to pay attention to his health and not to be excessively tired. But he shook his head and said, "I am enjoying it and do not feel tired."

We usually use this idiom to describe having interest in something specially, immersing into it without feeling fatigue or boredom.

It tells us that, if young people can always enjoy their study or work without feeling fatigue or boredom, they are sure to succeed.

31 鸱衔腐鼠

　　魏国的任城王曹彰,是魏武帝曹操的儿子,年轻刚毅,既学过阴阳占卜之术,又读过很多有关文韬武略的书。魏武帝想攻打吴国时曾咨询曹彰,以听取一些有利于用兵的策略。

　　曹彰善左右开弓射箭,好击剑,百步中能射中悬发。乐浪国献了一只老虎,身上斑纹很好看,用铁栏围着。一般的勇士不敢靠前,曹彰拽着虎尾巴绕在手臂上,虎却不叫不动,大家都佩服他的勇气。

　　当时,南越献了头白象,在武帝面前,曹彰用手敲打象鼻,大象便伏地不动。魏文帝曹丕铸了一口很大很重的钟,想放在崇华殿前,为了搬运,找了一百多名大力士,没拉动。曹彰却背起那钟走得很快。各国听说他这样神勇,都不敢轻举妄动。文帝说,若是用任城王曹彰领兵吞并吴蜀,就像猫头鹰叼个死老鼠一样简单。

　　我们现在用鸱衔腐鼠这个典故表示做事易如反掌。

An Owl Picking Up a Dead Mouse

　　Cao Zhang, King Rencheng, was the son of Cao Cao, Emperor Wu of Wei State. He was young and stouthearted. He not only learned augury but also read many books about the civil and military skills. When Emperor Wu of Wei State intended to attack Wu State, he ever consulted Cao Zhang to gain some tactical strategies.

　　Cao Zhang was good at shooting with both hands. He also did well in throwing sword. He could shoot a suspending hair in the distance of one hundred steps. One day, the state of Lelang offered a tiger as tribute. The tiger was surrounded by an iron fence and there were many beautiful stripes on it. The ordinary warriors dared not draw near while Cao Zhang could draw the tail of the tiger and wind it around his arm with the tiger not howling and moving. Everyone admired him for his courage.

In those days, the state of Nanyue offered a white elephant as tribute. In the presence of King Wu, Cao Zhang beat the nose of the elephant with his hand and consequently, the elephant lied still on the ground, face downwards.

Cao Pi, Emperor Wen of Wei State, casted a very big and heavy bell. It was intended to be put in front of the Chonghua Hall. In order to transport it, more than one hundred strong men were sent to drag it but in vain. However, Cao Zhang carried it on his back and walked very fast. All the other states at that time dared not take reckless military actions after hearing about his courage. For this, Emperor Wen said, "if Cao Zhang, King Rencheng of Wei, is appointed to lead troops to swallow up Wu State and Shu State, it is just like an owl picking up a dead mouse."

Today this idiom indicates that handling affairs is as easy as turning one's hand over.

代笔捉刀

三国时期，魏武帝曹操将要召见来自匈奴的使者，他自己感到相貌丑陋，不足以威慑边远小国，于是派相貌威武的大臣崔季珪代替自己坐在正位，曹操扮成卫兵，拿刀站立一旁。

召见完毕，曹操使人悄悄地问匈奴使者："魏王怎么样？"

使者回答："魏王风雅有度，然而一旁捉刀的人，像是个真正的英雄。"

我们后来把代别人做文章叫捉刀，也可以比喻代人做事。

这个典故给我们的启示是：代笔捉刀之事在这个世界上简直俯比皆是，我们要像那位匈奴使者一样，明察秋毫，方能不受欺骗。

Taking a Knife on Behalf of Others

During the Period of Three States, Cao Cao, Emperor Wu of Wei, would summon the messenger from the Huns. He worried that his ugly appearance was insufficient to deter the remote small country, so he appointed Minister Cui Jigui, who had an imposing appearance, to replace him and sit on his normal place. Cao Cao dressed himself up as a guard, standing by with a sword.

After the meeting, Cao Cao sent an underling to ask the messenger in private, "What's your opinion on the King?"

The messenger answered, "the King was elegant and graceful, but the guard, who took a sword, was likely to be a true hero."

We later describe somebody who ghostwrites for other people as a person taking a sword; we can also use this idiom to describe somebody who does things on behalf of others.

It tells us that such tricks are very popular in this world. We must be perceptive of the slightest like the Hun messenger in order to avoid being cheated.

谋略篇

谋 略 篇

按兵不动

春秋时期，卫国是一个弱小的诸侯国，被迫听命于晋国，为摆脱这种地位，卫灵公与齐景公结盟，与晋国绝交。

晋卿赵鞅立即调集军队，打算袭击卫国都城帝丘，同时派遣大臣史默前去了解情况，并要他一个月内返回。

但是，史默没有按期返回。有人建议立即出兵，但赵鞅坚决不肯草率行事。

半年后，史默回来了，讲述了卫灵公激励国人反抗晋国情绪的办法。

卫灵公派大臣王孙贾向国人宣告说，晋国命令卫国，凡是有姐妹儿女的人家，都要抽出一个人送到晋国做人质，引起国内一片痛哭声和怒骂声。

他又让王孙贾抽选出一批宗室大夫的女儿，准备送往晋国。结果出发时，成千上万的百姓拦路阻挡，并愤怒地表示要和晋军血战到底，宁死不屈。

另外，孔子已经来到卫国，他的弟子子贡正在为卫国出谋划策。

最后史默说："现在卫国贤臣很多，民气旺盛，要想使用武力让它屈服，恐怕要付出极大的代价。"

赵鞅认为进兵的时机未到，于是下令军队按兵不动，等待时机。

这则成语表示军队暂不行动，以待时机，也表示接到任务后不愿行动。

这个成语给我们的启示是：我们在做出重大决策前，要深思熟虑，绝不能草率行事。

Immobilizing the Troops and Not Throwing Them into Battle

During the Spring and Autumn Period, Wei State, small and weak, was forced to be the puppet of its powerful neighbor, Jin State. In order to put a final end to the humiliating position, Duke Ling of Wei State, planned a new alliance with Duke Jing, the ruler of Qi State.

Hearing that, the minister of Jin State, Zhao Yang, mustered troops and planned to attack Diqiu, the capital of Wei State. At the same time, he sent an official, Shi Mo, to investigate Wei State, and instructed him to return with information within a month's time.

But Shi Mo did not return on time. Some people of Jin called for an immediate military attack against Wei State, but Zhao Yang resolutely refused to act in haste.

Half a year later, Shi Mo returned and described how Duke Ling raised his people's resistant emotion against Jin State. The Duke assigned his minister Wang Sungu to send a declaration to the people that Jin had claimed a son or a daughter from each family as hostages, and it aroused widespread cries and snarls.

Later he assigned Wang Sungu to choose a number of imperial clans' and officers' daughters, and prepared to send them to Jin. Finally, tens of thousands of Wei citizens blocked in the way, and they indignantly vowed to fight against the Jin troops until death instead of a humiliating surrender.

In addition, Confucius had arrived there, and at present his disciple Zi Gong was offering advice and strategies for Wei State.

Finally, Shi Mo said, "Now there are a lot of virtuous officials in Wei State, and the Wei citizens' resistant emotion against Jin is very powerful. If Jin declares war against Wei at this point, Jin will be sure to suffer severe damage."

Zhao Yang agreed. He thought that it was not the time to attack Wei. So he decided to postpone military action and to wait for a more opportune moment.

This idiom means immobilizing the troops temporarily to wait for a more opportune moment. It can also express the hesitation to take action after an order has been given.

It tells us that we must keep a stiff upper lip before we make a great decision and never be imprudent.

谋 略 篇

百发百中

苏厉,是战国时期从事政治外交活动的谋士,听说秦国大将白起要统兵攻打魏国的都城大梁。而大梁一旦被攻占,附近的西周王室就会有危险。于是,他对周王说:"白起这几年打败过韩赵等国,夺取了大量土地。现在大梁一旦被攻占,周王室就会有危险,应该阻止白起出兵。"

于是,周王派苏厉前往秦国。苏厉对白起说:"从前楚国有一个叫养由基的射箭能手,距离柳树一百步,每箭都能射中柳叶的中心,百发百中,人人称赞。但是却有一个过路人说可以教养由基怎样射箭,养由基心中不悦,便让那人也来射柳叶。那人却说:'我无法教你射箭的本领,却要告诉你一点:你固然射柳叶百发百中,但却不善于休息,等一会儿一箭射不中,就会前功尽弃。'"

"将军现在已经打败了韩赵等国,夺取了许多土地,功劳很大。但你这次前去进攻大梁,一旦不能取胜,同样会前功尽弃。你还是称病不去为好。"

白起没有被苏厉说动,他率兵攻打魏国,大获全胜,夺取了数十座城池。

这则成语表示箭无虚发,泛指射击技术高明,每发必中。也比喻对事情的预料有充分把握,从不失算。

A Hundred Shots, a Hundred Bull's-Eyes

Su Li, a counselor in politics and foreign affairs during the Warring States Period, heard that Bai Qi, the general of Qin State, planned to command troops to attack Daliang, the capital of Wei State. If Daliang were occupied by Bai, the imperial court of Western Zhou would be in danger. Thus, Su said to the King of Zhou, "In recent years, Bai Qi has defeated Han State, Zhao State and so on, and captured a large amount of land. Once Daliang were occupied, the imperial court of Western Zhou would be dangerous. Your Highness should stop Bai."

So the King of Zhou sent Su Li to Qin State. Su Li said to Bai Qi, "Once upon a time, there was an expert archer in Chu State called Yang Youji. He could make every shot hit the center of each willow leave in a distance of a hundred paces from a willow tree. Everyone praised his marksmanship highly. But a passerby said that he could teach Yang how to shoot. Unpleasantly, Yang asked him to shoot the willow leaves. However the passerby explained. 'I can not teach you how to shoot, but I can tell you that though you make every shot hit the target, but you don't know how to have a good rest. Once you miss one shot, all your previous efforts are wasted.'"

"Now you have defeated Han State, Zhao State and so on, occupied a great amount of land and made great achievements. But if you could not win when attacking Daliang, all your previous efforts would be wasted, too. You'd better claim to your king that you can not lead troops to attack Wei State because of illness."

But Bai Qi did not follow Su Li's words. He attacked Wei State, won the battle and captured dozens of cities.

This idiom means that every shot hits the target. It generally describes excellent marksmanship in shooting, and also indicates assurance and no wrong move.

抱薪救火

战国时期，魏国不断受到秦国的侵略。魏国的安釐王即位后，秦国进攻更猛，魏国连连战败，城池不断丢失，秦军直逼魏国都城大梁。韩国派兵来救援，也被秦军打败，魏王只能割地求和，才算结束了战争。

两年后，秦军再至，不但打败了魏国的军队，还把前来救援的韩国和赵国的军队也打得大败，三国联军损失十五万人。

面对这种形势，安釐王坐卧不安，而魏国的大将段干子也十分恐慌，便向魏王建议割让南阳给秦国，请求罢兵议和。安釐王也害怕秦军，认为割让土地就可以换得太平，于是便答应了这个请求。

苏秦的弟弟苏代,极力主张各诸侯国联合起来,共同抗秦。他得知安釐王割地求和的事后,便去见安釐王说:

"侵略者贪得无厌,您想这样用土地去换取和平,是办不到的。只要你的国土还在,就永远无法满足侵略者的欲望。好比抱着柴草去救火,不断把柴投入火中,火怎么能够扑灭呢?柴草不烧完,火永远不会灭。"

但是安釐王不肯听从苏代的话,仍然不断地割地求和,这样没过多少年,魏国终于被秦国吞并。

这个典故的意思是抱着柴草去救火。比喻人想消灭灾害,但是由于所用的方法不当,反而使灾害扩大变得更严重了。

这个典故给我们的启示是:我们在学习与工作当中,要注意采取正确的方式与方法,才能够对症下药,真正地解决问题。

Carrying Firewood to Put Out a Fire

During the Warring States Period, Wei State suffered continual invasion from Qin State. During the reign of King Anxi of Wei State, because of Qin's more furious invasion, Wei State met a series of defeats and lost one city after another. And Daliang, the capital of Wei State, was in great danger. Han State sent troops to rescue Wei State and also met a defeat. In order to end the war, the King of Wei had no choice but end the war in ceding lands to Qin.

Two years later, Qin troops arrived again. This time, not only Wei troops, but also Han and Zhao troops who came to rescue Wei State, were greatly defeated by Qin troops, totally 150,000 soldiers were lost.

Facing such a situation, King Anxi was ill at ease. General Duan Ganzi, also in great panic, proposed ceding Nanyang to Qin so as to end the war. Fearing the powerful Qin troops, King Anxi also thought that ceding land to Qin was a feasible way to make peace and agreed to the proposal.

Su Dai, Su Qin's younger brother, made every effort to advocate that the kingdoms should ally in order to fight against Qin. Hearing that King Anxi planned to cede land for peace, Su Dai went to persuade him,

"The invaders are always greedy. You will never succeed in obtaining peace by ceding land because as long as you grasp any land in your hand, it will be impossible to meet the invaders' desire. Just like carrying firewood to put out a fire, how could the fire be put out? The fire will never be put out before the firewood is completely exhausted."

But King Anxi turned a deaf ear to Su Dai's words. He continued to compromise with the invaders by ceding territory for peace. So not many years later, Wei State was finally annexed by Qin State.

This idiom means carrying firewood to put out a fire. It is used as a metaphor for a behavior of adopting the wrong method to exterminate the disaster but end up making it worse.

It tells us that we must adopt the right methods in our study and work. Only in this way can we suit the remedy to the case and solve the problems.

 不可同日而语

战国时期，诸侯之间战争不断，因而出现了"合纵"和"连横"的政治活动。弱国联合进攻强国称为"合纵"，随从强国去进攻其他弱国称为"连横"，苏秦就是最著名的鼓动家之一。他到秦国和赵国游说都没有成功，但在燕国却获得了一定的资助，于是再次来到赵国，得到了国君赵肃候的接见。

苏秦分析了天下的形势，说道：

"如果赵国与秦国和齐国两国为敌，则百姓无法安宁；如果依靠齐国去攻打秦国，百姓还是没有安宁。如果您和秦国和好，秦国就会利用这一优势去削弱韩国和魏国；如果和齐国和好，齐国也会利用这种优势去削弱楚国和魏国。韩国和魏国被削弱，就会割地求和，这也会使楚国削弱。这样，大王就会孤立无援。

其实太行山以东没有比赵国更强的国家，疆土纵横两千里，军队数十万，战车千乘，战马万匹，粮食可以支用数年。西、南、东有山水险阻，北边燕国弱小，形不成威胁。秦国其实最忌恨赵国，但为何不来攻打呢？因为害怕韩国和魏国在后面下手，所以他们是赵国的南部屏障。但是秦国攻打韩国和魏国却很方便，而

谋略篇

他们抵挡不住，就会屈服。秦国一旦解除了后顾之忧，战火就会降临赵国。这正是我为大王所忧虑的。

我考察发现各诸侯国的土地和起来五倍于秦国，兵力十倍于秦国。如果结为一个整体，就一定可以并力向西打败秦国。如今大家反而向秦国称臣，打败别人和被别人打败，让别人向自己称臣和自己向别人称臣，怎么可以同日而语呢？"

于是赵肃候听从了苏秦的建议，给了他许多赏赐，让他去游说各国加入合纵联盟。

这个典故的意思是不可以放在同一时间来谈论，不能相提并论或互相比较。

No Comparison between the Two

During the Warring States Period, wars happened frequently among the feudal lords, resulting in the political activities of "Longitudinal Union" and "Horizontal Association". The former means that weaker nations united together to attack the stronger ones; and the latter means the weaker nations associated with the stronger ones to attack other weaker powers. Su Qin was one of the most famous agitators. Though he failed to persuade Qin State and Zhao State to follow his "Longitudinal Union" strategy, he gained a certain amount of pecuniary aid from Yan State. So once again he went to Zhao State and was summoned by Su Hou, the ruler of the state.

Su Qin analyzed the whole situation for him, and then said, "If Zhao fights against Qi State or Qin State, your people will not be able to live in peace. If you ally with Qi to attack Qin, your people will also not be able to live in peace. If you keep a friendly relationship with Qin, Qin will take this advantage to weaken Han State and Wei State. Being friendly to Qi, Qi will also take this advantage to weaken Chu and Wei. On condition that Han and Wei are weakened, they will compromise by ceding their territories and become weaker. Then, your majesty will be cut off from any help.

With a territory stretching two thousand li in length and breadth, hundreds of thousands of soldiers, thousands of chariots and steeds, food available for several years, Zhao is no weaker than any other countries to the east of the Taihang Mountains actually. To the west, south and east, surrounding mountains and rivers protect Zhao; to the north, Yan is too weak to threaten Zhao. In fact, Qin hates Zhao mostly. But why does it not attack Zhao? That is due to Han and Wei who will attack it in the back. So Han and Wei serve as the southern barriers of Zhao. However, since Han and Wei are within easy reach of Qin, they will yield to Qin when they cannot resist. What I am concerned with is that once Qin gets its trouble back resolved; it will launch a war against Zhao.

I have observed that the total amount of the territories of all the vassals is five times as that of Qin, their troops ten times. Uniting as a whole, they are able to march to the west and defeat Qin. Yet nowadays, all states submit themselves to Qin. Defeating others and defeated by others, submitted by others and submitting to others, can they be compared with each other?"

Therefore, Su Hou followed Su Qin's advice and presented him a lot of largess, sending him to persuade other states to join the "Longitudinal Union".

This idiom means that different matters can neither be mentioned at the same time and be placed at the same level, nor be compared with each other.

出奇制胜

战国时，燕国大将乐毅联合了秦、赵、燕、魏、韩等国的军队一起伐齐。齐国大败，最后只剩下莒和即墨两座城池。

由于即墨大夫守城身亡，田单被推为统帅。田单懂兵法，有计谋，深得民心，所以即墨得以坚守了三年。田单知道，要想打败强大的燕国军队，光靠武力是不行的。所以他设计让人到燕国去散布谣言，说乐毅有野心。燕惠王对乐毅产生了怀疑，便用骑劫替换了他。

骑劫才能低下，而且为人凶残，燕国军士对他十分不满，因而士气变得低落。

田单见时机已到，一边散步天神助齐的流言，一边把精兵隐藏，让老弱妇女守城的同时派人拿许多金子向骑劫请降，使燕军放松了警惕。

谋略篇

田单收集了一千多头牛,给它们披上各种颜色的布,牛角上绑上尖刀,尾巴上绑上浸过油的芦苇。夜深人静之时,点上牛尾巴上的芦苇,让它们向燕军营寨猛冲,同时后面的五千精兵也发起了攻击。

燕军被怪兽吓破了胆,有的被踩死,有的被尖刀扎死,也有的被后面的齐军杀死。骑劫被活捉后处死,燕军大败,田单率军追击,很快收复了原来齐国失去的疆土。

这则成语的意思是在战斗中利用奇妙的战术和策略,令敌人无法预料,从而战胜敌人。

To Defeat the Opponent with a Surprising Action

During the Warring States Period, Yue Yi, senior general of Yan State, united the troops from Qin State, Zhao State, Yan State, Wei State and Han State, to attack Qi State. Qi was defeated greatly and only kept two cities, Ju and Jimo, in hand.

Because the governor of Jimo died in a defending battle, Tian Dan was appointed commander of the Qi troops to defend the city.

He had succeeded in defending Jimo for three years because of his mastery of military science and strategies as well as his popularity among the people. But Tian Dan understood that it was impossible to defeat the powerful Yan troops totally by using military force alone. So Tian Dan then spread the rumor that Yue Yi, was very ambitious and it worked. The King of Yan suspected Yue Yi and replaced him with Qi Jie. Qi Jie, who knew little about war, was a savage and cruel man. The Yan soldiers were not satisfied with him. Needless to say, the soldiers' morale lowered.

Aware of this situation, Tian Dan felt it was the right time to counterattack. On the one hand, Tian Dan spread the rumor that the Heaven would bless Qi State. On the other hand, he hid all his best troops and sent the old and weak ones to guard the city with women. At the same time, he sent some people to Qi Jie with gold and bribed him to spare their lives if the Yan troops took over the city. All this lulled the Yan troops into a false sense of confidence.

Then Tian Dan gathered more than 1,000 oxen covered with cloth in various colors. Long, sharp knives were tied to their horns, and reeds soaked in oil to their tails. At midnight, Tian Dan's soldiers lit the reeds and drove all the oxen toward the Yan camps. And at the same time, Tian Dan's five thousand best soldiers launched a furious attack.

The Yan troops were terrified by the strange beasts, some trampled to death, some stabbed by sharp knives and some killed by the attackers. Qi Jie was captured and then sentenced to death. The Yan troops were greatly defeated and Tian Dan's army chased them and reoccupied the territory lost before.

This idiom means defeating the enemy in the war with unexpected and wonderful tactics and strategies.

6 推心置腹

西汉末年，王莽废除刘氏皇帝，建立了新朝，由于实行暴政，引起天下大乱。各地农民为了生存纷纷举行起义，各路豪杰共同讨伐王莽。公元23年初，刘玄被声势浩大的绿林农民起义军立为天子，刘秀被刘玄委任为偏将军。

王莽曾经多次派兵攻打刘玄的军队。在与王莽的政府军的多次战役中，刘秀屡立战功。在著名的"昆阳之战"中，绿林军一举歼灭了王莽军队的主力，奠定了推翻王莽的基础。刘秀因功勋卓著而被刘玄封为"萧王"。

后来，刘秀被派往河北去平定各地的豪强势力。刘秀与另一自称天子的邯郸人王郎曾在今河北省中南部的滹沱河、滏阳河流域交战多年，最终艰难取胜，平定了河北南部，有了自己的根据地，为后来扫荡群雄、登上皇位打下了基础。

公元24年秋，刘秀奉命率兵攻打铜马农民起义军，大破之，招降数十万人，封降兵的将领们以官职。但降者并不放心，担心刘秀是否出于真意。刘秀获悉这一情况后，为使其放心，便采用安抚之计，下令降者各归其本部，原来的将领继续统领其原来的兵马。刘秀本人则轻骑巡行各部，无丝毫戒备之意。这样一来，降者都开始相信刘秀，只听他们经常三三两两地在一起低语："萧王推己之红心，置他人之腹中，我们还担心什么？还能不为他打天下出死力吗？"

谋略篇

后人根据这段历史，将"推赤心置人腹中"句概括为"推心置腹"成语，以喻真心待人之意。

这个成语给我们的启示是：我们如果能够在为人处事时做到推心置腹，则会赢得别人对自己的信任与爱戴。

To Repose Full Confidence in People

In the end of West Han Dynasty, Wang Mang dethroned the emperor of the Liu Family. Then he became the emperor himself and set up his New Dynasty. However, because of his despotic rules, the whole country was in turmoil. The farmers, in order to survive, rebelled here and there. In the beginning of A.D.23, Liu Xuan was enthroned by the powerful peasant uprising troop called Lulin Army as emperor, and Liu Xiu was appointed as Junior General.

Wang Mang sent the government troops to attack Liu Xuan's army many times. Among the battles, Liu Xiu made great contributions. In the famous Kunyang Battle, the Lulin Army annihilated the main body of the enemy, which paved the way for overthrowing Wang Mang. So Liu Xiu was granted the title King Xiao.

After that, Liu Xiu was ordered to put down the local powers in Hebei. Liu Xiu fought with Wang Lang, another man who called himself emperor, in the fields between the rivers of Hutuo and Fuyang for years. At last, he won the hard battle, captured the south of Hebei as his base area which laid foundation for his later defeating the other powers and becoming the emperor.

In the fall of A.D. 24, Liu Xiu was sent to attack Tongma Army. He won a great victory and summoned tens of thousands enemies to surrender. Liu Xiu conferred official titles to the leaders who surrendered. But they were worried about if Liu Xiu treated them by heart. To convince them, Liu Xiu decided that the leaders could command their own soldiers and he inspected every camp with few guards, showing no alert. Those who surrendered started to believe in him and often whispered in small groups, "King Xiao takes out his own heart and put it into the other's chest. What should we worry about? Shouldn't we fight to death for him?

After that, people used "To Put One's Heart into the Other's Chest" to mean reposing full confidence in people.

It tells us that we must be good at dealing with others. If you can repose full confidence in others, you will get respect, love and esteem.

7 价值连城

由于秦昭襄王愿以十五座城换取"和氏璧",因此便有了"价值连城"这样一条成语。

"和氏璧"是以战国时期楚国一名樵夫的名字命名的。这位樵夫,名叫卞和,他有高超的识玉眼力。一天,卞和在荆山打柴时,发现了一块玉璞。他想,国库里缺宝少玉,空然如洗,为此,楚国常常受到列国诸侯的鄙视。那么,为何不把拾来的玉璞献给当今楚国的国君楚厉王呢?

谁知楚厉王有眼无珠,非但不奖赏卞和,还说卞和以石充玉欺骗君王,当即砍下了卞和的一只脚。

楚厉王死后,楚武王继位,卞和再次进殿献宝,谁知,由于鉴玉官从中作梗,二次献宝又没成功。这次卞和又被砍掉了另一只脚。

虽然失去了双脚,但卞和献宝之心仍未泯灭。当武王暴死文王继位后,卞和再一次踏上了去往郢都的路途。

楚文王果然是位有道明君,具有识玉的慧眼,当卞和献上玉璞之后,他一眼便认定这是块珍宝。经人稍加琢磨,玉璞便宝光四射,美妙无比。

楚文王为了表彰卞和三次冒死献宝的壮举,遂将此宝命名为"和氏璧"。

后来,"和氏璧"几经流传,落到了赵惠文王手里。秦昭襄王也想要这"和氏璧",便差人下书,愿以十五座城作为代价来换取和氏璧。这样一来,和氏璧的价值便昂贵起来。

现在人们用"价值连城"来形容物品十分贵重。

这个成语给我们的启示是:只要你有真正的价值,总有被人发现的时候。

A Jade Worth Cities

This idiom "A Jade worth Cities" derives from the story of King Zhaoxiang of Qin State wanted to get Jade of Heshi at the cost of 15 cities.

Jade of He Shi is named after Bian He, a woodchopper of Chu State of the Warring States Period. Bian He knew jades well. One day, when he was chopping wood on Jing Mountain, he found a raw jade. He knew the state treasury was almost empty, let alone jades, for which other states always looked down upon Chu on this respect. So he decided to dedicate this raw jade to the country, namely to King Li of Chu State.

He contributed it to King Li. But the King didn't appreciate it and said that Bian He cheated him by a stone to pretending to be a jade, not to say to reward him, and ordered to chop off one of Bian's feet.

After the death of King Li of Chu, King Wu succeeded the throne. Once again Bian He contributed the jade to the new King. This time the jade-appreciating official created some difficulties and the contribution failed again. Bian He was cut off the other foot.

Bian He still desired to contribute the jade to the country even though he lost his two feet. After the sudden death of King Wu, King Wen of Chu succeeded the throne. Bian He headed for Ying, the capital of Chu, to contribute the jade for the third time.

King Wen of Zhao was a real smart king and he knew jade well. As soon as Bian He showed the jade, the king recognized it was a real treasure at the first sight. After some carving and polishing, the jade was shining beautifully.

In order to reward Bian's brave behavior to dedicate the jade to the country, King Wen of Chu named the jade "Jade of Heshi".

As time flied, Jade of He Shi was passed down around and at last came to King Huiwen of Zhao. King Zhaoxiang of Qin wanted to get the jade too, so he sent a letter to King Huiwen of Zhao to say that he wanted to trade the jade with 15 cities. So the value of Jade of Heshi appeared extremely rocketing up.

Today, people use Jade of Heshi to express that something is valuable and priceless.

It indicates that college students will always be appreciated only if you have your real value.

8 完璧归赵

战国时期，赵国的赵惠文王得到了世间罕见的美玉"和氏璧"。秦国的秦昭襄王听说后，想将和氏璧据为己有，他写信给赵王，说愿意拿十五座城池交换和氏璧。

赵王明知这是秦王的诡计，想骗取美玉，可如果不给他，又怕他发兵进攻赵国。这件事弄得赵王很犯愁，一时拿不定主意。

正在赵王犹豫不决的时候，蔺相如来见赵王。请求送和氏璧到秦国去，"假如秦国把城池割给赵国，我就把玉留给秦国；若是他们不把城池给赵国，我再把玉带回来交给大王。"赵王没有别的办法，只好派蔺相如到秦国去献和氏璧。

蔺相如到秦国，进宫见了秦王，献上和氏璧。秦王双手捧着美玉，满心欢喜，早将交换城池的事情忘掉了。蔺相如看秦王并无诚意，便对秦王说："这块美玉有点小毛病，让我指给您看。"秦王信以为真，就把美玉交给蔺相如。蔺相如手捧美玉，背靠柱子，疾言厉色地说："我看您并不想交付十五座城池，所以把和氏璧拿了回来。您要是逼我，我的脑袋和美玉就一块儿撞碎在柱子上！"秦王怕损坏了美玉，连忙劝阻，答应过几日举行盛典，正式交换和氏璧。

蔺相如知道秦王又在设骗局，回到住处以后，他便将和氏璧交给随从亲信，偷偷地送回赵国去了。

到了举行典礼那天，蔺相如沉着地向秦王说："和氏璧已经送回赵国了，您如果有诚意，先把十五个城池交出来，我马上把和氏璧给您送来。不然的话，您即使杀我的头也无济于事。因为天下的人都知道秦国是从来不讲信义的！"秦王恼怒万分，但又毫无办法，只得放他回国。

因为蔺相如完璧归赵,立下了功劳,赵王封他为"上大夫"。

后来人们就用"完璧归赵"这句成语,比喻把原物完整无缺地归还本人。

这个成语给我们的启示是:我们要严守自己的承诺,如果不断做出承诺却不断食言的话,就会失去他人对自己的信任。

Returning the Jade Intact to Zhao State

During the Warring States Period, King Huiwen of Zhao State was fortunate enough to obtain a piece of very rare jade, named Jade of He Shi discovered by Bian He of Chu State. Hearing this and wishing to take possession of this jade, King Zhao of Qin State sent a letter to Zhao State, offering fifteen cities in exchange for the treasure.

Knowing that it's King Zhao's cunning trick, King Huiwen of Zhao immediately sought counsel with his generals and ministers, confessing that he was worried he might thus lose the jade for nothing if King Zhao of Qin broke his promise and refused to give Zhao the cities, and on the other hand, if he did not let the jade go, Qin might come to attack Zhao. This greatly troubled King Huiwen of Zhao. Much discussion went on, but the matter was not settled.

At that time, Lin Xiangru was recommended to the King. He told the King that he was willing to be the messenger and escort the jade to Qin. He promised that he would leave the jade in Qin if Qin really offered the cities to Zhao and he would take it back to the King if Qin tricked to possess the jade without offering the cities. King Huiwen of Zhao had no choice but dispatch Xiangru to Qin with the jade.

On arrival, Xiangru was received by the King of Qin in the palace. Xiangru offered the jade to the King of Qin who was greatly pleased when holding the jade in his hands. Seeing that the King of Qin had no intention of giving the promised cities to Zhao, Xiangru stepped forward and said, "The jade has flaws. Please let me show it to Your Highness." Without a shadow of doubt, the King of Qin handed the jade over to Xiangru, who, with the jade in hands, retreated a few steps to lean on a column, and in great fury rebuked the King's perfidy and addressed, "I guess that Your Highness doesn't want to offer the promised cities, so I take back the jade. If Your Highness chooses to put pressure on me to submit it, I will immediately knock both the jade and my head against this column, and smash both." Afraid that he was going to smash the jade, the King of Qin entreated Xiangru not to do so and promised to perform a solemn ceremony of reception in the main palace to exchange for the jade with the promised cities in an official way.

Noting that the King of Qin was only playing another trick, when coming back in the guesthouse, Xiangru ordered his trusted attendant to disguise himself as a commoner and return to Zhao with the jade by a short-cut.

On the day of the solemn ceremony, Xiangru said calmly to the King of Qin, "The Jade of He Shi has been sent back to Zhao. If Your Highness has great faith to offer the promised fifteen cities to Zhao first, I will submit the jade to Your Highness. Otherwise, it is of no avail even though my head is cut off. Qin is known by all to be lack of honesty and faith." Although he was raged, the King of Qin had no choice but let Xiangru back to Zhao.

Because of returning the jade intact to Zhao, a great meritorious deed to Zhao, Xiangru was entitled as the Senior Official of Zhao State.

Later, people usually use this idiom to refer to returning something to its owner perfectly intact.

It tells us that we must always keep our promises whenever we have made them. If you break them, you will lose your credit and trust from others.

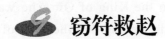

窃符救赵

战国时，秦国军队在白起率领下，在长平大破赵军，接着秦军包围并攻打赵国的都城邯郸。赵国向魏国求救，魏国派兵十万前去救赵。秦国听说魏国派兵救

谋 略 篇

赵一事，派人去魏国威胁魏王，魏王屈服于秦国，下令让前去救赵的魏兵统帅晋鄙按兵不动，坐观成败。

由于魏国公子信陵君的姐姐是赵惠文王的弟弟平原君赵胜的夫人，所以赵王和平原君不断向信陵君写信求救。信陵君无法说服魏王进兵，就准备率领自己的门客们与秦兵决一死战。

信陵君曾为魏王的宠妃如姬报了杀父之仇，因此信陵君请求如姬从魏王那里盗出了兵符，但兵营中的晋鄙却拒不从命，信陵君的随从朱亥用铁椎击死晋鄙，从而夺取了兵权。

信陵君统率了晋鄙的军队，约束兵士，下令军中说："父子都在军中的，父亲回去；兄弟都在军中的，哥哥回去；独子没有兄弟的，回家奉养父母。"他率领经过挑选的精兵八万人攻击秦军，秦军撤退了。于是救了邯郸，保存了赵国。

比喻用计谋达到目的，不正面交兵。

这个成语给我们的启示是：当我们面临困难时，我们是否可以采取一种迂回的方式来解决问题呢？

Stealing the Military Tally to Save Zhao State

During the Warring States Period, the army of Qin State, under the leadership of Bai Qi, soundly defeated the army of Zhao State in Changping. Then Qin's army surrounded and attacked Zhao's capital Handan. Zhao State prayed for rescue to Wei State. Under Zhao's request, Wei dispatched troops of one hundred thousand soldiers to go to save Zhao. When the King of Qin State heard of this news, he sent some messengers to Wei State to threaten the king. The King of Wei submitted and issued an order to Jin Bi, the commander of Wei's army which had been sent to rescue Zhao State, to stand by, wait and see which side wins.

Since the sister of Lord of Xinling, a nobleman in Wei, was the wife of Zhao Sheng, Lord of Pinyuan and he was also the younger brother of King Huiwen of Zhao State, the King of Zhao and Lord of Ping Yuan unceasingly wrote mails to pray for rescue to Lord of Xinling. Lord Xinling was unable to convince the king to save Zhao State, so he prepared to lead his own disciples to wage a life-and-death battle.

Lord of Xinling had revenged the death of Ru Ji's father on the murderer. Ru Ji was the favorite imperial concubine of the King of Wei. Lord of Xinling asked Ru Ji to steal the military tally from the king. However, Jin Bi, the commander of the army refused to obey their orders simply because of the military tally. Zhu Hai, an attendant of Lord of Xinling killed Jin Bi with an iron and won the military leadership.

Lord of Xinling commanded Jin Bi's army and issued an order, "If both father and son are all in the army, the father should go back home; if brothers are all in military service, elder brother should return; if one family's only son is in the troop, he should head back home to take care of his parents." He led eighty thousands elite soldiers to attack Qin troops and defeated them. Qin troops retreated. Handan was rescued and Zhao State was saved.

This idiom expresses the meaning of achieving—one's goal by wits and strategy instead of frontal attack.

When falling into trouble, shall we adopt a circuitous method?

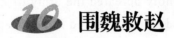

围魏救赵

战国时期，魏国大将庞涓领兵攻打赵国，包围了赵国的都城邯郸。赵王派人向齐国求救，请齐国出兵解围。

齐王任命田忌为大将，孙膑为军师，领兵援救赵国。

田忌打算直接去救邯郸，给赵国解围。孙膑却不赞成，他说："要解开乱丝，不能强拉硬扯；要劝解双方停止搏斗，不能进去帮打。现在魏军主力正在围攻邯郸，魏国内部一定空虚。如果我们直接去救邯郸，恐怕不等大军赶到，邯郸就被魏军攻下来了。我看不如率军攻打魏国的首都大梁。大梁受到威胁，庞涓必然从赵国撤兵来救，这样就给赵国解了围。另外，魏军攻打赵国已经很疲劳，再长途跋涉返回大梁，更加筋疲力尽。我军占领要地，以逸待劳，一定能够打败魏军。"

谋略篇

田忌很佩服孙膑的高见,就率领大军去攻打大梁。

魏将庞涓听说大梁危急,解除了对邯郸的包围,回兵救援大梁。魏兵退到桂陵的时候,田忌、孙膑指挥埋伏在深山峡谷中的齐兵,突然冲杀出来,把疲惫不堪的魏兵打得落花流水。庞涓在乱军中突围逃跑,魏军几乎全军覆没。齐军获得大胜,赵国得到了解救。

我们现在用它比喻在战争中避实击虚,迫使敌人撤兵,变被动为主动的战法。

这个成语给我们的启示是:我们正面解决问题无法成功时,可以转向对方的其他弱点进攻。

Besieging Wei to Rescue Zhao

During the Warring States Period, Pang Juan, General of Wei State, led his troops to attack Zhao State and besiege its capital Handan. Zhao State turned to Qi State for military help.

The King of Qi appointed Tian Ji as the Top General and Sun Bin as Military Counselor to lead the Qi troops to rescue Zhao.

Tian planned to rescue Handan and save Zhao directly, but Sun disagreed. Sun said, "You'd better not pull toughly when undoing a thread knot; you'd better not help fighting when persuading two parties to stop. The main force of the Wei troops is besieging Handan and Wei State must be empty and weak. Now if we march directly to rescue Handan, it's sure that Handan has been occupied by the Wei troops before our arrival. It's much better for us to attack Wei's capital Daliang. Once Daliang is in great danger, Pang Juan must retreat his troops from Zhao to rescue Wei. Thus, Zhao will be out of danger. What's more, the Wei troops are very exhausted when attacking Zhao; after a long and hard march back to rescue Daliang in haste, they must be more exhausted. If we occupy the strategically important places and wait at our ease for the greatly exhausted Wei troops, I am sure we can defeat them completely."

Tian admired Sun for his excellent idea and led his troops to attack Daliang.

Hearing that Daliang was in great danger, Pang Juan removed the siege to Handan and withdrew withdrew his troops in haste to rescue Daliang. When the Wei troops reached Guiling, Tian and Sun commanded the Qi troops hiding in deep valleys to ambush the Wei troops. The greatly exhausted Wei troops were heavily defeated, nearly all destroyed, and Pang Juan escaped fortunately. The Qi troops won a great victory and Zhao State was out of danger.

Now we use this idiom to describe a strategy in a battle, which emphasizes avoiding the vital points and dwelling on trivialities or turning passivity into initiative.

It tells us that we should attack the weak points of our opponents when we cannot solve a problem directly.

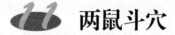

两鼠斗穴

赵惠文王二十九年（公元前270年）秦国派大军攻打韩国，韩国是赵国的西邻，而且秦国军队在这次的军事行动中还包围了赵国的重要边境城池阏与。阏与如果被秦军占领，赵国则会失去天险，处于危险的境地。

赵惠文王就战事问计于群臣，大将廉颇和乐乘都说"道远险狭，难救。"而赵奢却说："其道险狭，譬之有两鼠斗之于穴中，将勇者胜。"

赵惠文王认为赵奢的话有道理，于是封赵奢为大将，领大军前去解围。赵奢率赵军先是慢行军使秦军麻痹，后急行军赶至阏与，居高临下，然后突然向骄横的秦军发起攻击，大败秦军，顺利地解了阏与之围，从此成为赵国著名的将军，因战功被封为马服君，被尊为"赵国七贤"之一。

现在我们用这个典故比喻敌对双方在地势险狭的地方相遇，只有勇往直前的一方才能获胜。或者用来形容交战双方困在狭小的空间里，没有回旋的余地，只能以拼斗决死生的紧迫态势。

这个典故给我们的启示是：当我们面对强敌，无法回避时，要敢于与强敌做最后的决斗。

谋 略 篇

Two Rats Fighting in the Hole

In the 29th year of King Huiwen of Zhao State (270 B.C.), Qin troops invaded Han State, the west neighbor of Zhao State, and they also besieged Yuyu, Zhao's important strategic post at the frontier. If this city were captured by Qin, Zhao would lose the natural barrier and be in great danger.

King Huiwen of Zhao asked his ministers for countermeasures about the warfare. The senior generals Lian Po and Yue Sheng both said, "The rescue is almost impossible since the place is too remote with narrow and dangerous paths." While Zhao She said, "When two parties are fighting in a narrow and dangerous path, it is just like two rats fighting in a hole, the braver one will win."

King Huiwen agreed with Zhao She and appointed him as the senior general to raise the siege of Yuyu. Zhao She first led his troops to march slowly so as to make the Qin troops slacken their vigilance, and afterwards made a rapid march to Yuyu to occupy a commanding height, and then launched a sudden attack against the arrogant Qin troops. The enemy was defeated completely and the siege of Yuyu was successfully raised, for which Zhao She became a famous general of Zhao State and was rewarded the title Lord Mafu and was respected as one of the Seven Sages of Zhao State.

This idiom now means that only the braver one will win when two opposing forces fight in a narrow and dangerous place or the situation of having to wage a desperate struggle since there is no room to maneuver.

It tells us that we must have the courage of fighting to death when we meet an unavoidable enemy.

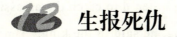

燕易王的母亲，是燕文侯的夫人，与苏秦私通。燕易王知道这件事，却对苏秦的待遇更加优厚。

苏秦恐怕被杀，就劝说燕王："我留在燕国，不能使燕国的地位提高，假如我在齐国，就一定能提高燕国的地位。"燕王说："一切听任先生去做吧。"

于是，苏秦假装得罪了燕王而逃跑到齐国。齐宣王便任用他为客卿。

齐宣王去世，齐湣王继位后，齐国大夫中有许多人和苏秦争夺国君的宠信，因而派人刺杀苏秦，苏秦当时没死，带着致命的伤逃跑了。齐王派人捉拿凶手，然而没有抓到。

苏秦将要死去，便对齐王说："我马上就要死了，请您在人口集中的街市上把我五马分尸示众，就说：'苏秦为了燕国在齐国谋乱'，这样做，刺杀我的凶手一定可以抓到。"

当时，齐王就按照他的话做了，那个刺杀苏秦的凶手，为了邀功，果然自动出头露面了，齐王因而就抓捕了他并把他杀了。

燕王听到这个消息说："齐国为苏先生报仇，做法也太过分啦。"

苏秦死后，他为燕国破坏齐国的一些事实才泄露出来。

这个典故的意思是人虽然已死，却仍然能为自己报仇。

To Take Revenge after One's Death

The mother of King Yi of Yan State, wife of Wenhou of Yan, committed adultery with Su Qin. Although the king learned of this, he treated Su Qin even better. In fear of being killed, Su Qin offered advice to the king, "If I stay in Yan, I cannot raise the status of Yan; but if I go to Qi State, I am bound to do so." The king said, "All is up to you."

Thus Su Qin pretended to have offended the King of Yan and escaped to Qi, where he was employed as an alien minister by King Xuan of Qi. After King Min of Qi succeeded King Xuan, many officials strived for the king's favor with Su Qin, and even plotted to assassinate him. Su escaped with deadly wounds. The king ordered to catch the assassin, but failed.

As Su Qin was dying, he said to the king, "I'm going to die. You might have me dismembered by five horses in a crowded street, declaring 'Su Qin conspired against Qi for Yan'. If so, the assassin is bound to be captured."

Then the king did as Su had said. As expected, the assassin showed up in order to seek rewards. Thus the king had him caught and executed.

Hearing this, the King of Yan said, "Qi has gone too far to revenge Mr. Su in this way."

After the death of Su Qin, some facts of his sabotage in Qi for the sake of Yan were disclosed.

This idiom indicates that a person can revenge even after he dies.

13 唇亡齿寒

公元前259年,秦国攻打赵国,齐国和楚国应赵国的请求出兵救赵。秦王盘算道:"如今齐、楚前来救赵,如果他们团结一致,寡人退兵未迟;假如他们一盘散沙,则乘势攻之。"

这时,赵军粮食告急,于是派人向齐国借粮,可是齐王不理睬。谋臣周子对齐王说:"大王不如把粮米暂借赵国,让他击退秦兵,如果不加理睬,秦兵就会无所忌惮,不会退去。这样,就正中了秦国的计策。赵国是齐、楚的一道屏障,这正像牙齿跟嘴唇的关系,没有了嘴唇,牙齿就会感到寒冷。今天秦国灭了赵国,明天祸患就会降临到齐、楚。救赵应当像捧着漏缸去浇烧干的锅一样急切,是高尚的德义;打退秦兵会使我们大显威名。不去显示正义张扬威名,却一味地吝啬粮食,这是战略决策的错误啊。"

这个成语的意思是嘴唇没有了,牙齿就会感到寒冷。比喻双方休戚相关,荣辱与共。

If the Lips Are Gone, the Teeth Will Be Cold

Qin State attacked Zhao State. Qi State and Chu State dispatched troops to rescue Zhao by Zhao's request. The King of Qin cast about in his mind, "Now Qi and Chu come to rescue Zhao. If they hold together, I will retreat temporarily; if they are just like a heap of loose sand, I will exploit the opportunity to attack them."

At that time, Zhao troops reported an emergency in food supplies. So a messenger was sent to borrow grain from Qi. But the King of Qi shut his ears to the appeal. Zhou Zi, the adviser of Qi, said to the King, "Your majesty, I think it would be better to lend the grain to Zhao to help beat back Qin troops. If we turn our back on it, Qin troops will stick at nothing and have no intention of retreating. In that case, Qi and Chu will take a false step and be caught in the trap set by Qin. Furthermore, Zhao is a natural barrier of Qi and Chu against Qin. It is just like the relationship between the teeth and the lips. If the lips are gone, the teeth will be cold. If today Zhao is ruined by Qin, tomorrow the calamity will befall Qi and Chu. We should rescue Zhao as urgently as holding a leaking jar to pour water on the burn-out pan. Rescuing Zhao is a magnanimous act and retreating Qin will show our power and prestige. If we do not demonstrate our justice and show our power, but to be mean on lending grain to Zhao, we will make a false decision."

This idiom means if the lips are gone, the teeth are exposed to cold. It indicates that mutual dependency of neighboring countries, when confronted with a powerful and aggressive enemy, share a common lot.

14 退避三舍

春秋时候，晋献公听信谗言，杀了太子申生，又派人捉拿申生的异母兄长重耳。重耳闻讯，逃出了晋国，在外流亡19年。

经过千辛万苦，重耳来到楚国。楚成王认为重耳日后必大有作为，就以国君之礼相迎，待他如上宾。

一天，楚王设宴招待重耳，两人饮酒叙话，气氛十分融洽。忽然楚王问重耳："你若有一天回晋国当上国君，该怎么报答我呢？"重耳略一思索说："美女侍从、珍宝丝绸，大王您有的是，珍禽羽毛，象牙兽皮，更是楚地的盛产，晋国哪有什么珍奇物品献给大王呢？"楚王说："公子过谦了，话虽然这么说，可总该对我

谋略篇

有所表示吧？"重耳笑笑回答道："要是托您的福，果真能回国当政的话，我愿与贵国友好。假如有一天，晋楚两国之间发生战争，我一定命令军队先退避三舍（一舍等于30里），如果还不能得到您的原谅，我再与您交战。"

四年后，重耳真的回到晋国当了国君，就是历史上有名的晋文公。晋国在他的治理下日益强大。

公元前633年，楚国和晋国的军队在作战时相遇。晋文公为了实现他许下的诺言，下令军队后退90里，驻扎在城濮。楚军见晋军后退，以为对方害怕了，马上追击。晋军利用楚军骄傲轻敌的弱点，集中兵力，大破楚军，取得了城濮之战的胜利。

成语"退避三舍"比喻不与人相争或主动让步。

这个成语给我们的启示是：在现实生活中，有时候让步并不代表着懦弱，而是一种策略，双赢才是最好的结局。

To Give Way to Avoid a Conflict

In the Spring and Autumn Period, Lord Xian of Jin State believed some slanderous words and killed Prince Shen Sheng. Then, he sent some persons to capture Chong Er, Shen Sheng's elder half brother. Chong Er heard the news and escaped from Jin. He was forced to leave his native land for nineteen years.

After suffering all conceivable hardships, Chong Er arrived in Chu State. King Cheng of Chu State believed that Chong Er would have great achievement in the future, so he welcomed Chong Er according to the etiquette of a king. Chong Er was treated as a distinguished guest.

One day, the King of Chu State gave a banquet to entertain Chong Er. They were drinking and talking; the atmosphere was quite harmonious. Suddenly, the King of Chu State asked Chong Er, "If you become the King of Jin State, how can you repay my favor?" Chong Er thought for a while and said, "You have plenty of treasure and silk, beauties and retinues. Chu State also abounds with rare birds and feathers, ivory and leather. There aren't so many precious treasures in Jin State, so I don't know what I can tribute to you." The King of Chu State said, "You are too modest. Even if your words are true, you should repay something to express your regards." Chong Er smiled and said, "Thanks for your concern, if I can go back to be the King, I would like to be friendly with your country. If there is a battle between Chu and Jin, I would order my army to withdraw three "she" first (one "she" equals ten miles) to give way to avoid a conflict. If I can't attain your forgiveness, I will fight with your army."

Four years later, Chong Er really went back to Jin State and became the King. He was the famous King Wen of Jin State in history. Jin State became powerful under his rule.

In 663 AD, Jin troops encountered Chu troops in the battlefield. In order to realize his promise, King Wen of Jin State ordered his troops to withdraw ninety miles. They stationed in Chengpu. Chu troops thought that Jin troops must be afraid of them, so they pursued to attack Jin roops. Jin troops brought the military together to defeat Chu troops by using their disadvantages of arrogance and the underestimation of the enemy. Jin won the battle of Chengpu.

The idiom "To Give Way to Avoid a Conflict" means avoiding competing with others or to give way voluntarily.

It tells us that in practical life, concession does not mean cowardice, but a sort of strategy. The best result is the win-win situation.

15 前事不忘，后事之师

春秋末年，晋国的大权落到智、赵、魏、韩四卿手中，晋定公实际上成了傀儡。公元前458年，晋定公派使者去请求齐、鲁两国出兵讨伐四卿。四卿得到消息后，联合出兵攻打晋定公。定公无力抵抗，只好被迫出逃，结果病死在路上。

晋定公死后，智伯独揽了朝政大权，成为晋国最大的卿。其他三卿赵襄子、魏桓子和韩康子都不敢和他抗衡。智伯分别向魏桓子和韩康子要了土地。当他要谋略篇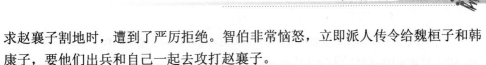

求赵襄子割地时，遭到了严厉拒绝。智伯非常恼怒，立即派人传令给魏桓子和韩康子，要他们出兵和自己一起去攻打赵襄子。

赵襄子估计智伯会攻打他，忙找谋臣张孟谈商量。张孟谈建议到晋阳去抵抗。到了晋阳，赵襄子发现能够打仗的武器很少。张孟谈劝道："这里的围墙是用一丈多高的楛木做的，殿柱是用铜铸的，这些都是制造武器的好材料。"智伯率魏、韩两家攻打晋阳，由于魏、韩不愿为智伯卖命，智伯无法取胜。

晋阳被智伯用水淹，围困了整整三年。由于地面积水，老百姓都在树上搭起棚子来居住，城里粮食也快要吃完，很多人冻饿成病，军心也开始动摇了。一天，张孟谈面见赵襄子，说："魏、韩两家是被迫的，我准备去向他们说明利害，动员他们反戈联赵，共同消灭智伯。"赵襄子听了非常高兴，连连拱手表示感谢。

当天夜晚，张孟谈潜入魏、韩营中，说服了魏桓子和韩康子，决定三家联合起来消灭智伯，事成之后平分智氏之领地。到了约定的那一天，赵、魏、韩三家联合进攻，杀得智军四散逃窜，智伯被擒。从此，晋国成了赵、魏、韩三家鼎立的局面。

一天，张孟谈向赵襄子告别，赵襄子急忙挽留。张孟谈说："你想的是报答我的功劳，我想的是治国的道理，正因为我的功劳大，名声甚至还会超过你，所以才决心离开。在历史上从来没有君臣权势相同而永远和好相处的。前事不忘，后事之师。请你让我走吧。"赵襄子只好惋惜地答应了。张孟谈辞去官职，退还封地，隐居起来，平安地度过了自己的晚年。

这个成语给我们的启示是：我们有成绩时不能骄傲，要时刻记住谦虚是人最大的美德之一，它会为我们带来他人的理解和尊重。

Past Experience Is a Guide for the Future

In the late Spring and Autumn Period, the real power of Jin State lay in the hands of the four ministers of Zhi, Zhao, Wei and Han, and Duke Ding, the ruler of Jin, had been reduced to a puppet. In 458 B.C, Dinggong sent envoys to petition the States of Qi and Lu to send troops to suppress the four ministers. Learning this, the four families joined hands and attacked Dinggong, who died of illness during his escape since he was powerless to resist.

After the death Dinggong, Zhi Bo arrogated all powers to himself and became the strongest. The other three ministers Zhao Xiangzi, Wei Huanzi and Han Kangzi didn't dare to contend with him. Zhi Bo demanded lands from Wei Huanzi and Han Kangzi. However, Zhao Xiangzi firmly refused to cede territories to Zhi Bo. Thus Zhi Bo, in fierce anger, formed an alliance with the families of Wei and Han to attack Zhao.

Zhao Xiangzi suspected that an attack from Zhi Bo was imminent, so he hurried to consult Zhang Mengtan, his adviser. Zhang suggested preparing the defense in Jinyang. Once in Jinyang, Zhao found that there were not enough weapons available for the war. Zhang said, "The walls here are made of a kind of thorn more than three meters high, and the pillars are made of bronze, both of which are the best materials for weapons." Zhi Bo attacked Jinyang but could not succeed because the other two families were reluctant to exert their full strength for him.

Jinyang was inundated by Zhi Bo and was besieged for three years. Since the buildings were submerged, the people of Jinyang were forced to live in the shacks built in the trees. Supplies were short, many people fell ill due to cold and hunger, and the army's morale began to waver. One day, Zhang Mengtan said to Zhao, "The families of Wei and Han are forced into the war. I intend to go and explain the gains and losses to them, and arouse them to hit back at Zhi Bo. And we can destroy him together." Zhao Xiangzi was greatly pleased at this and saluted with the hands folded several times as a sign of gratitude.

At the night, Zhang sneaked into the camps of Wei and Han, and persuaded them into an alliance to eliminate Zhi family and partition his lands fairly among them. On the appointed day, the families of Zhao, Wei and Han launched a sudden attack. Zhi Bo's troops suffered a severe defeat and dispersed, and he was taken prisoner. Thereafter Jin State was carved up into three parts by the families of Zhao, Wei and Han.

One day, Zhang Mengtan bade farewell to Zhao Xiangzi, and Zhao Xiangzi, repeatedly urged him to stay. Zhang said, "What you are thinking about is how to reward my service, while I am considering the principles of running a country. I decide to leave just because my great service has earned me a reputation even greater than yours. There is no such case in the past that the sovereign can always get along well with his minister when they possess almost the same power and influence. Past experience is a guide for the future. Therefore please leave me alone." Zhao Xiangzi had to agree regretfully. Zhang Mengtan resigned the post, returned his vavasory, and spent calmly his remaining years in seclusion.

It tells us that we must be modest instead of being proud when we have made achievements. Modesty is one of the best virtues of mankind, and it will bring us respect and understanding from others.

丛台置酒

这个典故也可以叫做"置酒丛台"。

马武字子张，南阳人，更始政权建立后，马武被任为侍郎，与刘秀一起在历史上著名的以少胜多的昆阳之战中击败王莽的大将王寻，因战功被封为振威将军，也曾经与尚书令谢躬一起攻克邯郸，打败王郎。

邯郸被攻克后，刘秀请谢躬与马武在邯郸丛台上喝酒，想要图谋谢躬，没有成功。于是刘秀单独与马武登丛台饮酒。

我们用这个典故来比喻别有用心的酒宴。

Giving a Feast on Congtai

Ma Wu, alias Zi Zhang, was born in Nanyang Prefecture. After the regime of Emperor Gengshi of Han Dynasty was found, Ma Wu was appointed as an assistant minister. He, together with Liu Xiu, defeated Wang Xun who was sent by Wang Mang, the Emperor of Xin Dynasty, with a force inferior in number in the famous Kunyang Battle. Because of his military achievement, he was appointed as General Zhenwei. He, together with Xie

Gong, the Director of Imperial Secretariat captured Handan city and defeated Wang Lang.

After capturing Handan city, Liu Xiu invited Xie Gong and Ma Wu for a drink on Congtai of Handan, intending to seize the opportunity to kill Xie Gong. But he failed. Consequently, only he and Ma Wu mounted Congtai and had a drink.

This idiom indicates a feast with ulterior motives.

 独智之虑

战国时期，赵国的赵武灵王为增强赵国的实力，大胆地进行改革创新，采用穿胡服学骑射的办法，大大地增强了赵国的军事力量，但是却招来了赵国旧贵族和一些大臣的反对。

赵武灵王说："有超过常人的伟大功劳的人，一定受到旧习惯势力的反对；有独特的智慧、超人的谋略的人，一定受到傲慢而不讲理的人的怨恨。我想让大家改穿胡人的服装、练习骑马射箭，你看这是为什么？"

我们通常用这个典故来比喻独特的智慧、超人的谋略。

这个典故给我们的启示是：当我们确定自己的想法或计划正确时，就不能过多地去考虑其他人的看法，而应该毫不犹豫地坚持自己的做法。

Consideration from a Person with Unique Wisdom

During the Warring States Period, in order to enhance Zhao's strength, King Wuling of Zhao State carried out reform and innovation by adopting the approach of wearing Hu tribe's clothing and learning their cavalry archery. This policy enhanced Zhao's military force, but attracted the opposition from some old aristocrats and ministers.

King Wuling said, "Persons with greater achievements than ordinary people will definitely receive the opposition from those who hold out-of-date customs; persons with unique wisdom and superb strategy will definitely get the hatred from arrogant and unreasonable people. Could you tell me why I'd like to ask everybody to wear Hu's clothes and learn their cavalry archery?"

We often use this idiom to indicate unique wisdom and superb strategy.

It tells us that we must be not hesitate to stick to our ideas when we are sure of our rightness without thinking about too much of other people's opinions.

18 不翼而飞

战国时期，秦兵包围并攻打赵国的都城邯郸，但是邯郸城池坚固，赵国士兵勇猛，秦军经过17个月的苦战也没有将其攻下。

秦国人佚庄对秦将王稽说："您为什么不赏赐下级军官呢？"

王稽说："我和君王之间，彼此互相信赖，他人的谗言就起不了作用。"

佚庄反驳到："我认为你说的不对，即使是父子关系，也有令在必行和不必行之分。比如说'丢掉娇妻，卖掉爱妾'，这就是一道必行的命令，'想也不要想自己的妻妾'，就是一道必然不能实行的命令。对父子关系来说，娇妻已经走了，爱妾也已经卖了，而父亲不应该说不许有思念之情。现在阁下虽然很得君王的宠信，但是君臣关系不能超过父子的骨肉至亲。阁下仰仗君王的宠信，平日一直轻视属下。常言道：'三个人说有虎，大家就会相信有虎；十个人说大力士可以折弯铁椎，大家也会相信是事实；众口一词，就可以使事物迁移变化，让真相不翼而飞。'所以你应该赏赐并优待诸将。"

它的原意是没有翅膀却飞走了，比喻物品忽然丢失。

Disappearing Without Trace

During the Warring States Period, the army of Qin State besieged Handan, the capital of Zhao State. But on account of the solidity of the city wall and the valor of the soldiers of Zhao, Handan was still not subdued by the Qin troops even after seventeen months.

Yi Zhuang, one soldier of Qin said to Qin's general Wang Ji, "Why don't you bestow prizes and rewards upon the officers of the army?"

Wang Ji said, "The King and I trust each other so much that others' slanders won't work."

Yi Zhuang retorted, "Not so. In the relationship between a father and his son there are some commands which the son will certainly carry out and some which he will certainly not. If the father says, 'Send away your beautiful wife, and sell the lovely concubine', that command will certainly be carried out. But if he says, 'Do not think of them', that command will never be carried out. Although the son has already sent away the beautiful wife and sold out the lovely concubine, the father should not require that his son cannot miss them. Now although the King favours you, your relationship does not go beyond that of a father and his son. Moreover, based on the king's favour, you are always looking down upon your subordinates. It is said that 'if three men say that there is a tiger on the street, people will believe it. And if ten persons claim that a strong man can bend a mallet, people will also believe it.' The unanimous voice will twist the facts and make them disappear without trace. Therefore the best way is to reward the officers and treat them courteously."

The original meaning of the idiom is to disappear without trace. Today, it means an object vanishes suddenly.

唱筹量沙

南朝宋文帝元嘉七年（公元430年）十一月，檀道济被授予督征讨诸军事，奉命率众伐北魏。

他率领军队在二十多天里，与北魏军进行三十余次战斗，并多次获胜。

不久，道济军抵达历城，遭叔孙建等骑兵部队的截击，所带粮秣也被焚烧，因而难以继续前进。

这时，北魏部将安颉，司马楚之等乘机专攻滑台。

滑台守将朱修之坚守数月，终因供应不继，困顿不堪，滑台为北魏所占，修之被俘。道济得知滑台失陷，又无粮秣接济，欲救不能，准备撤返。

此时，道济部下有投降北魏的士兵，将宋军缺粮的情况据实告诉以后，魏军立即追赶，企图一举歼灭道济军。

当檀道济率军撤退到邯郸市曲周县境内时，被追击上的魏军包围。

檀道济命令士卒唱着数筹码来发放沙子，把仅有的粮食盖在沙上来显示粮食很多，以迷惑魏军。

魏军望见宋军一堆一堆的"粮食"，以为宋军并不缺粮，故将投降过来的宋兵视为"间谍"而杀掉。

为了扭转局势，道济又心生一计，让士卒全穿上盔甲，唯有他一人穿白色衣服，带领部队从容出走。

魏军认为，道济及其部队在被包围的情况下，如此不慌不忙地撤走，一定预设有伏兵，故不敢近前聚歼。就这样，道济军得以安全返回。

这个典故比喻为安定军心，制造假象，迷惑敌人。同时它也告诫我们看事情不能只看表面，要学会透过现象看本质。

To Count Aloud the Chips of Meting Out the Sand

In the Southern Dynasty, Tan Daoji was dispatched as the commander-in-chief to attack Northern Wei in November, 430 AD, the seventh year of King Wen of Song State.

Under his leadership, his soldiers fought more than thirty battles with the army of Northern Wei and won most of them.

Daoji's army arrived at Licheng (in modern Ji'nan, Shandong Province) soon, where he was intercepted by the cavalries of Shusun Jian and the provisions were burnt away. Thus he could hardly advance on.

At this moment, the Northern Wei general An Jie and Sima Chu concentrated to attack Huatai. Although Huatai's commanding general Zhu Xiuzhi held fast to the town for several months, it soon fell since the supply route was cut off, and Zhu was captured. Hearing the fall of Huantai, Daoji began to retreat due to the lack of provisions.

Some of Daoji's soldiers surrendered to the Northern Wei and disclosed the fact of food supply in the army of Song. So the army of the Northern Wei tracked him down, ready to wipe them out.

Daoji's army was surrounded by the enemies when he retreated to the place which is now in Quzhou County, Handan. Daoji had his soldiers mete out sand by counting aloud the chips, and then covered the sand with grain so as to pretend they had enough food supply and to confuse the enemy.

When Northern Wei forces saw piles of sand covered with grain, they mistakenly thought that Daoji's forces did not lack food at all, and therefore killed the surrendered soldiers as spies.

In order to change the situation, Daoji came up with another trick. He had his soldiers all wear amour and he himself was dressed in white clothes. Then he led the army to move on unhurriedly. Northern Wei forces thought they must have laid an ambush since Daoji's army made such an orderly retreat under siege, and therefore they didn't dare to pursue further. Thus Daoji withdrew his forces safe and sound.

This idiom means creating a false impression to confuse the enemy so as to keep the army's morale. What's more, it also warns us that we should not just focus on superficial things; we must learn to see through their essences.

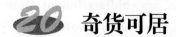

26 奇货可居

阳翟大商人吕不韦在邯郸遇到了秦国留在赵国的人质——秦昭襄王之子安国君的儿子异人。吕不韦凝思片刻，大笑着说道："他真是奇货。可先囤积起来，然后作一笔大生意。"

吕不韦先以重金结交监守人,后又结识异人。

吕不韦说:"我可以设法救你回国!"

异人说:"如能救我回国,日后倘能得到荣华富贵,你我共享!"

为了帮助异人回国,吕不韦来到了秦国的京都咸阳。

吕不韦费了很多的钱财与精力,到处行贿,最终秦昭襄王表示愿接异人回国。这时他想:"异人回国,日后继位为王,对自己来说,最大不过是从一位秦王身上得利。如何能长久呢?将来异人驾崩或者退位,又如何能从下一代秦王身上得利呢?"

他便想到了赵姬这位身姿艳丽,善歌善舞的美女。吕不韦很喜欢她,他俩早已暗中同居,赵姬已怀有两个月的身孕。

吕不韦想:"应该把赵姬献给异人。日后生下我的骨肉,长大继位。到那时,秦国的天下便是我吕氏的天下。那样,我做的这生意,其利可就无穷了。"

于是,他让赵姬出面勾引异人,最终,异人与赵姬结成了夫妻。

后来,赵姬生下了一个男孩,给男孩取名叫"政",他便是日后兼并其他六国的秦始皇。

昭襄王五十年,秦兵重围邯郸。吕不韦领着化了妆的异人,混出邯郸,回到了咸阳。

后来异人成为秦王,便请吕不韦做了丞相,并封号文信君,到河南洛阳,坐享十万户的奉养。再后来,异人逝世,立政为王。政尊吕不韦为相国,号称仲父。

这个成语的原意是指把少有的货物囤积起来,等待高价出售。现在我们通常用这个成语来指拿某种专长或特有的东西作为资本,等待时机,以获取成功。

Hoard as a Rare Commodity

Lu Buwei, the leading merchant in Yangdi, met Yi Ren in Handan, the hostage from Qin State, the son of Lord of Anguo and the grandson of King Zhaoxiang of Qin State. Lu Buwei meditated for a while and laughed, "He is a rare commodity. We can hoard him and then do a very profitable business."

Lu Buwei first spent a large sum of money to become the warden's friend and then got to know Yi Ren.

Lu Buwei told Yin Ren, "I may be able to rescue you to return to your motherland."

Yi Ren said, "If you could do so, I will share with you all the fortunes and power I could get in the future."

In order to assist Yi Ren back to his motherland, Lu Buwei went to Xianyang, the capital of Qin State. He offered bribe to a lot of officials and finally King Zhao Xiang of Qin State became willing to take Yi Ren back. Lu Buwei thought, "When Yi Ren gets back, he will succeed to the throne in the future. To me, the biggest profits I can get are the benefits from one king. How can it last long? When Yi Ren dies or abdicates in the future, how can I obtain profits from the next king?"

He had then thought of Zhao Ji, a stunning lady with gorgeous figure and great skills in singing and dancing. Lu Buwei was very fond of her. They had lived together in secret for a long time and Zhao Ji was pregnant with his baby for more than two months.

Lu Buwei thought, "I should marry Zhao Ji to Yi Ren. She will give birth to my baby. When my child grows up and succeed the throne, Qin State will be mine. If this becomes true, I will profit infinitely."

Therefore, he requested Zhao Ji to seduce Yin Ren. Finally, Yi Ren and Zhao Ji got married.

After the marriage, Zhao Ji gave birth to a baby boy. They named the baby boy Zheng. He was known as Ying Zheng, the future Emperor Qin Shihuang who gobbled up the other six states.

It had been fifty years since King Zhao Xiang ruled Qin State. In that year, his army encircled Han Dan. Lu Buwei led Yi Ren in disguise to leave Han Dan secretly back to Xian Yang.

Later, Yi Ren became King of Qin, appointed Lu Buwei the Prime Minister and entitled him Lord of Wenxin. Lu Buwei was also granted a territory in Luoyang, Henan province, with one hundred thousand households as his subjects. Later, the passing-away of Yi Ren made Zheng the new king. Zheng respected and made Lu Buwei the Prime Minister and called him as

谋 略 篇

my father's oldest brother.

This idiom means that the rare and hoarded goods are stored for a higher price. Now we usually use this idiom to indicate to take one's specialty and peculiar things as one's own advantage to waiting for an opportunity to succeed.

21 嫁祸于人

公元前262年，秦国攻打韩国，切断了韩国的上党郡与本土的通道，韩国想割让上党郡求和，上党的郡守冯亭拒绝了。

他来到赵国，说："韩国不能守住上党，但是如果把上党割让给秦国，这里的官员和百姓都不愿意，他们情愿归顺赵王。"

赵孝成王召见平阳君赵豹商量对策，赵豹认为，秦国采取逐步蚕食的策略，已经切断了上党与韩国的联系，有把握占领上党。上党人不愿意归顺秦国，是想嫁祸于赵国。

但是赵国的相国平原君赵胜贪图这块土地，劝说赵王接受了上党。

秦王大怒，派兵进攻赵国，爆发了长平之战。

由于赵国将领赵括只善于纸上谈兵，造成了赵军的重大失败，四十万大军全军覆没。上党郡最终被秦军占领，冯亭自杀身亡。赵国也因此而元气大伤。

我们用这个成语来表示把灾祸推到别人身上。但在现实生活中我们做人应以诚信为本，切勿嫁祸于他人。

Shifting Calamity to Others

In 262 B.C., Qin State invaded Han State, and Qin cut the access of Han's Shangdang County to its mainland. Han would like to cede Shangdang County for peace, but Feng Ting, the chief in the county, refused.

He came to Zhao State and said, "Han can not defend Shangdang. The officials and the people do not want Shangdang to be ceded to Qin State. They would rather to pledge allegiance to Zhao."

King Xiaowen of Zhao summoned Zhao Bao, Lord of Pingyang, to discuss the countermeasures. Zhao Bao believed Qin State adopted the gradual nibbling strategy and had cut off the ties between Shangdang and Han State. Qin State must be confident in the occupation of Shangdang. The people in Shangdang did not wish to pledge allegiance to Qin and they wanted to shift the calamity to Zhao State.

However, the Prime Minister Zhao Sheng, Lord of Pingyuan, coveted this piece of land and persuaded the king to accept Shangdang.

The King of Qin was furious and dispatched troops to attack Zhao State. The War of Changping broke out.

Zhao Kuo, the general of Zhao, was only an armchair strategist. He caused the significant defeat of Zhao troops. The army with 400,000 soldiers was annihilated, and Shangdang County was occupied by Qin eventually. Feng Ting committed suicide. And Zhao State was also vitally hurt.

We often use this idiom to indicate somebody shifting calamity to other people. But in reality we should be honesty and should not shift the blame onto others.

22 金城汤池

秦朝末年，陈胜、吴广率领起义军建立了张楚政权。陈胜派遣武信君武臣率人马进攻燕赵之地，第一个目标是范阳城。

蒯通去见范阳县令徐公，劝说道："你做官期间得罪了太多的百姓，如今大兵压境，百姓若向你复仇，你必死无疑。

武臣将军礼贤下士，定会向我询问平定燕赵的策略。我打算对他说，靠血战来攻城掠地，不是好办法。而采纳我的计策，不费一兵一卒，只需要发一张文告，就可以平定千里之地。

谋略篇

现在范阳县令徐公要献城投降，如果你不接受而杀了他，那么燕赵大地上其他城池的守将就会知道投降必死，他们防守的城池就会变得坚不可摧。

如果接受他的归顺，给徐公优厚的待遇，让他在燕赵大地上走一圈，其他人就会纷纷归顺，所以只要再发一个文告，就可以平定千里之地。"

于是徐公立即送蒯通去见武臣，武臣果然采纳了蒯通的意见，接受徐公的归顺并给与重赏，结果三十多座城池不战而降，武臣很快平定了燕赵之地。

这个典故的意思是形容据守的城市极其坚固。有时候它也形容某人或团队在比赛中防守很好，无法攻破。

Being Secure Against Assault

In the last phase of Qin Dynasty, Chen Sheng and Wu Guang led the uprising army to establish the Zhangchu Coutry. Chen Sheng dispatched Lord Wuxin, Wu Chen to lead troops to attack the land of Yan and Zhao. The first objective is the town of Fanyang.

Kuai Tong went to visit Xu Gong, the magistrate of Fanyang and advised him, "You have offended too many common people here. Now a large enemy force is approaching the border, if the common people revenge on you, you are certain to die.

General Wu Chen treats worthies and scholars with courtesy; he is bound to inquire me about the strategy on how to conquer the land of Yan and Zhao. I plan to tell him that it is not a good idea to occupy a town by bloody fight. But if he accepts my proposal, he can conquer vast land without damaging one soldier. What he needs to do is only to send a proclamation.

Now Xu Gong, the magistrate of Fanyang, would like to surrender by offering his town. If you do not accept and kill him, the garrison commanders of Yan and Zhao will know that surrender means death, and the towns they are defending will become indestructible.

But if you accept his pledging allegiance, give him favorable treatment and ask him to travel around Yan and Zhao, others will come over and pledge allegiance one after another. So to send a proclamation can conquer a thousand li."

Then Xu Gong sent Kuai Tong to meet Wu Chen, and Wu Chen really followed Kuai Tong's advice, he accepted Xu Gong's pledging allegiance and gave him favorable treatment. As a result, more than 30 cities and towns surrendered peacefully; Wu Chen occupied Yan and Zhao soon.

This idiom means an impregnable city or stronghold, which is hard to conquer. Sometimes it also indicates a person or a team who can not be broken through because of good defence in the game.

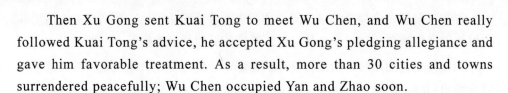# 挥汗如雨

战国时期,苏秦从赵国来到齐国,对齐宣王宣传他的"合纵"主张,其中谈到了齐国的地势、兵力和齐国都城临淄的情况:

"临淄有七万户人家,我大概估计,平均每户有男子三人。不用到外面去征兵,就可以得到二十一万人。临淄地方很富庶,老百姓家道殷实,日子过得快活。街上熙熙攘攘,行人、车辆难以计数。车碰轴木,人碰肩头。众人把袖子举起来,就像帐幕一般;每人挥一把汗,天上就像下了雨。以您的贤德,加上齐国的强大,天下没有能够和您为敌的。可是现在,您竟然屈服于秦国,我实在替您感到羞耻。"

然后,苏秦又进一步分析了当时各国的形势。齐宣王被苏秦说动,表示愿意加入"合纵"的阵营。

这则成语用来表示人多拥挤,也形容出汗很多,挥洒的汗水如雨一样。有时候它也形容人们在劳动中付出的辛勤劳动。

To Drip with Sweat

In the Warring States Period, Su Qin came from Zhao State to Qi State to advocate his "Longitudinal Union" ideas to the King of Qi. He talked about Qi's terrain, military strength and situation of its capital, Linzi.

"There are about 70,000 families in Linzi. I estimate that on average there are three men in every family. You can get 210,000 soldiers without levying soldiers outside. Linzi is a rich and populous place. People here have well-off families and they live a happy life. Uncountable vehicles and pedestrians are bustling on the streets. Carts are in collision with axles and pedestrians jostle each other in crowd. People's lifting of sleeves will shade the sunlight and people's wiping of sweat will look like dripping in the sky. With the virtues of Your Majesty and the power of Qi State, no one can rival you. But now, you yield to the power of Qin, I really feel ashamed for you."

Then, Su Qin made a further analysis of the situation in other countries. King Xuan was persuaded by Su Qin, so he expressed his willingness to be a member of the "Longitudinal Union".

This idiom is used as a metaphor to indicate a lot of people gather together. Literally it also means that sweat wiped off drips like rain. Sometimes it also indicates people's much hard work in their labor.

不绝若绳

"不绝若绳"也可以叫做"不绝如线"。

荀卿劝齐国相国孟尝君田文道：

"现在庞大的楚国摆在我们的面前，强大的燕国紧逼在我们的后面，强劲的魏国牵制了我们的西面，西面的领土虽然没有断送，也危险得像根细绳一样了，楚国则还有襄贲、开阳两座城监视着我们的东面。"

"在这种形势下，如果其中有个国家出谋划策，那么这三个国家就必然会一同来欺凌我们。如果这样，那么齐国一定会被分割成三四块，国土将像借来的城池一样而不属于自己，这就一定会被天下人大大地嘲笑一番。"

一般用"不绝若绳"这个典故比喻局势之危急。亦比喻技艺、学说等继承者稀少，但未失传；声音等细微，但未中断。后来还以此比喻子孙衰落，后继乏人。

As Precarious as a String Which Is Going to Break

This idiom can also be called as "As Precarious as a Thread Which Is Going to Break".

Xunzi, also respectfully called as Xunqing, once persuaded Tian Wen, the Prime Minister of Qi State, who is also called as Lord of Mengchang and said, "Now giant Chu State is glaring at us in front; powerful Yan State is pressing hard at our back; strong Wei State is tying down our west. Although the west territory has not been lost, it is as precarious as a string which is going to break. Moreover, Chu State is watching our east by the two cities Xiangbi and Kaiyang."

"Under the circumstances, if one of them gives counsel, the three countries are bound to come together to bully our state. In that case, Qi State will surely be divided into several parts and the territory, just like the borrowed cities, will no longer belong to us. Then we will be sneered by people all over the world."

We often use this idiom to indicate the critical situation. It also indicates that the successors of some crafts or theories become almost extinct, and that the sound lingers on faintly. Later on it also means lacking successors and becoming declined.

25 食不甘味

战国后期，有齐、秦、楚、赵、燕、韩、魏七国，称为战国七雄。

其中七雄之一的秦国最为强大，它经常侵犯其他国家。

有一年，秦惠文王派使者去见楚威王，要挟说："如果楚国不服从秦国，秦国就要出兵伐楚。"

楚威王闻听大怒，下令把秦国使者驱逐出境。但楚威王又因实力不足而焦虑不安，如果强秦发兵入侵该如何办呢？

恰在这时，说客苏秦前来拜见。

他劝楚威王与赵、魏等国联合起来抗秦。楚威王一听，十分高兴，说："非常感谢你的妙计，我正为这件事'卧不安席，食不甘味'呢，现在就按你的计策去做。"

这个典故形容心里有事或身体不好，吃东西也不香。我们在日常生活和工作中会经常因为各种挫折导致食不甘味，应该学会及时调整心态。

To Have No Appetite for Food

During the late Warring States Period, there were seven states: Qi, Qin, Chu, Zhao, Yan, Han and Wei, which were called the Seven Powers.

Among the seven powers, Qin State was the most powerful and it invaded the other states regularly.

One year, King Huiwen of Qin State sent an emissary to call on King Wei of Chu State and threatened him, "If Chu State doesn't yield to Qin State, the Qin troops will come to attack your state."

Hearing that, King Wei of Chu State was very infuriated and drove the emissary out of his state. But he was quite worried and anxious owing to his lack of strength. What would he do if the powerful the Qin troops came to invade?

Just at that time, a persuasive talker Su Qin came to visit.

He persuaded King Wei of Chu State to ally with Zhao, Wei and other states against Qin State. King Wei of Chu State was pleased and said, "Thank you very much for your wonderful idea. I cannot go to sleep in bed and have no appetite for food just for this problem. Now I will follow your strategy."

Now we often use this idiom to mean having no appetite for food for being worried about something or being unhealthy. In our daily life and work we often encounter a variety of setbacks and have no appetite for food. We should learn to adjust our mentality timely.

26 鸡口牛后

战国时期，苏秦在游说了赵国和齐国之后，又来到韩国游说韩宣惠王抗秦：

"韩国的地理位置非常优越，国土方圆千里，甲兵数十万众。天下的强弓劲弩，大多数出于韩国。一些著名的弩机，射程都在六百步之外；士兵脚踏发射，可以连射上百发，杀伤力非常强。韩国的剑和戟，也极有威力，再坚硬的东西也抵挡不了；而且韩国士兵勇猛，可以以一当百。

韩国如此强盛，大王如此贤明，却准备向西面的秦国屈服。这样做，不但国家受辱，天下人也要笑话。臣听说过一个俗语：宁当鸡的嘴巴，也不当牛的肛门。鸡的嘴巴虽小，但是比较干净；而牛的肛门虽大却很臭。如今大王向秦国称臣，和当牛的肛门有什么区别？大王如此贤明，又拥有如此多的雄兵，却背负如此臭名，臣私下为大王感到羞耻啊！"

宣惠王听到这里，勃然变色，拔剑仰天叹息道："我虽然没有什么出息，也不能像秦国臣服，就照先生说的办吧。"

这个典故的意思是宁可在局面小的地方自主，也不在局面大的地方听从别人支配。比喻做事要有自己的主见，不能受制于人，任人摆布。

Fowl's Beak and Ox Buttocks

In the Warring States Period, after canvassing in Zhao State and Qi State, Su Qin went to Han State, trying to persuade King Xuanhui against Qin.

"Han has superior geographical location, a thousand li of land in length and breadth，with hundreds of thousands of first-rate soldiers. Most of the powerful bows and crossbows are made in Han. The range of some famous crossbows can reach farther than six hundred steps; soldiers can discharge about one hundred arrows by pedaling at one time, with a terrible execution. The swords and halberts of Han are also powerful enough to penetrate any hard objects. And the Han soldiers are so brave that each of them can defeat many.

Han State is so powerful and Your Majesty is so wise and virtuous, however you are ready to yield to Qin in your west. If you do so, not only the country is humiliated, but also others will laugh at you. I have heard of a proverb going as "It is better to be the beak of a chicken than the anus of a cow". Although chicken's mouth is small, it is quite clean; cow's anus great but smelly. Now you submit yourself to the rule of Qin, what is the difference from a cow's anus? Your Majesty is so wise and able, with so many powerful soldiers, but you have to shoulder such a bad reputation, I feel ashamed for you in privately！"

Hearing these, the king was badly infuriated. He drew his sword out, looked up at heaven and sighed, "Although I am good-for-nothing, I can not submit myself to the rule of Qin. Let's act according to what you said."

This idiom means it is preferable to lead in a petty position than to follow behind a greater leader. This idiom also indicates that one wants to act with a mind of its own instead of being controlled by others or under the mercy of others.

27 以卵投石

荀况，人称荀卿，也叫荀子，是战国时期赵国人。

有一次，荀子同楚将临武君谈论军事，临武君认为："善用兵者如能再用攻夺变诈，就可以无敌于天下。"

荀子不同意临武君的说法，荀子反对侵夺、欺诈，而主张仁人之兵。认为必须重礼、贵义、好士、爱民……这样，军队和国家才能强大无敌。荀子说："以桀诈饶礜之若以卵击石，若赴水火。"

荀子这句话是说：如果是暴君桀的不义之师，以攻取诈骗为主要战略，去攻击圣王的仁义之师，结果一定失败。那就好比是用鸡蛋攻打石头，用手指去搅沸汤，也好比是跳进深水热火，一进去就只能被烧焦和淹没了。

该成语意指用鸡蛋打石头，比喻自不量力，自取灭亡，也说"以卵击石"。这个成语也告诫我们当我们遭遇实力悬殊的对手时，不应以卵击石，而是承认差距，先依靠强者活下来，然后再逐步创建自己的新天地。

Knocking an Egg Against a Stone

Xun Kuang, who was called as Xun Qing, also known as Xun Zi, was a citizen of Zhao State in the Warring States period.

Once, Xun Zi discussed military affairs with Lord of Linwu. Lord of Linwu said, "If a good commander of the armed forces knows how to devise the military tactics of attacking, seizing, changing and cheating, he will be invincible in the world."

Xun Zi did not agree with Lord of Linwu. He supported virtuous army and opposed to the tactics of seizing or cheating. He thought that in order to make his army and country invincible, a leader must value virtue and righteousness, respect and take good care of capable talents, and love his people. He said, "Using the intrigue of Jie to attack a holy army is like knocking an egg against a stone or jumping into water and fire."

Xun Zi meant that if Jie, a tyrant, sent his evil army to assault a holy king's virtuous army, by adopting attacking and cheating as its major strategy, he was doomed to be defeated. It was just like knocking an egg against a stone or stirring boiling water with a finger, or jumping into deep water or fire. Once one got into the water or the fire, he would be drowned or burned.

We often use this idiom to mean some behaviour like knocking an egg against a stone. It expresses the meaning of over-evaluating one's ability and inviting destruction. It is also known as "Hitting an Egg Against a Stone". The idiom also reminds us that when we encounter an unequal opponent, we should not break recklessly, but first make a recognition of the gap, and then depend on the strong to survive, and gradually create our own new world.

谋略篇

28　自陈功过

苏秦入齐之后,燕昭王对他产生了怀疑,因为他以时机未到为由,几次劝阻燕昭王对齐的进攻,于是昭王打算让别人替换苏秦回国。

苏秦感到非常委曲,向燕王写信申辩。这封信可以说是他对自己一生功过的一个评说。他说:

"燕和齐仇恨由来已久。我为燕齐的邦交奔走,本来就难以获得各方面的信任。齐是燕国的心腹大患,我在齐国,大可使齐不谋攻燕,小可使齐赵关系破裂,以此为大王的大事做准备。五国伐秦,燕虽然出兵出粮,但一来免去齐称帝燕称臣的耻辱,二来没有齐赵攻燕的祸患。后来奉阳君接受齐的封地,将我扣在赵国。大王救臣下出于水火,现在齐赵都不谋攻燕,燕得以修饬国力,我虽无功,但自以为可以免罪了。

我作为燕臣,在齐国活动,本来就会有流言蜚语。我如在齐显贵,燕国大夫就不信任我,我在齐作贱,世人就看不起我。我如受齐王重用,燕大夫就会对我抱有希望,希望达不到又徒增埋怨。齐国如有不利于燕的地方,就把责任都归到我头上,天下人不攻齐,就说我善于为齐谋划。我的处境也可以说是够危险的了。我不畏死报效于大王,大王却怀疑怪罪于臣下,我实在感到恐惧。尽管我自以为可以列于天下公卿之中也无可愧疚,如大王只是重用有才的贤人,我愿在齐与他认真合作;如大王不放心我,我就回燕国侍奉大王,以宽解大王的忧虑。"燕昭王最终没有撤换苏秦。

这个典故的意思是自己陈述自己的功劳和过失。

这个典故从另外一个角度说明作为领导者应该知人善任,用人不疑,疑人不用。

To Manifest One's Merits and Demerits

When Su Qin was in Qi State, King Zhao of Yan State began to doubt him and planned to send someone else to substitute him since he prevented the king from attacking Qi several times; making an excuse that it was not the best timing.

Su Qin felt wronged, and wrote to the king to defend himself. This letter could be regarded as a comment on the merits and demerits of his whole life. It read as follows:

"Yan and Qi have a deep-rooted enmity towards each other. I have been keeping busy with the diplomatic relationship between them, but it is hard to gain trust from both sides. Qi was the serious hidden danger for Yan. If I were here, I could dissuade Qi from planning to attack Yan at most, or I could break off the relationship between Qi and Zhao at least so as to prepare for Your Majesty's ambition. Although Yan had provided soldiers and provisions when the five states united to attack Qin, the result is that, on the one hand, we avoided the disgrace of being subjected to Qi; on the other hand, we would not worry about the danger of being attacked by Qi and Zhao. Later Lord Fengyang accepted the vavasory from Qi, and detained me in Zhao. At this time Your Majesty saved me from all the troubles. Since neither Qi nor Zhao intends to attack Yan at present, it is high time for Yan to strengthen itself. Though I have no great merits, I think at least I should be free from faults.

As a minister of Yan doing his job in Qi, various kinds of rumours spreading about me are inevitable. If I gained a great reputation in Qi, those officials of Yan would not trust me. If I got humiliated in Qi, the world would look down upon me. If I was offered a high position by the King of Qi, the officials of Yan would build some hope on me and there would be complaints when it couldn't be achieved. If Qi did something harmful to Yan, they would blame it on me. If no state attacked Qi, they would say that I made successful scheme for Qi. I was in so dangerous a situation. I have rendered service to Your Majesty fearlessly, but I am suspected and blamed now, and it scares me indeed. I do not think that I will feel uneasy to rank with other lords or ministers; and if you wished to put talent of virtue in an important position, I would like to remain here to cooperate with you earnestly. If you had no confidence in me, I would return to Yan to serve Your Majesty so as to eliminate your anxiety." At last King Zhao of Yan didn't replace Su Qin.

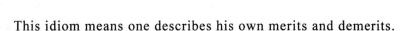

This idiom means one describes his own merits and demerits.

From another point of view, it indicates as a leader one should know one's men well enough to assign them jobs according to their abilities and do not suspect the man you use or do not use the man you suspect.

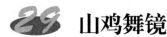 山鸡舞镜

曹操有个小儿子叫曹冲,从小聪明过人。曹操特别宠爱他,想立他为继承人。

有一年,南方献给曹操一只极美丽的山鸡,可是它在殿堂上不肯鸣舞。众人束手无策,认为请曹冲来也许有办法。

曹冲被请到殿堂上,他一看到山鸡,就命人取一面铜镜来。山鸡在铜镜前看到自己美丽的形体,仿佛置身于明净的湖面,居然连连欢叫、翩翩起舞。山鸡越舞越得意,竟不知停歇,直至倒地死去。

可惜,聪颖无比的曹冲只活到13岁便死了。曹操痛悼爱子早亡,失去了理想的继承人。

典故"山鸡舞镜"比喻顾影自怜,自鸣得意。这个典故也暗示现实社会中切勿因一时成就孤芳自赏。

The Pheasant Dancing in Front of the Mirror

Cao Chong, the youngest son of Cao Cao, was exceptionally bright. Cao Cao was very fond of him and had the intention to make him his successor.

One year, a beautiful pheasant was sent as tribute to Cao Cao from the south, but it did not sing or dance in the palace. All the people were nail-biting, so they sent for Cao Chong.

As Cao Chong came to the palace and saw the pheasant, he asked to bring a bronze mirror. Seeing its beautiful body in the mirror, the pheasant thought it was on the surface of a clear lake, and then started to sing happily and dance trippingly. The pheasant got more and more proud as it kept dancing until it was exhausted to death.

Unfortunately, this smart Cao Chong died at the age of thirteen. Cao Cao mourned over his death and his loss of an ideal successor.

This idiom means admiring oneself or show self-satisfaction. It also implies in reality one that has got temporary achievements should not be smug and narcissistic.

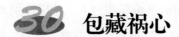

包藏祸心

建安15年（公元210年），曹操56岁。那时，曹操挟天子以令诸侯，先后击败了袁术、吕布、袁绍等地方割据势力，完成统一中国北方的大业后，定都邺城，政权逐渐巩固，继而希望能够统一全国。但是南方的刘备和孙权两大军事势力仍然是他的巨大威胁。

他们除在军事上联盟抗曹外，在政治上则抨击曹操"托名汉相，实为汉贼"、"欲废汉自立"。

在这种政治形势下，曹操发布了这篇令文，借退还皇帝加封三县之名，表明了自己的本志，反击了朝野谤议。文中概述了曹操统一中国北部的全部过程，表达了作者以平定天下、恢复统一为己任的政治抱负。

这个典故的意思是不怀好意。

我们在日常生活和工作中不可包藏祸心，心怀恶意，应诚信待人，与人坦诚相处。

To Conceal the Evil Intention

In the fifteenth year of Jian'an (210 AD), Cao Cao was fifty- six years old. At that time, Cao Cao was usurping power by holding the emperor as a hostage and acting in his name. After he defeated Yuan Shu, Lu Bu and Yuan Shao who controlled the separatist regimes, he unified the north of China.

Then, he established the capital in Yecheng and his political power was strengthened gradually, so he planned to unify the whole country. However, Liu Bei and Sun Quan who had powerful military forces in the south were a great threat to him.

In addition to resisting Cao Cao with allied military force, Liu Bei and Sun Quan also politically attacked him that "although he was under the name of the Prime Minister of Han Dynasty, in fact, he was a treacherous court official of Han Dynasty", and that "he wanted to abolish Han Dynasty and establish his own state political power."

Under such political circumstances, Cao Cao published an autobiographical article. He seized the opportunity to return the fief of three counties to Emperor to express his real intention and attack the slanderous words from the government and the public. The lyric contains the whole process of Cao Cao's unifying the north of China. It expresses Cao Cao's political ambition of quelling the whole country and regaining the unification.

In our daily life and work, we should not have evil intentions and ill will, but be honest with people and get along with people honestly.

31 反侧自安

公元24年，刘秀奉命率兵平定河北，他的第一个强敌就是在邯郸自称天子的王郎。

经过多次激战，刘秀的军队终于攻克邯郸城并追斩王郎。

在搜查宫室时，刘秀发现了在过去几次与王郎交战失利时，其部下毁谤他并表示愿意归附王郎的大批信件。

刘秀让人把这些信件当众烧毁，说道："让心神不安的人自然而然地安下心来。"这一方法果然很奏效，朝野平定，大家彼此相安无事。

现在我们一般用"反侧自安"来表示安抚人心的措施很奏效。

这个典故也可以说成"反侧获安"或"反侧自消"。它常用于比喻作为管理者善运用有效策略来安抚众人。

From Tossing about in Bed to Obtaining a Peaceful Mind

This idiom is also known as "From Tossing about to Getting a Peaceful Mind" or "Vanishment of a Troubled Mind".

In the year 24, under the order, Liu Xiu commanded troops to pacify the rebellion in Hebei. His first powerful enemy was Wang Lang, who proclaimed himself as the Son of Heaven.

Through many fierce combats, Liu Xiu finally conquered the city of Handan and killed Wang Lang.

When searching Wang Lang's royal palaces, Liu Xiu discovered large quantities of letters, which his subordinates wrote to Wang Lang to slander him and indicate their desire to change their allegiance to Wang Lang when Liu Xiu encountered several defeats in the battle.

Liu Xiu asked his subordinates to burn down those letters in public and said, "This can help those who tossed about in bed to get a peaceful mind naturally." This approach was very effective. The government remained steady and the officials worked in peace with each other.

Now we often use this idiom to indicate that the measures to appease people are very effective. It is often used as a metaphor of good managers using effective strategies to appease the people.

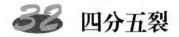

四分五裂

战国后期,七雄争霸。七国之中,秦国最为强大。面对强国和弱国纷争不休的形势,出现了以苏秦为首的"合纵"的主张和以张仪为首的"连横"主张。各国为了自己的利益,纷纷派出说客,游说列国。

谋略篇

张仪到了魏国，对魏王说：

"魏国的地理条件不好，处于楚、韩、赵、齐中间，打起仗来无法固守是致命的弱点。如果联合楚国而不联合齐国，齐国会从东面进攻；联合齐国而不联合赵国，赵国会从北面进攻；如果不和韩国和好，韩国会从西面进攻；不亲近楚国，它会从南面进攻。这就是四分五裂的道理啊！"

魏王听了这番话，感到非常焦虑。

张仪又说："我真为大王担心，一旦秦国和韩国联合攻打魏国，魏国的灭亡就是旦夕之间的事了。为大王着想，依我之见，还是联合秦国为好。秦国强大，联合了秦国，楚国和韩国一定不敢进犯，魏国就没有亡国的忧虑了。"

在张仪的威逼利诱下，魏王终于依附了秦国。

这则成语的意思是很分散，极不完整，也形容一个国家或一个集团支离破碎、不团结、不统一的情况。人们常用"四分五裂"从另一个角度说明团结的力量和集体主义的重要性。

To Be Split

In the last years of the Warring States Period, seven states struggled for supremacy. During the seven states, Qin State was the most powerful one. In the constant discordant situation between the powerful ones and the weak ones, two kinds of views emerged: one is "Longitudinal Union" represented by Su Qin and the other is "Horizontal Alliance" advocated by Zhang Yi. In order to defend themselves, each state sent their persuasive talkers to persuade different nations.

Zhang Yi arrived in Wei State, and talked with the King, "Your Country is not in a good geographical position, for it is surrounded by the States of Chu, Han, Zhao and Qi. Once there is a war, the biggest disadvantage is that it can't be defended tenaciously. If you unite Chu State but not Qi State, Qi will attack you from the east; if you unite Qi State but not Zhao State, Zhao will attack you from the north; if you don't get along well with Han State, Han will attack you from the west; if you are not close to Chu State, it will attack you from the south. That is the predicament to be split."

Hearing Zhang Yi's words, the King of Wei State was very anxious.

Zhang Yi continued, "I am really concerned about you. Once Qin State unites Han State to attack you, your state will be conquered immediately. In my opinion, for your sake, you should unite with Qin State. Qin is powerful. If you unite with Qin State, Chu State and Han State dare not to invade you. Wei State will not become a conquered nation."

Zhang Yi's threat and promise of gain made the King of Wei State attach to Qin State.

This idiom means being scattered and incomplete. It expresses that a country or a group is fragmented, disunited or decentralized. From another angle people often use this idiom to imply the power of solidarity and the importance of collectivism.

励志篇

志在四方

孔穿,字子高,是孔子的第五代子孙,出游赵国(今河北省南部一带)。

在赵国都城邯郸,他和赵胜(即平原君)门下的宾客邹文、季节两人结成了好朋友。

后来孔穿要回鲁国了,邹文、季节两人上路相送,一直送了三天,陪着走了不少路,总是恋恋不舍。

临别的时候,邹文、季节难过得流下眼泪,而孔穿只躬身向他俩轻轻一揖,就转身而去。

与孔穿同行的人不理解他为什么如此不近人情。孔穿说:"起初我以为他们都是大丈夫,想不到这两个人却如此婆婆妈妈,'人生则有四方之志',怎么能儿女情长、长期聚在一起呢?"

"四方之志"现在一般说作"志在四方",用来形人们的远大志向。该成语也提示大家应有远大的抱负和理想,敢于勇往直前闯天涯。

Having a Great Ambition

Kong Chuan, the fifth-generation descendant of Confucius, styled Zigao, went on a journey to Zhao State (around the southern part of Hebei Province now).

In Handan, the capital of Zhao State, he made good friends with Zou Wen and Ji Jie, hangers-on of Zhao Sheng (Lord of Pingyuan).

Later, Kong Chuan would go back to Lu State, so Zou Wen and Ji Jie had to see him off. They accompanied him for three days on the road and traveled a long journey, but were still reluctant to part with him.

When they had to part, Zou Wen and Ji Jie were in such a deep sorrow that they burst into tears. But Kong Chuan only bent forward and bowed with his hands clasped, and then he turned about and left.

Kong Chuan's companions could not understand why he paid so little attention to human feelings, Kong Chuan explained, "In the beginning I regarded them as great men, but I have never expected that they two are so womanishly fussy. 'When a man lives in the world, he should have a great ambition', how can we be immersed in love and always stay together?"

Now we use this idiom to mean that a person has great ambitions for the interests of his motherland or people. The idiom also inspires that everyone should have lofty aspirations and ideals, and dare to move forward arround the world.

取而代之

秦始皇灭了燕、赵、韩、魏、齐、楚六国，建立了统一强大的秦朝。他为了宣扬威德，进一步巩固统治，经常出巡全国各地。

有一次，秦始皇南巡会稽（在今浙江），当他的车马仪仗，浩浩荡荡地经过南江（今江苏吴县附近）时，大路两旁伫立着无数观看的人群，少年项羽和他的叔父项梁也在其中。

这时，项羽忽然说了这么一句："彼可取而代之也！"

"彼"，即"他"，这里指秦始皇的统治、权势和地位"可以夺取过来并且代替他！"

项梁听了，不禁大吃一惊，急忙伸手去捂住项羽的嘴，小声责备他道："别乱说！你不怕全家合族都要被杀头吗！"但是，项梁却也暗暗赞赏他这个小侄子的胆识。

原来项梁也早在心里盘算着怎样推翻秦朝、恢复楚国的事，不过他没有透露罢了。后来他叔侄俩就在陈胜、吴广领导的农民起义运动中投入了反秦的战斗。

项梁阵亡后，项羽统领项梁的军队继续战斗，在救援赵国的巨鹿之战中，破釜沉舟，一举歼灭秦军主力，成为各路诸侯中赫赫有名的西楚霸王。

取而代之是指排除别人或别的事物而代替其位置。这则典故告诉我们，在现实生活中要有远大志向，不断付出自己的努力，才能有最后的成功。

To Supersede Somebody

After Qinshihuang (the First Emperor of Qin) exterminated the six states of Yan, Zhao, Han, Wei, Qi and Chu, he set up the powerful Qin Dynasty. In order to publicize his power and benevolence and to strengthen his domination, he often went on tours of inspection.

Once upon a time, Qinshihuang went on a south tour of inspection to Kuaiji (now in Zhejiang Province). When the carriages and honor guards that were arranged in formidable array passed Nanjiang (now around Wu County in Jiangsu Province), there were crowds of people watching along both sides of the roads. Among them were young Xiang Yu and his uncle Xiang Liang.

Suddenly, Xiang Yu said, "He can be superseded!"

"He" stood for Qinshihuang. It meant that power and status of the Emperor could be taken over.

Xiang Liang was shocked by Xiang Yu's words. He covered Xiang Yu's mouth and blamed him in a low voice, "Don't talk wildly! Don't you fear our clan will be wiped out?" However, Xiang Liang appreciated his nephew's courage and insight inwardly.

In fact, Xiang Liang had already planned how to overturn Qin Dynasty and recover Chu State in his mind, but he never revealed his thoughts. Later on, they both threw themselves into the peasants' uprising launched by Chen Sheng and Wu Guang to fight against Qin Dynasty.

After Xiang Liang died in the battle, Xiang Yu took over Xiang Liang's army to continue fighting. In the Julu Battle where he rescued Zhao State, he burnt all his boats so as to cut off all the means of retreat and destroyed the main force of Qin. He became the famous King of Western Chu among the feudal countries.

This idiom means getting rid of someone or something so as to replace it. This idiom indicates that in real life only having great ambition and taking continuos efforts can one succeed finally.

励志篇

鹿死谁手

东晋时代，十六国中后赵的开国皇帝名叫石勒。有一天，他设宴招待高丽的使臣，喝酒喝到快醉的时候，他大声地问臣子徐光道："我比得上自古以来的哪一位君王？"

徐光想了一会儿，说："您非凡的才智超过汉代的高祖，卓越的本领又赛过魏朝的始祖，从三王五帝以来，没有一个人能比得上您，您恐怕是轩辕黄帝第二吧！"

石勒听后笑着说："人怎么能不了解自己呢？你说的也太过分了。我如果遇见汉高祖刘邦，一定做他的部下，听从他的命令，只是和韩信、彭越争个高低；假使碰到光武帝刘秀，我就和他在中原一块儿打猎，较量较量，未知'鹿死谁手'？"

后来，人们用"鹿死谁手"这个典故来表示双方争夺的对象不知道会落在谁手里，引申指比赛双方还不知道谁胜谁负。

In Whose Hands Will the Deer Die?

In the era of Eastern Jin Dynasty, Shi Le was the founding emperor of Later Zhao Dynasty in the 16 States. One day he gave a banquet in honor of the envoy from Korea. After drinking for a while, Shi Le asked his minister Xu Guang loudly, "which ancient emperor can I be compared with?"

Xu Guang thought for a moment and said, "Your extraordinary talent can transcend the founding emperor in Han Dynasty and your excellent skill can surpass the first emperor of Wei Dynasty. No one can match you since the three sage kings and five virtuous leaders. You are the second Chinese Xuanyuan Huangdi！"

Hearing these, Shi Le laughed and said, "How come people do not know themselves? You have exaggerated too much. If I met Liu Bang, the founding emperor of West Han Dynasty, I would be under his command and just compete with his famous generals Han Xin and PengYue; if I met Liu Hsiu,

Emperor Guanngwu, the founder of the Eastern Han Dynasty, I would chase the deer and compete with him on the Central Plains. But no one knows the deer will die in whose hands."

Later, we use the idiom "In Whose Hands Will the Deer Die" to indicate it is not known that the target object will fall into whose hands of the two parties; then it is extended to refer to it is unknown which one of the two sides will win the prize.

不让肉食

刘赞，河北魏州（今邯郸魏县）人氏，他的父亲刘玭是县令。刘赞开始读书时，穿的是青布衣衫，每次吃饭时刘玭自己吃肉，而只给刘赞吃蔬菜。

刘玭对刘赞说："肉，是皇上给我的俸禄。你如果想吃，就得勤奋学习挣得俸禄，我吃的肉不是你能吃的。"

因此刘赞更加努力地学习，考中了进士。他做官奉公守法，有权有势的人也不能够从他这里谋求好处。

我们用"不让肉食"这个典故表示不让儿子吃肉，以激其刻苦学习。这则典故表示我们应该有勤俭节约并激发进取的精神。

Not Being Allowed to Eat Meat

Liu Zan was born in Weizhou, Hebei (in today's Wei county of Handan city in Hebei province). His father Liu Pin was a county magistrate. When Liu Zan began to receive education, he was dressed very plainly. At every meal time, only his father ate meat, while Liu Zan was allowed to eat only some vegetables.

His father said to him, "Meat is my official's salary paid by the Emperor. If you want to eat it, you have to study hard to earn the salary. The meat I ate isn't the food that you are qualified to eat."

Consequently, Liu Zan studied harder than before and passed the highest imperial examination. When he held office at court, he carried out official duties and abided by the law. People who had high rank or influence could not reap any benefits from him.

This idiom means not allowing one's son to eat meat so as to encourage him to study hard. This idiom means to stimulate one's enterprising spirit by living an industrious and thrifty life.

5 争先恐后

晋国有个很有名的驾驭能手叫王子期。有一次卿大夫赵襄子（赵国国君的先人）向他学习驾车的技术，不久就自以为了不起，要同王子期比比高低。

比赛开始了，赵襄子刚把车赶到平原上，就挥鞭催马，同王子期双双飞快地追赶起来。

一开始赵襄子遥遥领先，可越跑他的车速度越慢，结果，他换了三次马，还是远远地落在了王子期的后面。

赵襄子不高兴，便把王子期叫到跟前，责备道："你教我驾车，为何不把技术全都教给我？"

王子期解释道："我的技术都毫无保留地全教给您了，可您在运用上有毛病。驾车最重要的是要让马和车协调一致，要让马感到舒服。这样马才能跑得快，跑得远。"

接着，王子期又具体地指出赵襄子的毛病，说："在比赛中，当您跑在前面的时候怕我赶上您，落在后面的时候又拼命想追上我，总是把注意力放在我身上，试问，您哪里还有心思来驾车呢？这就是您落后的原因。"

赵襄子虚心接受了王子期的批评，并认真地按照王子期的指点练习驾车技术，终于成为一位驾车能手。

后来人们用"争先恐后"这个成语来形容争着向前，唯恐落后。在自己的工作岗位上人人应该创优争先。

To Rush on to Be the First

In the ancient Jin State, there lived a famous chariot driver named Wang Ziqi. Zhao Xiangzi (forefather of the rulers of the later Zhao State), Prime Minister of the state, once learned driving from Wang Ziqi. Soon Zhao Xiangzi thought his driving skills outstanding and wanted to have a match with Wang Ziqi.

The match started. As soon as Zhao Xiangzi drove his chariot to the plain, he began to whip his horses to speed up, and chased each other with Wang Ziqi.

At first Zhao Xiangzi kept far ahead, but as time went, he became slower and slower. Although three times he changed his horses, he was far behind Wang Ziqi.

Zhao Xiangzi got angry. He called Wang Ziaqi to him and blamed, "Now that you agree to instruct me to drive, why haven't you taught all your skills to me?"

Wang Ziqi explained, "I have really taught you all my driving skills, but there was something wrong in your exertion. The most important driving skill is to keep the chariot and the horses in harmony and at the same time keep the horses comfortable. Only in this way can the horses run faster and farther."

Then, Wang Ziqi pointed out Zhao Xiangzi's shortcomings concretely, "During the match, when you ran ahead, you were afraid that I would catch up. When you were behind, you tried your best to catch me up. Now that you have paid all your attention to me, how could you have any mind on your driving? That is the basic reason for your falling behind."

Zhao Xiangzi accepted the comment modestly and practiced the driving skills conscientiously according to Wang Ziqi's instructions. At last he became an excellent chariot driver.

Later we use the idiom to indicate that people strive forward and are unwilling to fall behind. In their workplace, everyone should compete with each other to excel in their performances.

青出于蓝，而胜于蓝

南北朝时期，李谧拜孔璠为师，他非常用功好学。过了几年，他的学问就超过了孔璠。孔璠因有这样的好学生而感到高兴。李谧觉得孔璠是老师，因此解答孔璠的问题时吞吞吐吐，很不自然。于是，孔璠诚恳地对他说："我向你请教问题，不要不好意思回答。凡在某一方面有学问的人，都可以做我的老师，何况是你呢！"

孔璠虚心向学生求教的佳话传出后，人们深受感动。有人编了一首短歌，颂扬孔璠不耻下问的精神："青成蓝，蓝谢青，师何常，在明经。"

这首短歌的大意是：靛青这种染料，是从蓼蓝中提炼出来的，然而它却比蓼蓝蓝得更深，颜色更浓。同样，师生关系也不是固定不变的，谁的知识多，谁就可以当老师。

现在我们用这个成语来比喻学生胜过老师或后人胜过先人。只要我们坚持不懈地刻苦学习，艰苦训练，就能够超过老师。

Indigo Blue Is Extracted from the Indigo Plant But Bluer than the Plant

During Southern and Northern Dynasties, Li Mi learned from Kong Fan as a student. Because of very hard study, several years later, Li was more knowledgeable than Kong who was proud of such a talented student. But thinking that Kong was his teacher, Li often minced the words and felt uncomfortable when answering Kong's questions. Thus Kong said sincerely to Li, "Don't be ashamed to answer my questions when I ask for your advice. Everyone with great learning in some aspect can be my teacher, let alone you."

Later, people were greatly moved when hearing that Kong open-mindedly consulted with Li. A short song was composed to praise Kong's merit of not feeling ashamed to learn from his subordinate, whose main idea was that indigo blue was extracted from the indigo plant, but bluer than the plant it came from; teacher-student relationship was not fixed unchangeably, namely, one with more knowledge could be able to be another's teacher.

Now we take this idiom as a metaphor for a student surpassing his teacher or a descendant surpassing his forefathers. As long as we consistently study deligently and train hard, we may exceed our teachers.

7 破釜沉舟

秦朝末年，秦始皇死后，胡亥继位，历史上称为秦二世。秦二世上台后，派大将章邯率大军打败了陈胜、吴广的起义队伍，然后又向北渡过黄河，进攻赵国。赵国招架不住，就派人去楚国求援。楚怀王答应了赵国的请求，派宋义做上将军，项羽做副将，领兵救赵。

楚国的兵马行到安阳，就安营下寨，因为宋义害怕和秦军决战，就一连46天按兵不动。项羽非常气愤，一怒之下杀了宋义，自己代理上将军。项羽夺了兵权，立即派英布和蒲将军，率两万人马过漳河援救赵国，但是没有取得重大胜利。于是项羽就亲自统率部队作战。大军刚过漳河，他就命令全军凿沉全部渡船，砸破所有做饭的大锅，烧掉营房，每个人只带三天的干粮，以此向士卒表示不打胜仗决不回来，非决一死战不可。项羽对部下声色俱厉的大声疾呼："我们这次进军，只能前进，不能后退。要和敌人血战到底，不获全胜誓不罢休！"士兵看到锅都砸了，船都沉了，一点退路也没有，因此都抱着死战到底的决心和秦军拼杀。结果，楚兵以一当十，喊声震天，锐不可当，大败秦军，救了赵国。

后来，人们就用"破釜沉舟"这个成语，来表示只能前进、绝不后退的决心，或是绝不更改、毫不动摇的坚定意向。作为当代大学生，我们一旦做出正确决定，就应该全力以赴，不遗余力地实现它。

To Break the Cauldrons and Sink the Boats

In the late Qin Dynasty, Huhai, Emperor II of Qin State, succeeded to the crown after the First Emperor's death. After he came into power, Emperor II of Qin ordered General Zhang Han to lead the Qin troops to suppress Chen Sheng and Wu Guang's uprising peasant troops. Later the Qin troops crossed the Yellow river to the north and attacked Zhao State. Zhao was unable to withstand the attack and asked reinforcement from Chu State. King Huai of Chu accepted Zhao's request and appointed Song Yi as the Top General and Xiang Yu as the Vice General to lead the Chu troops to rescue Zhao.

Chu troops camped when they arrived in Anyang because Song Yi was afraid to make a decisive battle with the Qin troops and took no action for forty-six days. Xiang Yu was so raged that he killed Song Yi and made himself the deputy Top General. After getting the control of the troops, Xiang Yu immediately ordered General Ying Bu and Pu to command 20,000 soldiers to cross the Zhang River to rescue Zhao, but it played little part in rescuing. Thus Xiang Yu himself led all his troops forward. As soon as his troops had crossed the Zhang River, he ordered them to sink all the boats, smash all the cauldrons, burn down all the barracks, and carry food for only three days, indicating that they would never retreat and have to fight to death. Xiang Yu shouted in stern voice and countenance to all his troops, "This time we will only go ahead and never retreat. We'll fight against the enemy to the last drop of blood and victory is our only choice." Seeing all the boats sunk, all the cauldrons smashed, all the barracks burned down and no way to retreat, powered by this strong-willed determination in a "make-or-break" situation, all the soldiers fought heroically and irresistibly against the Qin troops to the bitter end. Finally, they defeated the Qin troops completely and won the battle. Zhao State was rescued at last.

This idiom indicates one's firm determination to achieve one's goal at any cost. As college students, once we make the right decision, we should go all out and spare no effort to achieve it.

军事篇

军事篇

1 背水一战

公元前204年,汉王刘邦派大将韩信和张耳,率领汉军去攻打赵国。赵王赵歇和赵军统帅陈余,率领20万兵马,集结在井陉口,即现在的河北省井陉山上的井陉关,准备迎战。

赵国谋士李左车向陈余献计说:

"韩信这次领兵前来,一路上打了许多胜仗,他乘胜而来,其锋不可挡。但是他们经过长途跋涉,必定粮草不足,士兵吃不饱,战马也缺乏草料。我们井陉地方的山路很窄,车马很难通过,汉军走不上一百里路,他们的随军粮草必然要落在后面。因此,我有个主意,派三万兵从小路截断他的粮车。你再把沟挖得深些、墙垒得高高的,坚守营寨,不与他们交战。这样一来,他们前不得战、后不得退,用不了十天,我们就可以捉住韩信。"

李左车虽然说得条条在理,可是陈余是一个书呆子,不肯听从他的意见,反而说:"我读过不少兵法,兵书上说,兵力比敌人大十倍,就可以包围它,兵力比敌人大一倍,就可以和他对阵。现在汉军号称几万人,其实不过几千人,况且远道而来,疲惫不堪。我们的兵力超过汉军许多倍,难道还不能把他们消灭掉吗?如果今天避而不战,别人会讥笑我胆小。"他没有采纳李左车的正确意见。

韩信探知陈余不用李左车的计策,十分高兴,就把兵马驻扎在离井陉口30里的地方。到了后半夜,韩信派两千名轻骑兵,每人带一面汉军红旗,从小路迂回到赵营的侧后方,埋伏起来,准备袭取赵营。然后,韩信派一万人马作先头部队,沿着河岸摆开阵势。陈余等人见韩信兵马沿河布阵,都哈哈大笑,说:"韩信空有虚名!背水作战,不留退路,这是自己找死!"

天亮后,韩信带领后队兵马,打出帅旗,大张旗鼓地向井陉口杀来。赵军立即迎战。交战后,汉军假装败退,抛掉旗鼓,向河岸阵地退去。陈余不知是计,指挥赵军拼命追赶。

这时,韩信埋伏的两千轻骑兵,见赵军倾巢而出,立即杀入赵营,拔掉赵军旗子,换上汉军的红旗。

赵军追到汉军背靠河水的阵地后,汉军后退无路,只能背水拼命死战。赵军

119

久战不能获胜，士气开始低落，忽然又发现背后自己的营垒都插上了汉军的红旗，军心顿时大乱，纷纷溃逃。汉军前后夹攻，大破赵军，陈余被杀，赵歇被活捉。

现在我们用"背水一战"比喻没有其他选择，只有决一死战。当代大学生在学习和工作中，面临各种选择或困境时，要排除万难的决心，这样才能到达胜利的彼岸。

To Fight with One's Back to the River

In 204 BC, King Liu Bang of Han State ordered his generals Han Xin and Zhang Er to lead the Han troops to attack Zhao State. King Xie of Zhao State and his commander-in-chief Chen Yu gathered 200,000 troops in Jingxingkou (around Jing- xingguan on Mountain Jingxing in Hebei Province now) to wait for the coming battle.

Li Zuoche, an adviser of Zhao, made a suggestion to Chen Yu, "This time Han Xin's troops have marched forward in many triumphs and wished to make an irresistible attack against Zhao. But after a long and hard journey, the Han troops must be short of military provisions and food and their horses lack of straws. Because in Jingxing the rough and rugged mountain paths make horses and carts very difficult to pass though, the Han troops' military provisions can't keep up with their main force after marching forward 50 kilometers. So in my opinion, you can send 30,000 soldiers to cut off their transportations of military provisions through tortuous trails, and then get our ditches deepened and walls heightened, and hold our camps and positions without meeting their challenges. Thus, we can capture Han Xin within ten days because they have no chance to fight and no way to retreat."

Although Li's suggestion was very reasonable, Chen Yu, a typical pedant, did not follow Li's suggestion. On the contrary, Chen Yu asserted eloquently, "I have read quite a few books on military science. According to the strategies of war, we can besiege the enemy if our troops are ten times more than the enemy; we can make a face-to-face fight against the enemy if our troops are twice as the enemy. Thousands of Han troops, claiming to be tens of thousands, must be extremely exhausted because of a long and hard journey. With overwhelming numbers of troops, we have full confidence to defeat them. Today, if we avoid fighting, others will jeer at my cowardice." Chen Yu failed to adopt Li's advice.

Hearing that Chen didn't take Li's strategy, Han Xin was very pleased and then camped his troops 15 kilometers away from Jingxingkou. After midnight, 2,000 Han cavalry troops with light equipment, everyone with a red Han flag, wound through tortuous trails to the rear beside the Zhao camps and laid in ambush. Later, Han Xin ordered 10,000 troops as vanguards to lay out battle array along the river bank. Seeing such a display, Chen Yu burst into laughter and said, "Han Xin is unworthy of his name! Fighting with his back to the river and leave no way to retreat, Han Xin is sure to meet his death!"

After dawn, with the flag of commander-in-chief flying in the sky, Han Xin commanded his rear army to rush towards Jingxingkou in a big way. After meeting a face-to-face battle with the Zhao troops, the Han troops pretended to fall back, discarded their flags and drums, and finally retreated to their river bank position. Not noting it's a trick, Chen Yu commanded the Zhao troops to chase the Han troops with might and main.

At this moment, seeing that all the Zhao troops rushed out of camps to the battlefield, the 2,000 Han cavalry troops dashed into the Zhao camps at once, removed the Zhao flags and stuck up the Han flags.

When the Zhao troops perused the Han troops to the position on the riverbank, the Han troops had to fight against the enemy to the last drop of blood because they had no way to retreat. The Zhao troops' morale became low because of no chance to win after a long-time fight, and they began to flee in disorder when finding the Han flags flying over the Zhao camps. The Han troops attacked the enemy both from the front and in the rear. Finally, the Zhao troops were completely defeated, with Chen Yu killed and King Xie of Zhao captured.

Now we take this idiom as a metaphor of fighting to one's last drop of blood with no other choice to achieve one's goal. When facing a great many difficulties and choices in study or life, college students should have the confidence to overcome all obstacles so as to be more successful.

拔旗易帜

这则成语的故事内容和前面的背水一战相同。

楚汉战争期间,韩信率汉军数万,东下井陉,攻击赵国。赵国国王和主将陈余率领大兵20万在井陉口聚集,准备迎战。

赵国谋士李左车向陈余献计说:

"韩信一路打了许多胜仗,其锋锐不可当。但是他们经过长途跋涉,必定粮草不足。我们井陉地方的山路很窄,车马很难通过,汉军走不上一百里路,他们的随军粮草必然要落在后面。因此,我有个主意,派三万兵从小路截断他的粮车,你们在此坚守不战。这样一来,他们前不得战、后不得退,用不了十天,我们就可以捉住韩信。"

李左车虽然说得条条在理,可是陈余不肯听从他的意见,反而说:"我读过不少兵法,兵书上说,兵力比敌人大十倍,就可以包围他们,兵力比敌人大一倍,就可以和他们对阵。现在汉军号称几万人,其实不过几千人,况且远道而来,疲惫不堪。我们的兵力超过汉军许多倍,难道还不能把他们消灭掉吗?如果今天避而不战,别人会讥笑我胆小。"他没有采纳李左车的正确意见。

韩信探知陈余不用李左车的计策,十分高兴,就把兵马驻扎在离井陉口三十里的地方。到了后半夜,韩信派两千名轻骑兵,每人带一面汉军红旗,从小路迂回到赵营的侧后方,埋伏起来,准备袭取赵营。

天亮后,韩信带领兵马,大张旗鼓地向井陉口杀来。赵军立即迎战。汉军假装败退,抛掉旗鼓,向河岸阵地退去。陈余不知是计,指挥赵军拼命追赶。

这时,韩信埋伏的两千轻骑兵,见赵军倾巢而出,立即杀入赵营,拔掉赵军的旗子,换上汉军的红旗。

赵军追到汉军背靠河水的阵地后,汉军后退无路,只能背水拼命死战。赵军久战不能获胜,士气开始低落,忽然又发现背后自己的营垒都插上了汉军的红旗,军心顿时大乱,纷纷溃逃。

汉军前后夹攻,大破赵军。陈余被杀,赵王歇被活捉,赵国被汉军攻占。

这则成语的意思是指一事物取代另一事物。

To Pull the Enemy's Flags and Let One's Own Flags Fly

It shares the same story with another idiom: "To Fight with One's Back to the River".

During the Chu-Han War period, Han Xin led tens of thousands of soldiers of the Han Dynasty to advance east to Jingxing and Planned to attack the Zhao State. King of Zhao State and his commander-in-chief Chen Yu gathered 200,000 soldiers in Jingxingkou to wait for the coming battle.

Li Zuoche, an adviser of Zhao, offered a suggestion to Chen Yu, "This time Han Xin's troops have marched forward in many triumphs and will make an irresistible attack against Zhao. But after a long and hard journey, the Han troops must be short of military provisions. Because in Jingxing the rough and rugged mountain paths make horses and carts very difficult to pass through, Han troops' military provisions can't keep up with them after marching forward 50 kilometers. So in my opinion, we can destroy the transportations of their military provisions, and you station here without meeting Han's rival. Thus, we can capture Han Xin within ten days because they will have no chance to fight and no way to retreat."

Although Li's suggestion was very reasonable, Chen Yu did not follow it. On the contrary, Chen Yu asserted eloquently, "I have read quite a few books on military science. According the strategies of war, we can besiege them if our troops are ten times more than the enemy; we can make a face-to-face fight against them if our troops are twice as the enemy. Several thousands of Han troops, with a big talk of tens of thousands, must be very exhausted after such a long and hard journey. With overwhelming numbers of troops, we have full confidence to destroy them. Today, if we avoid fighting, others will jeer at my cowardice." Chen failed to adopt Li's advice.

Han Xin was very pleased after hearing that Chen didn't take Li's strategy, and camped his troops 15 kilometers away from Jingxingkou. After midnight, 2,000 Han light-horsemen, with a red Han flag for each one, wound through tortuous trails to the rear beside the Zhao camps and hid in ambush.

After dawn, Han Xin commanded his troops to rush towards Jingxingkou in a big way. The Han troops pretended to fall back and discarded their flags and drums, and finally retreated to the river bank. Not noting this trick, Chen Yu commanded the Zhao troops to chase the Han troops with might and main.

At this moment, seeing that all Zhao troops rushed out of camps to the battlefield, the 2,000 Han cavalry troops immediately rushed into the Zhao camps, removed the Zhao flags and stuck in the Han flags.

When the Zhao troops forced the Han troops back to the position on the river bank, the Han troops with their backs to the river fought against the enemy to the last drop of blood because of no way to retreat. The Zhao troops' morale became low because of no chance to win after a long-time fight, and they were routed away disorderedly when finding the Han flags flying over their camps. The Han troops attacked the Zhao troops both from the front and in the rear. Finally, the Zhao troops were heavily defeated, with Chen Yu killed, King Xie of Zhao captured and Zhao State occupied.

This idiom means the replacement of someone or something.

3 秋风落叶

东汉末年，天下大乱，群雄互相争斗不休。

曹操在官渡之战中，以少胜多，战胜了北方最强大的敌人袁绍。袁绍死后，他的儿子们为了争夺地盘而互相攻打。

公元204年，袁绍的小儿子袁尚攻打其哥哥袁谭，袁谭抵挡不住，就派使臣辛毗去向曹操求援。

曹操问辛毗："袁尚能不能被我打败？"辛毗说："袁氏兄弟互相残杀，现在连年攻战，百姓穷困，而袁尚严重缺粮，凭借你的强大军力去攻打困乏而没有战斗力的袁尚，无异于秋风扫落叶。"

果然，曹操大军一到，袁氏的势力立即灰飞烟灭，曹操顺利地统一了中国的北方。

我们通常用"秋风落叶"来比喻一扫而光，不复存在。

军 事 篇

Autumn Wind Sweeping the Fallen Leaves

In the end of the East Han Dynasty, the society was out of order; all the warlords were busy fighting each other.

Cao Cao, in the Battle of Guandu, commanded fewer soldiers to defeat a much larger army of Yuan Shao, the most powerful enemy in the north. After he died, Yuan Shao's sons began to fight with each other in order to occupy more territories.

In 204 A.D., Yuan Shang, the youngest son of Yuan Shao, went to attack his elder brother Yuan Tan who could not withstand and sent an emissary named Xin Pi to ask for help from Cao Cao.

Cao Cao asked Xin Pi, "Can I defeat Yuan Shang?" Xin Pi answered, "The Yuan brothers are fighting with each other for years, so that the common people are suffering a lot and becoming poorer and poorer. In addition, right now Yuan Shang is facing with severe grain shortage. If you are going to attack him with your strong military force, the campaign must be like the autumn wind sweeping the fallen leaves.

As expected, when Cao Cao's army came, the powers of the Yuan Family were completely defeated. Therefore, Cao Cao successfully unified the north of China.

Now we usually use this idiom to indicate to get rid of something completely.

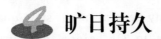

战国时期，燕国打算派高阳君荣蚠率军进攻赵国。荣蚠善于打仗，赵孝成王非常害怕，他与平原君赵胜商量，准备以割让三座城池给齐国为条件，请求齐国大将军田单来担任赵军统帅，抵御燕军的进攻。

赵国名将马服君赵奢坚决反对这样做，他对掌握着国政的赵胜说："难道我们赵国就没有能够胜任的大将吗？仗还没有打，就提出割三座城池给齐国，这成什么话！大王为何不命我为统帅呢？我曾在燕国做过官，那里的情况我很熟悉，派我领兵作战，一定能够取胜，为何要去求助田单呢？"赵奢继续说道，"第一，假如田单愚蠢，那他便打不过荣岔；相反，假如田单聪明，我看他是不会为赵国出力的，因为赵国强盛对齐国称霸极为不利。现在请田单统领赵军，依我看，他一定会把军队拖在战场上，荒废时间，拖延很多年。这样，我国的人力、财力将会消耗殆尽，后果不堪设想。"

赵王没有听取赵奢的意见，仍把赵军交给田单指挥。结果，事情的结局正像赵奢所预言的那样，战争拖延了很长时间，赵国的兵马死伤无数，却只夺到燕国三座小城，没有取得预计的胜利。

成语"旷日持久"即由此而来。现在人们引用这个成语，来比喻荒废时间，拖延很久。我们要不断地在知识、能力方面提高自己，遇到困难要自强自立，要善于把握机遇，不能盲目拖延而使自己陷于困境。

A Long-Drawn-Out Situation

During the Warring States Period, Yan State intended to send Rong Fen, Lord Gaoyang, to attack Zhao State. Rong Fen was quite acquainted with the military art. King Xiaocheng of Zhao State was scared, so he talked it over with Zhao Sheng, Lord Pingyuan. King Xiaocheng intended to cede three cities to Qi State provided that Tian Dan, the great general of Qi, could be the commander of Zhao troops to resist the invasion of Yan.

Zhao She, Lord Mafu, was the famous general of Zhao State. He was strongly against this idea. He said to Zhao Sheng who managed the whole state affairs, "Isn't there any general in our state qualifying for the position? We will cede three cities to Qi before the battle begins. That's really ridiculous! Why not appoint me to be the commander in chief? I once was an official of Yan, so I know clearly about the circumstances there. If you send me to the battle as the general, I'm sure we will win. Why should we ask for help from Tian Dan?" Continued Zhao She, "If Tian Dan is stupid, he will not defeat Rong Fen; on the contrary, if he is wise, I don't think he will do his best to help us, because our prosperity means disadvantage to Qi. Now if you ask for Tian Dan to be the commander of Zhao troops, in my point of view, he will let grass grow under their feet and waste time on the battlefield for many years. Then it will cost most of our energy and wealth. There will be the devil to pay."

However, the King of Zhao State didn't take Zhao She's advice. He still made Tian Dan the commander of Zhao troops. At the end, the result was just as Zhao She had foretold. The war had been lasting for a long time. The troops and the horses of Zhao State died and injured in large number, yet they only got three little towns of Yan. They didn't achieve the victory as they expected.

Now people use "A Long-Drawn-Out Situation" to mean the waste of time or delay for a long time. We need to enrich our knowledge and enhance our abilities to get over any possible difficulties by ourselves and grasp the favorable opportunities, instead of landing ourselves into a predicament by blind delay.

5 攻难守易

战国时，长平之役惨败后的赵国，想通过掠夺燕国国土，来弥补损失。

赵国相国平原君就此问题，向大将冯忌征求意见。

冯忌说："秦国凭借七战七胜的军威，在长平之战后，乘胜围攻邯郸城，而我们只靠散兵败卒坚守，秦军不仅没有攻破，反而消磨了锐气。这是什么缘故？就是由于攻起来难而守起来易。"

冯忌继续分析到："赵国既没有屡战屡胜之威风，而燕国也没有遭受像长平之战那样巨大的损失，拿我们疲惫不堪的军队，去攻打燕国，不仅占不到什么便宜，还会让秦国钻我们的空子。那样做，其后果是不堪设想的。"

平原君赵胜觉着冯忌的话很有道理，便取消了攻打燕国的想法。

"攻难守易"这个典故是比喻坚守以逸待劳，与攻取相比更为容易。

It Is Difficult to Attack but Easy to Defend

During the Warring States Period, after the disastrous defeat in the war of Changping, Zhao State attempted to take possession of the Yan State to recuperate. At this point Lord of Pingyuan, the Prime Minister of Zhao asked General Feng Ji for advice.

Feng Ji said, "With the army prestige of sweeping seven wars, Qin State exploited its victories to siege Handan after the war of Changping. However, in the tough defending by our skirmishers, Handan city wasn't captured by the Qin troops, what's more, we have weakened our opponent's dash. Why? It goes that way simply because it is difficult to attack but easy to defend."

Then Feng Ji made a further analysis and said, "Our country has not the ever-victorious army prestige, and Yan has not suffered such enormous losses as the war of Changping. Sending our exhausted army to attack the powerful Yan State will not do good to us. On the contrary, the mighty Qin State will exploit an advantage of it and attack us. In that case, the consequence is inconceivable."

Considering what Feng Ji said was reasonable, Lord of Pingyuan, Zhao Sheng, gave up the idea of attacking Yan State.

The idiom "It Is Difficult to Attack but Easy to Defend" means that compared with immediate attack, strong defending and waiting at ease for an exhausted enemy is easier.

不遗余力

战国时候，秦国攻打赵国，赵国大将廉颇率军在长平与秦军交战，赵军失利。赵孝成王急忙将大臣虞卿和楼昌召来，商量对策。

孝成王说："我决意集中兵力与秦军打一仗，如何？"楼昌主张求和。虞卿虽不赞同赵王的意见,但他却不主张求和。虞卿说:"大王,您认为秦军是一定要将我们打败吗?"

赵王说:"秦军这次是一点力量也不留,看来是想将我们一举打败!"

虞卿说:"依臣之见,秦国既然想将我们一举击败,那么他们是一定不会轻易收兵讲和。我有个主意,我们派使者带重礼向楚王和魏王求救,秦国害怕我们和楚、魏联合起来,就会要求同我们讲和。那时候再讲和,我们才不会吃亏。"

但是,孝成王过于担心会被秦军彻底打败,没有听从虞卿的劝告,急忙派特使向秦军求和。结果不出虞卿所料,秦国认为赵国害怕,没有轻易答应赵王的求和要求,反而再次出击,不仅攻下长平,而且连赵国的都城邯郸也被包围起来。后来秦国虽然撤军,但提出必须割让六座城池,才肯答应与赵国讲和。

孝成王又召来虞卿商量此事。

虞卿说:"秦国这次集中数十万兵力攻打我国,是倾尽了全力的。现在他们因疲惫而撤军,您却轻易地答应他们的讲和条件,把六座城池拱手送给他们,这不等于帮助敌人来进攻自己吗?"

赵王点头称是,但却想不出对策。

虞卿说:"依臣之见,这六座城池还不如赠送给齐国。齐和秦素来有仇,齐王得到城池后一定会帮我们攻打秦国。到那时,秦王必定会主动向我们求和的。"

这次,赵王听从了虞卿的劝告,派虞卿到齐国谋划去了。

果然又不出虞卿所料,秦国很快派使者主动向赵国讲和了。

"不遗余力"形容用尽全部力量,不保留一点剩余的力量。青年人要有不遗余力地为实现自己的理想而努力的精神。

Sparing No Efforts

During the Warring States Period, Qin State invaded Zhao State. General Lian Po of Zhao led the army to resist the Qin troops at Changping city, but got no advantages.

King Xiaocheng of Zhao called his ministers Yu Qing and Lou Chang together to ask for some countermeasures. The King said, "I have made the decision to fight a final battle against the Qin army, what you think of that?"

Lou Chang was for negotiation for peace, but Yu Qing was for neither the idea of the King nor Lou Chang's proposal. Yu Qing said, "My lord, do you think the Qin troops want to beat us by all means?"

The King sighed and said, "The Qin troops now do their best to fight against us, and it seems that they want to beat us at one stroke."

Yu Qing said, "I think if Qin state wants to defeat us completely they won't easily change their mind and retreat their troops through negotiation. I have got a good idea we can send an envoy taking tribute to ask for help from King of Chu State and King of Wei State. In fear of our ally with Chu and Wei, Qin will negotiate a truce with us. At that time, it is advantageous to our negotiation."

Worrying about being defeated thoroughly, King Xiaocheng instantly sent an envoy to ask for peace negotiation with the Qin army. Just as Yu Qing said, Qin thought Zhao was scared, so the negotiation was refused. The Qin troops launched one attack after another and captured Changping and surrounded Handan, the capital city of Zhao State. Later the Qin army agreed to negotiate with Zhao for peace and retreat, provided Zhao ceded six cities to Qin.

King Xiaocheng consulted with Yu Qing again.

Yu Qing said, "Qin has assembled hundreds of thousands of soldiers to invade us, which means they have done their endeavor to do this. Now they agree to retreat because their army is exhausted. Your agreement to cede six cities to them means nothing but to help the enemies to invade ourselves!"

The King nodded but didn't know the countermeasures.

Yu Qing said, "In my opinion, the six cities can be presented to Qi State because there is always enmity between Qi and Qin. If we give the six cities to Qi, we can get the assistance of Qi to fight against Qin. Under such circumstances, Qin must sue for negotiation with us."

This time the King took Yu Qing's advice and sent Yu Qing to Qi to bring the plan into effect.

军 事 篇

Just as Yu Qing expected, in no time Qin sent an envoy to ask for peace negotiation with Zhao.

Sparing no efforts is an idiom that means trying one's best to do something. Young people should keep the determination to spare no efforts to pursue their ideals.

7 扬兵戏马

王莽的新朝被起义军推翻之后,刘秀由于功勋卓著,被更始帝封为萧王,并被派往河北去平定各路地方豪强势力。刘秀在河北得到了大将吴汉和彭宠。

吴汉,字子颜,河南南阳人,曾以贩马为业。他劝说当时的渔阳太守彭宠一起投奔了刘秀,任偏将军。

在刘秀与邯郸人王郎交战时,吴汉率领精锐骑兵绕邯郸城驰骋,使敌军为之胆寒。后来攻克邯郸,击杀王郎,吴汉因功封为建策候。

吴汉后来又参加了镇压铜马农民起义军,并袭杀更始政权的尚书谢躬,攻占邺城和其他地区,因功封广平候,成为东汉的开国功臣之一。

"扬兵戏马"这个成语的意思是高举兵器,策马驰骋,比喻耀武扬威,嘲弄敌人。

这则成语告诉我们要在工作和学习中勇于展示自己的实力。

Displaying One's Strength

During the end of the West Han Dynasty, Wang Mang established the New Dynasty, but was soon overthrown by the uprising army. Liu Xiu performed meritorious deeds repeatedly in the campaigns against Wang Mang's troops. For his outstanding performance, Liu Xuan entitled him Lord Xiao by Emperor Gengsh and was dispatched to Hebei to suppress the local powers, where he gained two outstanding generals Wu Han and Peng Chong.

Wu Han, styled Ziyan, came from Nanyan of Henan Province and his former occupation was buying and selling horses. He persuaded Peng Chong, the prefect of Yuyang to submit to Liu Xiu, and was appointed assistant general.

During the battle between Liu Xiu and Wang Lang from Handan, Wu Han led the crack cavalry troops galloping outside Handan with their weapons held high, making the enemy frightened. Later Wu Han conquered Handan and killed Wang Lang. And he was therefore granted as Marquis of Jiance.

Then Wu Han took part in suppressing the Tongma's uprising army, attacked and killed Xie Gong, the minister of Gengshi government, and occupied the Yecheng and other vast areas. Because of his achievements, Wu Han was granted as Marquis of Guangping and became one of the founding generals of the Eastern Han Dynasty.

This idiom means holding weapons high and galloping, which refers to displaying one's strength or power.

It tells us that we should be good at displaying our strength ability in study and work.

8 作壁上观

秦朝末年，大将章邯领兵攻打赵国，赵军大败，逃到巨鹿（即现在的河北省平乡县）死守。章邯派将领王离、涉间把巨鹿紧紧包围起来。

赵王一边死守鉅鹿，一边派人向各国求救。前来救赵的各国军队，在距鉅鹿城很远的地方修筑十多个营垒，他们按兵不动，没有一个敢出来同秦军作战。

为了解救赵国，项羽率领楚军渡过漳河，赶到鉅鹿城外，立即把秦军包围起来，与秦军进行决战。

楚军与秦军展开了激烈的搏斗，战场上战鼓齐鸣，杀声震天。项羽挥戈跃马，

军 事 篇

带头冲入敌阵,斩秦将苏角。楚军将士以一当十,拼命死战。项羽指挥楚军连续向秦军发起进攻,杀得秦军血流成河,尸积如山。

各国将士见楚军与秦军奋勇血战,都站在自己的营垒上观看,惊得目瞪口呆。

巨鹿之战,项羽消灭了秦军的主力。秦将王离被俘,涉间自杀,章邯被迫投降。各国军队的主将一起来拜见项羽,表示愿意服从项羽指挥。项羽从此威震天下,成了统帅各国军队的上将军。

我们现在往往用这句成语比喻坐观成败,不去帮助;置身事外,持观望态度。

To Stay Behind the Breastworks and Watch Others Fight

In the late period of Qin Dynasty, General Zhang Han commanded his troops to attack Zhao State. Zhao troops were defeated utterly, and retreated to Julu (around Pingxiang County of Hebei Province) to make a last-ditch defense. Zhang Han assigned General Wang Li and She Jian to surround Julu closely.

King of Zhao made a last-ditch defense and at the same time dispatched messengers to ask help from other states. The troops from other states came to save Zhao, built more than ten camps at the place far away from Julu. They held their troops in the camps, but no one dared to fight with Qin troops.

In order to rescue Zhao, Xiang Yu led Chu troops across Zhang River immediately to surround the Qin troops at the outside of Julu city. He carried out a decisive battle with Qin troops.

The Chu troops and the Qin troops engaged in a fierce battle. Riding on his horse and brandishing his weapon, Xiang Yu took the lead into the enemy positions. He killed Su Jiao who is one of the generals of Qin State. The soldiers of Chu State fought desperately, they pitted one against ten. Under Xiang Yu's directing, the Chu troops launched continuous attacks to the Qin troops. Their attacks made the blood of soldiers flow like river and their corpses piled up into a mountain. The losses of the Qin troops were great.

The generals and soldiers from other states were all struck dumb with fear as standing on their camps and watching the fight between the Chu troops and the Qin troops.

In the battle of Julu, Xiang Yu annihilated main strength of the Qin troops. General Wang Li was captured, She Jian committed suicide and Zhang Han was forced to surrender. The chief commanders of all the states came to visit Xiang Yu to express their willings to obey his direction. From then on, Xiang Yu was well-known and became the chief general of all the states.

Now we often use this idiom to mean sitting idly by without lending a helpful hand and staying aloof from the affair.

犹豫不决

战国时，有一年秦军围困了赵国都城邯郸，赵王派人前往魏国请求援救。魏王派大将晋鄙领兵救赵，但又害怕强大的秦军，让军队在汤阴停留下来，不再前进；又派将领辛垣衍暗中潜入邯郸，通过赵国的相国平原君赵胜告诉赵王说，秦国之所以急迫地包围邯郸，是因为秦昭王想称帝，而并非为了夺取城池，占据地盘。如果赵国能派使臣向秦昭王表明愿意尊他为帝，那么秦王必定很高兴，一定会休战离去。

平原君听了，一时拿不定主意，没有决定下来。

这时，齐国的谋士鲁仲连恰好在赵国游历，了解到这件事，就去见平原君。他请平原君介绍，会见了辛垣衍。鲁仲连向他解释了不能尊秦王为帝的理由，使辛垣衍改变了原来的看法。平原君也拿定主意，决定抗击秦军。他再次派人去魏国，请魏将晋鄙发兵救赵。

"犹豫不决"也称"犹豫未决"。这则成语的意思是迟疑，拿不定主意。人们要善于根据主客观情况，果断决策，适时采取行动，不能犹豫不觉而导致失去发展自己的机会。

To Be in Two Minds

During the Warring States Period, one year the Qin troops besieged Handan, the capital of Zhao State. The King of Zhao State dispatched a messenger to ask for help from Wei State. The King of the Wei sent general Jinbi lead Wei troops to rescue Zhao. For fear of the power of the Qin troops, the Wei troops didn't move on and stationed at Tangyin. At the same time, the king assigned General Xin Yuanyan sneak into Handan. Xin Yuanyan intended to tell the King of Zhao about Qin's reason for surrounding Zhao through Zhao Sheng's mouth, Lord Pingyuan who was the prime minister of Zhao. Xin Yuanyan said, "Qin's reason for surrounding Zhao is not to conquer the city and occupy the sites of Zhao, but that the King of Qin intends to proclaim himself as the emperor. If Zhao would like to send a diplomat to Qin and express the willing to respect King Zhao of the Qin State as the emperor, the King of Qin must be very happy and withdraw his troops.

On hearing these, Lord Pingyuan hesitated and didn't know what to do.

At that time, Lu Zhong, the adviser of Qi State was traveling in Zhao. On hearing this matter, he went to visit Lord Pingyuan. Lu Zhong asked Lord Pingyuan to introduce him to Xin Yuanyan. He went to visit Xin Yuanyan and explained to him the reasons why not to respect the King of Qin as the emperor. Lu Zhong even made Xin Yuanyan change his mind. Then Lord Pingyuan also set his mind to defend the Qin troops. He dispatched another messenger to Wei state to ask general Jinbi to lead his troops to rescue Zhao State.

"To Be in Two Minds" means being hesitating and can't make a decision. People should not hesitate to make decisions and take opportune actions in the light of objective circumstances and their own conditions, instead of letting go of the opportunities to improve themselves due to hesitation.

乘胜追击

前秦王苻坚派王猛攻击前燕，攻占晋阳后，与镇守邺城的慕容评的军队相持于邺城之外，经过激战，大败慕容评，斩首五万多人，于是趁着胜利的形势继续追击敌人，扩大战果。最终，指挥部队包围了邺城。

苻坚听说后，命李威留守长安辅佐太子，苻融镇守洛阳，他亲自率领精锐部队十万奔向邺城方向。

这个成语的意思是趁着胜利的形势继续追击敌人，扩大战果。我们在学习和工作中都应该有一鼓作气、不断自我完善的精神，决不能满足于已有的成绩而停止不前。

To Pursue Enemy Troops in Retreat

Fu Jian, the King of Qianqin appointed Wang Meng to attack Qianyan State. After capturing Jinyang city, outside Yecheng city they confronted the troops of Murong Ping who was guarding the city. After a fierce battle, they defeated utterly the troops of Murong Ping and beheaded more than fifty thousand enemy soldiers. Later on they continued to chase the enemy by taking advantage of a favorable situation and exploited the victory. Finally, the troops of Wang Meng besieged Yecheng city.

Hearing that, Fu Jian ordered Li Wei to stay in Chang'an city to assist the prince in governing the state and commanded Fu Rong to guard Luoyang city. However, Fu Jian himself led one hundred thousand crack troops to head for Yecheng city.

This idiom means continuing to chase the enemy by taking advantage of a favorable situation and exploiting the victory. We should press on without letup to acquire more achievements and to improve ourselves incessantly in our study and work, instead of resting on the achievements and hesitating to move forward.

军 事 篇

釜底抽薪

东汉末年,军阀混战,河北袁绍乘势崛起。公元199年,袁绍率领十万大军攻打许昌。当时,曹操据守官渡,兵力只有二万多人。袁绍和曹操两军隔河对峙。

袁绍仗着人马众多,派兵攻打白马。曹操表面上放弃白马,命令主力移往延津渡口,摆开渡河架势。

袁绍怕后方受敌,迅速率主力西进,阻挡曹军渡河。谁知曹操虚晃一枪之后,突派精锐回袭白马,斩杀袁军大将颜良,初战告捷。

由于两军相持了很长时间,双方粮草供给成了关键。袁绍从河北调集了一万多车粮草,屯集在大本营以北四十里的乌巢。曹操探听乌巢并无重兵防守,决定采取釜底抽薪之计,偷袭乌巢,断其供应。

他亲自率五千精兵打着袁绍的旗号,衔枚疾走,夜袭乌巢。乌巢袁军还没有弄清真相,曹军已经包围了粮仓。一把大火点燃,顿时浓烟四起。曹军乘势消灭了守粮袁军,袁军的一万车粮草,顿时化为灰烬,袁绍大军闻讯,惊恐万状,供应断绝,军心浮动,袁绍一时没了主意。曹操此时,发动全线进攻,袁绍士兵已丧失战斗力,十万大军四散溃逃。袁军大败,袁绍带领八百亲兵,艰难地杀出重围,回到河北,从此一蹶不振。

这则成语指从根本上解决紧急问题。

To Take Away the Firewood from under the Cauldron

In the late East Han Dynasty, wars frequently broke out among the warlords. Yuan Shao leapt at the chance and occupied Hebei. In 199 AD, he attacked Xuchang with one hundred thousand warriors. Cao Cao stationed and guarded Guandu with only more than twenty thousand soldiers. Thus the two armies confronted each other across the river. Taking advantage of his great forces, Yuan Shao attacked Cao Cao's fort at Baima. Cao Cao pretended to give up Baima and to have his main force march towards Yanjin Ferry, as if being ready to cross the river.

Yuan Shao was afraid that his rear might be threatened, and immediately commanded his main force to advance westwards to stop Cao Cao from crossing the river. With a feint of crossing the river, Cao Cao then struck back with his elite force and killed Yan Liang, one of Yuan Shao's senior generals, obtaining the victory at the start of the campaign.

Since the two sides had been in a stalemate for a long time, the key point was the supply of grain. Yuan Shao assembled ten thousand carts of provisions from Hebei, and reserved them at the depot in Wuchao, a place 40 li to the north of his main camp. Cao Cao learned that Wuchao was not heavily guarded, so he decided to adopt the strategy of "To Take Away the Firewood from under the Cauldron" and launch a sneak raid so as to destroy Yuan Shao's provisions.

Thus Cao Cao led a force of five thousand best soldiers with his enemy's banners to attack Wuchao at night. They marched in a fast pace with each soldier keeping a stick in his mouth. Cao Cao's soldiers had surrounded the depot in Wuchao before Yuan Shao's soldiers came to know what had happened. Soon fire broke out and heavy smoke blotted out everywhere. Cao Cao's soldiers seized the opportunity and wiped out Yuan Shao's guarding troops and all the supplies were reduced to ashes. Yuan Shao's army was seized with terror at the reports of the fire. His army's morale lowered sharply due to the loss of food supplies. For a moment Yuan Shao didn't know what to do. At this moment, Cao Cao's forces launched attack in all fronts. Yuan's soldiers had no ability to fight and the force of one hundred thousand scattered. Yuan Shao fled north to Hebei with only about 800 soldiers and suffered a complete collapse.

This idiom means taking fundamental measures to deal with an emergency.

教训篇

大儒纵盗

春秋时期，在上地（今陕西绥德县一带）住着一个知识渊博的儒者，名叫牛缺，人们都尊称他为大儒。

有一天，大儒到邯郸去，在渨水（古赵地，今邢台沙河）碰到一伙盗贼。

盗贼索要大儒口袋里的钱财，他便痛痛快快地全部给了他们。盗贼又索要大儒的车马，他也慷慨地给了他们。盗贼还要大儒的衣服和被褥，他还是痛痛快快地给了他们。

大儒把东西全部送得干干净净后，便步行而走。

盗贼们感到惊奇，私下议论道："这一定是天下杰出的人，今天我们侮辱了他，他一定会向大国的君主诉说我们的所做所为。君主也一定会用所有力量来对讨我们，那时我们就难以活命了。还不如现在就把他杀死，以消除后患。"

于是，盗贼们又向前追赶了三十里地，最后追上大儒，把他杀死了。

对此，秦国的相国吕不韦在其著作中评论说：大儒之所以被杀，是因为他纵容盗贼的结果。

"大儒纵盗"这个典故，常被用来讽喻那些不分是非曲直，一昧无原则地对犯罪分子讲善良宽容的人们。

Great Scholar Conniving the Robbers

During the Spring and Autumn Period, there lived a knowledgeable scholar in Shangdi (around Suide County in Shaanxi Province now), whose name was Niu Que, and the local people respected him and called him "Great Scholar".

One day, the great scholar went to Handan and met a group of robbers in Yushui (a place of ancient Zhao State, Shahe County in Xingtai City now).

The robbers wanted the money in his pockets and he gave to them racily.

The robbers wanted his carriage and horses and he gave to them generously.

教 训 篇

The robbers wanted his clothing and bedding and he gave to them without any hesitation.

The great scholar gave everything to the robbers and walked away.

The robbers felt astonished and discussed in private, "This must be an outstanding man under the sun. Today we have insulted him and he will be certain to pour out what we have done to the ruler of a great state; and the ruler will send all his forces to suppress us, then we will lose our lives. Therefore we had better kill him now, exterminate the traces and eliminate the future trouble."

So, the robbers chased the great scholar for 30 li, caught up and killed him.

Lu Buwei, the prime minister of Qin State, commented on this event in his works that the great scholar was killed because he connived the robbers.

We often use this idiom "Great Scholar Conniving the Robbers" to satire those people who are so good and tolerant to criminals without differing rights and wrongs and without principles.

邯郸学步

相传在战国的时候，赵国邯郸人走路的姿势，特别优美好看。在北方的燕国寿陵，有个青年人，不顾路途遥远，跋山涉水，到邯郸来学习当地人走路的姿势。

他整天在邯郸的大街上，观看人家怎样走路。他边看边琢磨人家走路的特点，又模仿着做，跟这个人后边走几步，再跟那个人后边走几步。可是学来学去，总是不像，始终没有学会邯郸人走路的步法。

这个青年人心想：也许自己多年来习惯了原来的走法，所以学不好。于是他索性丢掉原来的走法，从头学习走路。从此，他每走一步都很吃力，既要想着手脚如何摆动，又要想着腰腿如何配合，还得想着每一步的距离……把他弄得手足无措。

他越学越差劲，一连学了几个月，不但没有学会邯郸人的步法，而且把自己原来的步法也忘掉了。他的钱已经花光，不得不返回寿陵，可是他已经忘记怎样走路了，只好狼狈地爬回去。

后人用"邯郸学步"来讽刺那些自己无主见、无创造，胡乱模仿别人的人，不但学不成，反而把自己原来会的东西也忘掉了。我们要善于学习别人的长处，更要学会创新和发展自我。

Learning to Walk in Handan

During the Warring States Period, Handan, the capital of Zhao State, was famous for people's elegant walking style. A young man lived in the Shouling area of Yan State, who trudged over a long and hard journey to Handan to learn the local people's way of walking.

For a whole day, he observed how the people walked in the streets of Handan. While observing, he refined the style of Handan people's walking and then intimated. He kept intimating for several strides after a person and then another person. But however he learned with heart, he couldn't learn how to walk like the Handan people.

This young man thought that maybe he himself was used to walking in his original way for many years, so he couldn't learn another new walking style. Thus, he completely gave up his old way of walking and learned the new one from the beginning. From then on, he found it uneasy to learn each step because he should bear in mind how to sway hands and feet and how to cooperate his feet with his waist, and simultaneously reminding himself the distance of each step. Finally, he made himself at a loss and in a flutter.

He walked worse and worse. For several months, he had not only failed to learn the Handan people's walking gestures, but had also forgotten his original style. By this time, he had run out of all his money, so he had to return home. But he couldn't recall his original walking posture, so in the end, the young man had no choice but scramble on the ground all the way back to Yan State.

We use this idiom to describe someone who imitates others blindly only to lose his own individuality. As we learn from others, we also have to know how to bring forth new ideas to improve ourselves.

教 训 篇

纸上谈兵

　　战国时期，赵国大将赵奢曾以少胜多，大败入侵的秦军，被赵惠文王提拔为上卿。他有一个儿子叫赵括，从小熟读兵书，张口爱谈军事，别人往往说不过他。因此他很骄傲，自以为天下无敌。然而赵奢却很替他担忧，并且说："将来赵国不用他为将罢了。如果用他为将，他一定会使赵军遭受失败。"

　　公元前259年，秦军又来犯，赵军在长平坚持抗敌。那时赵奢已经去世，廉颇负责指挥全军，他年纪虽高，打仗仍然很有办法，使得秦军无法取胜。秦国宰相范雎知道拖下去于己不利，就施行了反间计，派人到赵国散布"秦军最害怕赵括领兵"。赵王上当，不顾蔺相如和赵奢夫人的劝阻，派赵括替代了廉颇。

　　赵括自认为很会打仗，死搬兵书上的条文，到长平后完全改变了廉颇的作战方案。那边范雎得到赵括替换廉颇的消息，知道自己的反间计成功，就秘密派白起为上将军，去指挥秦军。白起一到长平，布置好埋伏，故意打了几阵败仗。赵括不知是计，拼命追赶。白起把赵军引到预先埋伏好的地区，派出精兵切断了赵军的后路；另派骑兵直冲赵军大营，把赵军切成两段。

　　赵括这才知道秦军的厉害，只好筑起营垒坚守，等待救兵。秦国又发兵把赵国救兵和运粮的道路切断了。

　　赵括的军队，内无粮草，外无救兵，守了四十多天，兵士都叫苦连天，无心作战。赵括带兵想冲出重围，秦军万箭齐发，把赵括射死了。赵军听到主将被杀，也纷纷扔了武器投降，最后全部被白起所杀。四十余万赵军，就在纸上谈兵的主帅赵括手里全部覆没了。

　　这则成语是指在文字上谈用兵策略，比喻不联系实际情况，空发议论。

An Armchair Strategist

　　During the Warring States Period (475-221B.C.), Zhao She, a great general of Zhao State, was promoted to be the Secretary of the State by King Huiwen, for his defeat of the invading Qin State army which was stronger and much larger than Zhao army in number. He had a son named Zhao Kuo who had been familiar with the books of tactics since his childhood and enjoyed arguing about military affairs with others and he always turned out to be the winner. So he became very proud of that and thought he was invincible in the world. However, General Zhao She was worried about him in this respect because he thought his son was just an armchair strategist. So he said, "I hope he couldn't be appointed the general of Zhao State; otherwise, Zhao army will suffer fatal defeat."

In 259 B.C., Qin State launched the invasion to Zhao again. The Zhao army resisted the Qin army at Changping. At that time, General Zhao She had passed away, and the general in charge was Lian Po who was advanced in years but knew the art of war, so the Qin army couldn't get victory then. Fan Ju, the Prime Minister of King Qin, felt the disadvantage in this war if it lasted too long, so he made mischief and sent someone to Zhao to propagandize that the Qin army was only afraid of General Zhao Kuo. King of Zhao was caught with chaff and replaced General Lian Po with Zhao Kuo, ignoring the dissuasion of Lin Xiangru and Zhao Kuo's mother.

Zhao Kuo arrogantly thought that he was very skilled in military affairs and followed rigidly the rules in military books. When he arrived at Changping, he totally changed the battle plan of General Lian Po. Fan Ju learned that his mischief worked and he secretly sent General Bai Qi to command the army. When Bai Qi arrived, he instantly prepared the ambush and pretended to be defeated by Zhao Kuo for several times. Zhao Kuo didn't know it was a trap and chased the Qin army at full speed. The Qin army led Zhao Kuo and his army into the trap and sent strong soldiers to cut off the retreat of the Zhao army, and then sent the cavalry troops to attack the Zhao army battalion, which cut the Zhao army into two.

Zhao Kuo learned the power of Qin army, so he had to build rampart and wait for the reinforcements. Qin sent a troop to cut off the routes of Zhao army reinforcements and its logistics.

Having no reinforcements and no food, the Zhao soldiers lost their heart in this war and complained bitterly. Zhao Kuo led his army and tried to break the besiege but was killed by the Qin army's arrows. Learning the news, the

教训篇

Zhao army gave up their weapons and surrendered, but all the soldiers were killed by the Qin army despite their giving in. Zhao Kuo's engaging in idle theorizing killed 400,000 soldiers of Zhao State.

This idiom means talking about the art of war only on paper. It refers to the engagement in idle theorizing with no contact with reality.

4 铸成大错

唐朝末年，朱全忠在朝廷做节度使。他的势力非常大，曾领兵打败了许多大将，占了不少地盘，后来又阴谋杀了唐昭宗，很多人都依附于他。

朱全忠的亲家罗绍威，想借他的力量除掉魏州的田承嗣。田承嗣招募了五千骁勇善战的士兵，组成一支牙军，镇守魏州，十分骄横。罗绍威向朱全忠请求援军，朱全忠便派十万大军去攻打魏州。这时正巧赶上罗绍威的儿子罗廷规病故，朱全忠借吊唁女婿为名，将兵士乔装成家人，提囊挑担，混入魏州。罗绍威事先派人偷偷地把魏州军的武器库破坏了，结果魏州军被偷袭，城内八千户百姓被杀的一个不剩。

朱全忠带兵进入魏州，住了半年。罗绍威给他们杀了牛羊七十万只，粮食更是不计其数，又送给朱全忠金银百万，结果将魏州的积蓄挥霍一空。罗绍威虽然赶跑了敌手，可是自己的兵力却日渐衰弱了。他因此非常后悔，见人就说："我算是做错了，即使把魏州的六州四十三个县的铁全聚在一块，也铸不成我这么大的错啊！"

后人用"铸成大错"这则典故形容错误的重大。这个故事告诉我们无论做什么事，都要考虑周全，谨慎行事，以免铸成大错而悔之不及。

To Make a Gross Error

In late Tang Dynasty, Zhu Quanzhong was a higher official of the royal government. He had great influence and had led his troops to defeat many senior general and seized many places. Later he killed Emperor Zhaozong of Tang by plot. Many people attached themselves to him.

Luo Shaowei, Zhu Quanzhong's relative by marriage, intended to get rid of Tian Chengsi by using Zhu Quanzhong's power. Tian Chengsi was very domineering. He recruited an army of 5,000 soldiers who were brave and well versed in battles. They guarded Weizhou and were very arrogant. Luo Shaowei sought assistance from Zhu Quanzhong, so Zhu Quanzhong dispatched 100,000 soldiers to attack Weizhou. It was coincident that Luo Tinggui, Luo Shaowei's son, died of illness at that time. On the excuse of condoling over his son-in-law, Zhu Quanzhong let soldiers sneak into Weizhou, they are disguised as the servants to carry on the luggage. Luo Shaowei had sent someone to destroy the weapon storehouse of Weizhou in advance. As a result, the Weizhou troops launched a surprise attack and eight thousand families in the city were all killed.

Zhu Quanzhong led his soldiers to occupy the city for half a year. Luo Shaowei slaughtered 700,000 sheep and cattle, provided countless grain to entertain them. He even gave Zhu Quanzhong a million of treasures. As a result, the savings of Weizhou were all spent out. Although Luo Shaowei had driven away his enemy, his own military strength declined day by day. He was very regretted and said before everybody, "I had made a gross error. Even if gather together all the iron in the 6 prefectures and 43 counties of Weizhou, it couldn't make such a gross error."

Later, people began to use this idiom to indicate a tremendous mistake. This story tells us that no matter what we deal with, we should be circumspect in word and deed to avoid a gross error.

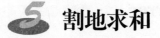

割地求和

秦国军队打败了赵国的军队后，围困了赵国都城邯郸，但是却久攻不下。

说客楼缓对赵王说：现在赵国被秦军围困，天下庆贺战争胜利的就一定都站

教 训 篇

147

在秦国一方。所以不如迅速割地求和，使各国揣测秦、赵两国的关系已经修好，不敢进攻赵国，而且可以缓解秦国的敌意。

我们通常用"割地求和"来比喻屈服于强势，把领土的一部分割让给他国，以图求苟合。

这则典故的启示是，遇到困难时和强敌时，退缩绝不能解决问题。

Ceding Territory for Peace

After Qin's army defeated Zhao's army, they besieged Handan, the capital of Zhao State, but could not capture it for a long time.

Lou Huan, a persuasive speaker, said to the King of Zhao, "Zhao State is sieged by Qin troops at the moment. The states which celebrate victory must stand on the side of Qin State. So I suggest we should cede some territory to Qin for peace. Then other countries may conjecture that Qin and Zhao have already repaired the relations and they do not dare to attack Zhao any more. We can also ease Qin's hospitality."

We often use this idiom to mean the action of succumbing to strong force and ceding part of the territory to other country for so-called peace.

It tells us that cowardice and escape will not help when facing difficulties or powerful enemies.

郭开之金

公元前 229 年，秦国派名将王翦攻打赵国，赵国派李牧、司马尚率领赵国军队抵抗秦国军队。

秦国靠军事进攻无法取胜，便设法用重金收买赵王的宠臣郭开。

于是郭开向赵王诬告李牧、司马尚欲谋反。

赵王听信谗言，委派赵葱、颜聚到军中代替李牧、司马尚。李牧不服从命令，赵王便派人秘密捕杀李牧，并废掉了司马尚。

三个月后，王翦加大进攻力量，大破赵国军队，攻克邯郸，赵王迁被俘，赵国灭亡。

我们现在用这个典故表示奸佞之人收受贿赂，陷害忠良。

这则典故的启示是，我们要忠于祖国和人民，绝不做无耻小人。

The Bribe Received by Guo Kai

In 229 B.C., Qin sent Wang Jian, a famous general, to attack Zhao State; Zhao sent Li Mu and Sima Shang to launch a counter attack against the Qin troops.

Qin State was unable to win through military attack, so it tried with a huge sum of money to bribe Guo Kai, the King of Zhao's minion.

So Guo Kai made a false charge against Li Mu and Sima Shang of rebellion.

The King of Zhao believed his slanderous talk and delegated Zhao Cong and Yan Ju to replace Li Mu and Sima Shang in the army. Li Mu did not obey his order, so the King of Zhao sent his underlings to secretly capture and kill Li Mu and also discarded Sima Shang.

Three months later, Wang Jian strengthened their attack power and crushed the Zhao troops and conquered Handan. The King of Zhao was captured and Zhao State perished.

We now use this idiom to indicate evil persons receiving the bribe and framing the faithful and the loyal.

It tells us that we must be loyal to our motherland and its people and never be evil persons.

---

7 中饱私囊

春秋后期，晋国的执政大臣赵简子（赵国君王的先人），派税官去民间征收赋税。临行前，税官问赵简子："这次收税的税率应该是多少？"

赵简子回答道:"不轻不重最好。税赋收得重了,国家是富了,但老百姓却变得穷了;税收得轻了,老百姓是富了,但国家却变得穷了。你们如果做事情没有私心,这件事就可以做得很好。"

这时,有个叫簿疑的人对赵简子说:"依我看,您的国家实际上是中饱。"

赵简子以为簿疑说自己的国家很富有,心中十分高兴,故意问簿疑是什么意思。

簿疑直截了当地说:"在您的国家中,上面的国库是空的,下面的百姓是穷的,而中间那些贪官污吏都富了。"

这个成语指以欺诈手段从经手的他人或公共钱财中牟利。

To Line One's Pockets with Public Funds or Other People's Money

In the late Spring and Autumn Period, the ruling minister of Jin State, Zhao Jianzi (ancestor of the kings of Zhao State) dispatched an official to collect taxes from people. Before leaving, the tax official asked Zhao Jianzi, "How much should the tax rate be this time?"

Zhao Jianzi answered, "Neither too high nor too low. If the tax is too high, the state will become rich while the common people will become poor; on the contrary, if the tax is too low, the common people can actually become wealthy, but the state poor. Without selfishness, you may handle this matter well."

At this moment, a man called Bo Yi told Zhao Jianzi, "In my opinion, actually your state's middle part is rich."

Zhao Jianzi thought that Bo Yi meant his country was very rich. He felt excited and intentionally asked Bo Yi what he suggested by saying that.

Bo Yi said straightforwardly, "The state treasury in the higher part is empty and the common people in the lower part are poor, only the corrupted officials in the middle part are rich."

This idiom refers to the act of battening on other people's money or public funds entrusted to one's care.

8 步履蹒跚

平原君家临街的楼房很高，在楼上可以俯瞰附近居民的房屋，平原君的妻妾，就住在楼上。有一天，众美人在楼上闲望，看到一个瘸腿的人到井台打水。美人们见到他行路缓慢，东摇西晃的样子，忍不住哄笑起来，有的还模仿他走路的姿态来取乐。

这个瘸腿的人，受到这番侮辱很是恼怒。第二天清早，就来登门拜访平原君，要求说："我听说你喜欢接纳贤士，而贤士所以会不远千里来投奔你，是因为你能看重贤士，轻贱美女的缘故。我不幸有了腰弯曲、背隆高的病，你的房里人在高处看到了，肆意笑弄我，这是不合礼的。我要得到笑我的人的头！"

平原君假笑着答应说："好吧。"等那个人走了后，平原君冷笑了一声，对左右的人说："瞧那个小子，想以一笑的缘故让我杀美人，这也太过份了！"最后平原君并没有杀。

过了一年多，住在平原君家里的宾客，一个接着一个的走了有一多半。平原君很奇怪，对留下未走的门客说："我对待各位，可以说是诚心诚意的，没有敢失过礼，为什么走了那么多的人呢？"

有一个门客上前直率地说："就因为你不杀那笑瘸腿的人，这说明你喜欢女色而看不起士人，所以宾客就走了。"

平原君听了大为后悔，立刻叫人杀了那些嘲笑过瘸腿人的美人，拿着头亲自到瘸腿人的家去谢罪。

不久，离开平原君家的宾客，才又一个接着一个的回来了。

这条典故，常用来形容腿脚不方便，行路艰难。这个故事告诉我们每个人各有长短，不可以己之长笑人之短。

Walking Staggeringly

The building of Lord of Pingyuan was very high and looking down into the street, where the nearby houses can be overlooked. His beautiful concubines just lived there. One day, his concubines overlooked the street idly in the building and saw a lame person who was drawing water from a well. Seeing the slow and teetering stance of the man, they could not help laughing. Some of them even imitated his stance for pleasure.

Being humiliated, the lame man was very angry. Early in the next morning, he called at Lord of Pingyuan's house. He said, "I have heard that you like to accept talented men as your retainers. These men went one thousand miles to your places for shelter just because you think more of the talented men than the beauties. It is unlucky that I have got an illness which made my waist stooped and my back bent. Seeing me in the high place, your beauties laughed at me wantonly. It is very indecorous. I want the heads of those who laughed at me!"

Lord of Pingyuan smirked and answered, "All right. I will do as you told me." After the lame man left, Lord of Pingyuan sneered and said to the men beside him, "Look at that man who dares to ask me to kill my beauties just for a laugh. Doesn't it go too far?" He didn't kill his beauties after all.

More than a year passed, a greater part of the retainers in Lord of Pingyuan's house left one after another. Lord of Pingyuan was very surprised and asked the remainders, "I can say I treat you all sincerely and I never dare to show any disrespect to you. But why did so many people leave me?"

One of them came over and spoke frankly,"The reason is that you did not kill those who laughed at the lame man. It indicates that you love beauties but look down upon the talented men. So they left."

Hearing that, Lord of Pingyuan felt great regret. He immediately ordered his men to kill the beauties who had ever laughed at the lame man and took the heads personally to the lame man's house to apologize for his offence.

Soon the retainers who left began to come back one after another.

We often use this idiom to describe one has disease on the leg and feet or has difficulty in walking. This story tells us that we should not laugh at others' shortcomings or defects since all have their own advantages and disadvantages.

人人自危

秦始皇晚年时到会稽游玩，丞相李斯、中车府令赵高随行。因为秦始皇很偏爱自己的小儿子胡亥，所以带了胡亥随车出游，其他的儿子都没跟他一起出游。

这年七月，秦始皇走到沙丘时，得了病，而且病得很重，他知道自己快要死了，便令赵高写封信给领兵驻扎在边境的大儿子扶苏，让扶苏立刻赶回都城咸阳，主持丧事。

赵高刚刚把诏书写好，秦始皇已经断了气，因为平常赵高负责掌管秦始皇的玉玺。这样，秦始皇的遗诏和玉玺都落到了赵高手里。于是，赵高和胡亥合谋，伪造了一道遗诏，说秦始皇立胡亥为太子，让胡亥继位。

丞相李斯起先不同意，后来在赵高的威胁利诱下，也被迫同意了。

接着，赵高又伪造另一道诏书，说扶苏不孝顺，赐给他一把剑，让他自杀，并派人夺了与扶苏一起镇守边境的大将蒙恬的兵权，也逼他自杀。经过一番阴谋活动，胡亥当上了皇帝，称为秦二世。赵高当上了郎中令。从此，朝政大权便全落到了赵高手里。

秦二世非常昏庸暴虐，他害怕别人识破他与赵高的阴谋，坐不稳皇位，便问赵高怎么办？奸诈阴险的赵高说："必须采用严刑酷法，把那些老臣全部除掉，用新人来代替他们。"秦二世听了，便下令处死了蒙毅等一批老臣，又把对自己皇位有威胁的十二个公子全部斩首，把十个公主也全部用酷刑处死。因受到牵连而被杀害的人更是不计其数，弄得上上下下一片恐怖，人人自危，朝廷中一片混乱。

秦二世和赵高用这种残酷的手段屠戮亲族和大臣，对老百姓更是凶狠残暴。广大人民群众的生活痛苦不堪，终于忍无可忍，激起了广大人民的反抗。

不久，陈胜、吴广揭竿而起，在大泽乡举行起义。三年后，秦王朝便被起义军灭亡。

这个成语形容政治形势险恶，人人感到自己处在危险之中。

Everyone Finds Himself in Danger

In his late years of, Qinshihuang travelled to Kuaiji. He was followed by the Prime Minister Li Si and the official Zhao Gao who was in charge of the Emperor's carriages. As the Emperor was partial to his youngest son Hu Hai, he took him to travel with him, and his other sons didn't have this opportunity.

In July of that year, Qinshihuang arrived at Shaqiu, where had a very serious disease. He realized that he would die soon, so he ordered Zhao Gao to write a letter to his eldest son Fu Su who was stationed at the frontier and asked Fu Su to go back to Xianyang quickly to take charge of his funeral arrangements.

When Zhao Gao just finished the imperial edict, Emperor Shihuang of Qin had already breathed his last. Zhao Gao had been in charge of the imperial jade seal, so both the imperial edict left by the Emperor before his death and his imperial jade seal fell to Zhao Gao's hands. Therefore, Zhao Gao conspired with Hu Hai to fabricate an imperial edict in which the Emperor said that he would make Hu Hai the prince and that Hu Hai should succeed the throne.

At first, the Prime Minister Li Si didn't agree. Threatened and bribed by Zhao Gao, he had to agree at last.

Then, Zhao Gao fabricated another imperial edict saying that Fu Su was not filial, so Qinshihuang gave him a sword to commit suicide. At the same time, Zhao Gao sent his men to take over the military power of the general Meng Yi who was stationed at the frontier with Fu Su and forced him to commit suicide, too. After a series of villainous schemes, Hu Hai came to the throne and was called the Second Emperor of Qin Dynasty. Zhao Gao was offered the position of Langzhongling whose job was to govern the guards of the palace. From then on, the power of court administration fell into Zhao Gao's hands.

The Second Emperor of Qin Dynasty was quite muddle-headed and tyrannous. He was afraid of his conspiracy with Zhao Gao being disclosed so as to threaten his throne, so he asked Zhao Gao what to do with it. The treacherous and insidious Zhao Gao said, "We must use cruel punishment to wipe out the old officials, and replace them with some new ones." The Second Emperor agreed and he gave orders to kill the old officials including Meng Yi. Then, he decapitated all the twelve princes who might threaten his throne and all the ten princesses were killed with cruel punishment. Other involved people were killed innumerably. At that time, terror pervaded the imperial palace and the common people. Everyone found himself in danger. The imperial court was in disorder.

The Second Emperor and Zhao Gao employed the cruel punishment to slaughter the imperial kinsmen and the high officials. They treated the common people even more ruthless. Numerous people lived a miserable and intolerable life which instigated their revolt.

Soon, Chen Sheng and Wu Guang raised the standard of revolt, and they started an uprising in Daze Town. Three years later, Qin Dynasty was conquered by the uprising military.

This idiom means that feels insecure due to the dangerous political situation.

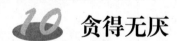

贪得无厌

春秋末年，周天子的权利已经不为大家所重视。各路诸侯都在纷纷扩展自己的领土。

晋国是一个大诸侯国，国中有六个上卿：赵、魏、韩、范、智和中行。其中智伯野心勃勃，一心扩张势力。

智伯联合韩、赵、魏攻打并消灭了范氏和中行氏，吞并了他们的土地。

几年后，智伯又要求韩康子割地。韩康子惧怕智伯，只好割地一万户给他。他接着又要求魏桓子割地，要求也得到了满足。智伯颇为得意，又要求赵襄子割地给他，却被严词拒绝。

智伯联合了韩康子和魏桓子攻打赵襄子，赵襄子寡不敌众，便采纳谋士张孟谈的计策，退入晋阳城中，坚守了三年。

城中粮食将尽，智伯又放水淹城，形势十分紧急。张孟谈出城游说魏桓子和韩康子，指出智伯贪得无厌，灭了赵氏对他们没有任何好处，不如三家联合，灭掉智伯，平分他的土地。

结果是韩、赵、魏三家联合，打败并杀死了智伯，贪得无厌的他落了一个可悲的下场。

这则成语的意思是贪心没有满足的时候。它告诉我们过度的贪欲最终会给自己带来毁灭。

To Have an Unlimited Desire for More

In the last years of the Warring States Period, the King of Zhou Dynasty's authority placed no importance on people. All the feudal barons expanded their territories.

Jin State was a big vassal country. There were six ministers in the country: Zhao, Wei, Han, Fan, Zhi and Zhonghang. Among the six ministers, Zhi Bo was the ambitious one. He hoped to expand the territory wholeheartedly.

Zhi Bo, allied with Zhao and Wei, attacked and conquered Fan and Zhonghang. They took possession of their territories.

Several years later, Zhi Bo demanded that Han Kangzi should demarcate some territory to him. Han Kangzi was afraid of Zhi Bo, so he had to demarcate ten thousand households to him. Then, he asked Wei Huanzi to demarcate territory to him, and again his demand was fulfilled. Zhi Bo was quite complacent, and he asked Zhao Xiangzi to demarcate some territory to him. But this time, he was declined in stern words.

Zhi Bo united Han Kangzi and Wei Huanzi to attack Zhao Xiangzi. Zhao Xiangzi fought against heavy odds, so he took his advisor Zhang Mengtan's plan to withdraw into Jinyang City and stay there for three years.

When there remained little food, Zhi Bo began to draw off the water to flood the city. The situation was very urgent. Zhang Mengtan went out of the city to persuade Wei Huanzi and Han Kangzi that Zhi Bo had an unlimited desire for more territories. If Zhao was defeated, there was no benefit to them. Therefore, they should unite together to conquer Zhi Bo, and then equally divide his territories.

At last, Han, Zhao and Wei united together to defeat and kill Zhi Bo, who met a miserable end for his unlimited desire for more.

This idiom means that the avarice can't be fulfilled.

It tells us that too much greed will destroy oneself in the end.

11 利令智昏

战国时代，各诸候国之间为了争夺土地，经常发动战争。

秦国派大将白起攻打韩国，占领了韩国的一块土地——野王。在野王邻近有另一块叫"上党"的土地，他们的地方官员看到野王轻易地就被秦军攻下，怕上党也守不住，就写信给赵国，表示愿意归顺，希望得到赵国的庇护。

赵国的君臣们对于要不要接受上党的归顺，意见不一，大家展开激烈的争论。平原君赵胜说："上党这么大块的地方，我们不用出一兵一卒，就可以得到，为什么不要呢？"平阳君反对说："就是因为不花力气得到好处，轻易要了，恐怕会招来大祸。"赵王因为不想失去这块到嘴的肥肉，便支持平原君的主张，并且派他去接收上党，把它划为赵国的领地。

秦国知道后，认为赵国存心和自己作对，就命令白起率大军去攻打赵国。结果赵国的四十余万大军全部被秦军歼灭，国都邯郸也被围困，后来平原君带毛遂去楚国，说服楚王联赵抗秦，最后楚国出兵，才解除了赵国的邯郸之围。

赵王和平原君因为贪图眼前可以获得上党土地的利益，而差点导致赵国灭亡。后人便形容他们的行为是"利令智昏"。这个故事提醒我们不能为了利益或私欲而丧失理智、不辨是非。

教 训 篇

To Bend One's Principles to One's Interest

During the Warring States Period, the kingdoms were always waging wars on each other to occupy the land.

Qin State sent senior general Bai Qi to invade Han State. Bai occupied a piece of land named Yewang. Not far from Yewang, there was another piece of land named Shangdang. The local officers of Shangdang thought that since the Qin troops can easily took over Yewang, Shangdang was in danger. So they wrote to Zhao State that they wanted to submit to them for the sake of Zhao's protection of Shangdang.

The King and the officials in Zhao State debated with each other about whether they should accept Shangdang. Lord Pingyuan said, "We can get such a large piece of land as Shangdang with no strength. Why not accept?" Lord Pingyang rebutted, "If we would possess it with no efforts, I'm afraid we might have great troubles." The King of Zhao didn't want to lose the chance, so he supported Lord Pingyuan and sent him to take over Shangdang as Zhao's territory.

When the King of Qin State got the news, he thought Zhao State was deliberately on the opposite of him, so he ordered Bai Qi and his troops to attack Zhao State. As a result, all Zhao troops, more than four hundred thousand soldiers, were annihilated by Qin troops. Handan, the capital of Zhao State, was also besieged. Later on, Lord Pingyuan went to Chu State with Mao Sui to convince the King of Chu to resist Qin. Until Chu troops arrived was Handan released.

The King of Zhao and Lord Pingyuan had an insatiable desire for the land of Shangdang. They almost led their state to an end.

Now we consider their behavior amount to bend one's principles to one's interest. This story reminds us not to lose our senses or confuse right and wrong for the sake of interest or selfish desires.

市道之交

廉颇被赵王免去了大将军的官职，他失势时众门客纷纷离他而去。后来，廉颇被赵王重用为大将军时，门客又纷纷复归。

廉颇对此现象很不满。一名门客说："您的见识已经过时了。现在天下是以市场买卖的方式交朋友，您有权势时我们就跟随您，您没有权势时我们就离开，这是市场买卖的道理，将军有什么可怨恨的呢？"

这个典故通常指买卖双方之间的关系。比喻人与人之间以利害关系为转移的交情。

他告诉我们人与人相处时必须要诚实，否则会被人鄙视。

The Fellowship of Opportunists

During the Warring States Period, the King of Zhao State relieved General Lian Po of his post. When he receded to the background, his retainers left him one after another. Later, when the King resumed Lian Po's post as the senior general, all the retainers who left him came back again.

Therefore, Lian Po was very unsatisfied with this phenomenon. One of his retainers said to him, "Your insight is out of date. Now in this society, making friends is like the way of marketing. That is to say, if you have the power and influence, we will follow you; but if you lose those, we will leave you. That is marketing principle. So what do you complain about?"

We usually use this idiom to refer to the relationship between the buyer and the seller and the changeable fellowship based on interests.

It tells us that we must be honest to one another, or we will be scorned.

13 胶柱鼓瑟

战国时期的赵国，有一位大将叫赵奢，他的地位与廉颇、蔺相如同样显赫，因为屡建战功，被赵惠文王赐予"马服君"的称号。

赵奢的儿子赵括，从小学习兵书，对兵法非常熟悉，与别人谈起打仗来，条条是理，谁也比不上他。连他的父亲赵奢，也难不住他。可是，赵奢从来不说儿子懂得指挥打仗。

赵括的母亲觉得有些奇怪，就问赵奢："儿子不是兵法不错吗？怎么没听见你夸奖过他呢？"

赵奢回答到："你不懂，他是纸上谈兵，打仗是生死的较量，可是赵括却把它说得太容易了。以后赵王不用他还好，如果让他领兵，那非得把军队毁了不可！"

有一年秦国和赵国在长平交战。那时赵奢已死，蔺相如重病在床，廉颇率兵打退了几次秦兵后，就坚守阵地，不再出战。这时秦国想出了一条离间计，散布流言说："秦国最怕的就是赵奢的儿子赵括当将军！"赵王听信了流言，便派赵括为将军，代替廉颇。蔺相如闻讯后，立即对赵王说：

"大王以这样的名义任赵括为将军，就如同用胶粘上琴的柱子然后拨琴一样，那是发不出来好的声音的。赵括只能背诵父亲的兵书，不会在战场上灵活运用兵法。"

可是赵王主意已定，没有听蔺相如的意见，让赵括率领赵军与秦兵交战。

赵括代替了廉颇，改变了他的军规，更换了他的军吏，便与秦国交锋。

秦军的大将白起，用了一个计策，假装败退，背地里断了赵军的粮道。赵军四十多天得不到粮食，饿得无法作战。赵括亲自临战搏斗，结果被秦军射死。赵军遭到惨败，损失四十余万士兵。

人们后来用胶柱鼓瑟这个成语比喻拘泥固执，不知变通。

它告诉我们做事情不能过分顽固，不听别人的意见。

Stubbornly Sticking to Old Ways in the Face of Changed Circumstances

During the Warring States Period, Zhao She, a famous general of Zhao State, shared equal political status with Lian Po and Lin Xiangru. Owing to his great victories of battles, Zhao She was entitled "Lord of Mafu" by King Huiwen of Zhao State.

Zhao She had a son named Zhao Kuo who was very fond of reading books on military science and discussing strategies of war. Zhao Kuo spoke so clearly and logically that it seemed that even his father was not his match. But his father didn't think that his son knew how to command the troops and fight a battle. Out of curiosity, Zhao Kuo's mother asked Zhao She, "Doesn't our son have a good mastery of military science? Why did you never praise highly over him about it?"

Zhao She answered, "You don't understand him. He just makes empty talks about warfare. He takes the battle so easily; however, battle is a contest between life and death. I wish that the King of Zhao should never order him to lead the troops, or he will ruin them."

In a later year, Qin troops set out to attack Zhao State. Troops from both sides fought in Changping. At that time, Zhao She had been dead and Lin Xiangru was badly ill in bed. General Lian Po was commanding the Zhao troops, who had repulsed Qin troops' several attacks. Lian saw that Qin troops was more powerful so he ordered his troops to stay in defense position and avoid fighting Qin troops' head-on. There was no fighting for four months. Later Qin brought out a strategy of sowing discord between the Lord of Zhao and the General Lian Po. The Qin troops spread the rumor widely that Qin was greatly afraid of Zhao She's son Zhao Kuo as the General but not Lian Po. Believing the rumor, the King of Zhao appointed Zhao Kuo as the General to replace Lian Po. Hearing this, Lin Xiangru immediately persuaded the King of Zhao, "Your Highness' appointment of Zhao Kuo as the General under such an excuse, is just like playing the se (an ancient

教 训 篇

musical instrument with 25 or 50 strings), with its string stands pasted with glue (stubbornly sticking to old ways in the face of changed circumstances), how can it make a pleasant sound? He can only recite his father's books on military science and cannot use strategies of war flexibly in the battlefield."

But the King of Zhao still insisted on his decision and didn't take Lin's advice. He ordered Zhao Kuo to command Zhao troops and fight against the Qin troops.

After taking the place of Lian Po, Zhao Kuo changed the military rules and replaced the subordinate officers, and then led his troops to fight against the Qin troops.

Bai Qi, the General of the Qin troops, made a strategy to pretend to retreat and secretly cut off the way for delivering provisions for the Zhao troops. Badly short of food for more than forty days, Zhao troops were too hungry to fight. Zhao Kuo himself charged Qin troops' lines and was finally shot down by Qin archers. Zhao troops were heavily defeated and Zhao State missed 400,000 troops.

People usually take this idiom as a metaphor of stubbornly sticking to old ways in the face of changed circumstances.

It tells us that we must never be too stubborn to accepting others' opinions.

14 前倨后恭

苏秦周游列国，向各国国君阐述自己的政治主张，但无一个国君欣赏他的想法。苏秦只好垂头丧气，穿着旧衣破鞋回到家乡洛阳。

家人见他如此落魄，都不给他好脸色，苏秦的嫂子不但不给他做饭，还狠狠训斥了他一顿。这件事大大刺激了苏秦，在一年的苦心学习和研究中，苏秦废寝忘食，困倦时就用锥子尖扎自己的大腿，最终彻底掌握了当时的政治形势。

然后他在周游列国时说服了当时的齐、楚、燕、韩、赵、魏六国"合纵"抗秦，并被封为"纵约长"，做了六国的丞相，身佩六国相印，名震天下。

苏秦衣锦还乡后，他的亲人一改往日的态度，都"四拜自跪而谢"，其嫂更是"蛇行匍匐"。面对此景，苏秦对嫂子说："为何前倨而后恭也？"意思是说为什么以前对我傲慢，而现在又如此恭敬呢？

这个故事告诉我们要以宽容、平等的态度待人接物，而不能以狭隘、势利的眼光看待别人。

Haughty Before and Reverent Afterwards

Su Qin traveled around many states to propagate his political views, but no king appreciated his ideas. He had to return to his hometown Luoyang in tattered clothes and worn shoes, with the tail between the legs.

His family found him completely down and out, and treated him coldly. His sister-in-law gave him a good dressing down instead of a meal. This strongly stimulated him. During one year's painstaking study and research, he was so absorbed as to neglect sleep and meals and even prodded his thighs with an awl to keep awake. Finally he obtained a good and complete command of the political trend of that time.

Then he lobbied the rulers of the states of Qi, Chu, Yan, Han, Zhao, and Wei into a "Longitudinal Union" against Qin from one state to another on mediating tours. He himself was appointed the chief of the union, wearing the prime minister's official seals of all the six states, with an unrivalled reputation.

After Su Qin returned home with all the pomp befitting his high rank, all his family members changed their attitudes towards him. They all kowtowed four times and made apologies, and his sister-in-law even crawled on the ground like a snake. At this sight, Su Qin asked her, "Why were you so haughty before and so reverent now?" In other words, this idiom means, "Why were you so arrogant before and so humble now?"

This story tells us to treat others tolerantly and equally instead of with a narrow and snobbish attitude.

15 兵破士北

汉文帝问冯唐匈奴之事。冯唐回答:"我的祖父说,李牧为赵将,屯住在边境,军市的租税都自行用来犒赏士卒,赏赐在外决定,不必受朝廷的牵制。"

"君主既然一切委托他,而但求他成功,因此李牧可以竭尽他的智能。派遣精选的兵车一千三百辆,能射的骑兵一万三千名,价值百金之良士十万人,所以他能够在北方驱逐单于,大破东胡,歼灭猎林,在西方抑制强秦,在南方抵抗韩、魏,那个时候,赵国几乎能够称霸。"

"后来,刚好赵王迁即位,竟然听信奸臣郭开的谗言,杀了李牧,而派颜聚代替他。因此军队被击败,士兵溃散奔逃,皆被秦兵所虏杀。"

"兵破士北"表示军队被击败,士兵溃散奔逃,用来比喻打了大败仗。

这个故事告诉我们相互信任是大家一起成功的关键所在。

The Defeated Army

Emperor Wen of Han Dynasty asked Feng Tang about the warfare against the Huns. Feng Tang answered, "My grandfather said Li Mu, a general of Zhao State, was stationed along the frontier. The revenue from the army's market was used for rewarding the soldiers. The reward could be distributed by the general without the containment of the imperial government."

"The King entrusted Li Mu to decide all the things, for the King only wished a success at any rate. Thus, Li Mu could display all his talent. He sent one thousand and three hundred carriages carefully chosen, thirteen thousand cavalries skilled in archery and one hundred thousand fine soldiers to the frontier, so he could expel Chanyu (the king of the Huns), defeat East Hu and destroyed Lielin in the north, restrain powerful Qin State in the west and resist States of Han and Wei in the south. At that time, Zhao State almost dominated the Central Plains."

"Then, King Qian of Zhao State ascended the throne. After he became the King, he believed in the treacherous court official Guo Kai's slanderous words. At last he killed Li Mu and Yan Ju was made to take the place of Li Mu. Gradually, the army was defeated, and the escaped soldiers were all killed or captured by the Qin troops."

This idiom indicates that the army is defeated, and the soldiers escape in every direction. It refers to a crushing defeat.

It tells us that mutual trust among a group of people is the critical point for success.

 人心难测

秦末汉初，常山王张耳（后为赵王）与成安君陈余两人曾经在反抗秦国暴政的时候结为刎颈之交。不料后来两人闹翻，张耳投奔了刘邦，陈余则加入了项羽的阵营。

在汉赵之间发生的井陉口之战中，陈余的军队被韩信和张耳打败，他本人也被斩首。

患难生于贪欲，可谓是人心难测啊！

我们通常用"人心难测"来比喻人的心思难以揣测。

它告诉我们，如果大家都能够忠于自己的朋友，就会避免很多悲剧的发生。

The Human Heart Is a Mystery

During the end of Qin Dynasty and the beginning of Han Dynasty, Zhang Er, the King of Changshan and later, the King of Zhao State, and Chen Yu, the Lord Of Chengan had been friends sworn to death when they fought together against the despotic rule of Qin Dynasty. Nevertheless, to our surprise, they finally broke off for personal interest. Then Zhang Er turned to Liu Bang, and Chen Yu joined Xiang Yu's camp.

Several years later, in the Battle of Jingxingkou between Han State and Zhao State, Han Xin and Zhang Er defeated Chen Yu and beheaded him.

Therefore, we can see that Zhang Er and Chen Yu's adversity was born from greed, from which we obtain this idiom "The Human Heart is a Mystery".

Now we often use it to indicate that the human heart cannot be estimated easily.

It tells us that, if everyone is faithful to his friends, many tragedies will be avoided.

和 谐 篇

1 路不拾遗

　　唐朝的时候，有一个做买卖的人途经武阳（今河北大名、馆陶一带），不小心把一件心爱的衣服丢了。

　　他走了几十里后才发觉，心中很着急，这时有人劝慰他说："不要紧，我们武阳境内路不拾遗，你回去找找看，一定可以找得到。"

　　那人听了半信半疑，心里想："这可能吗？"转而又一想，找找也无妨。于是赶了回去，果然找到了他失去的衣服。

　　这件事后来越传越广，人们就把"路不拾遗"变成一个成语。

　　"路不拾遗"又作"道不拾遗"，常用以说明国家安定，人们的思想品德高尚，社会风气很好。

　　这则成语告诉我们优良的社会风气对建设安定和谐社会的重要性。一个国家的发展要注重经济建设，更要注重高尚的品德和良好的社会风气的建设。

No One Picks Up and Pockets Anything Lost on the Road

　　In Tang Dynasty, there was a businessman who lost one of his favorite clothes by carelessness when he passed by Wuyang (in the region between Daming and Guantao of Hebei Province today).

　　It was not until he walked dozens of li that he found he had lost it. He felt worried. At that time someone soothed him, "Don't worry. People in Wuyang don't pick up and pocket anything lost on the road. You can come back to look for it and you are bound to find it."

　　Hearing that, the businessman was in dubitation. He thought to himself, "Is it possible?" Thinking better of his words, he felt there was no harm to look for it. So he hastened back and as things turned out, he found it on the road.

　　Afterwards, the news had been spread wider and wider. As a result, this story was turned into an idiom.

The idiom "No One Picks Up and Pockets Anything Lost on the Road" indicates the stability of a nation, the nobleness of the people's moral characters, and the good atmosphere of the society."

This idiom attaches importance to the good social conventions in building a stable and harmonious society. A nation should pay attention to economic development and more attention to the construction of people's noble characters and good social conventions.

奉公守法

春秋战国时期，赵国大将赵奢是个足智多谋的人，他英勇善战，屡战屡胜，建立了显赫的功勋。赵惠文王封赵奢为马服君，官列上卿。

赵奢原来是一个普通的收取田税的官吏。他一片忠心，收税时大公无私，一视同仁。有一次，他来到赵惠文王的弟弟平原君赵胜家收取田税，但是赵胜的管家却仗势欺人，戏弄赵奢，拒付税款。赵奢并不怕赵胜的权势，他毫不客气地处理了这件事，且依照赵国法令杀了那些无事生非的闹事者。

赵胜听说后，怒气冲天，一定要赵奢抵命，以显示他的权势。

赵奢得知赵胜的想法后，马上去找了赵胜，真心诚意的对他说："您是赵国栋梁之材，是受朝廷重用的大官。应该遵守国家法令，以昭示天下百姓。而现在您的管家却依靠您的权势，公然违反国家法令。如果百姓都拒不付税，那么天下还会太平吗？国家还会富强吗？到那时候，您还会有现在这样显赫的地位吗？但是，您要是能够奉公守法，那么百姓也会以您为榜样，天下就会稳定，国家就会富强，您怎么能轻视呢？"

赵胜听了这番话，惭愧万分。继而转怒为喜，将赵奢保举给赵惠文王，赵王封了他一个掌管整个赵国税收的官。赵奢上任后，没有仗着权势欺压百姓，仍然公正、无私的处理一切事务。

后来，赵奢又被赵王任命为大将，为赵国建立了很多战功。

"奉公守法"这则成语告诉我们，官员必须按照法令行事，不得违法乱纪。若无奉公守法的官员，则无安定和谐的社会。

To Be Law-Abiding

During the Spring and Autumn Period and the Warring States Period, Zhao She was a famous general in Zhao State. He was very wise, brave in battle, and had established one prominent achievement after another. King Huiwen of Zhao State ennobled him Lord of Mafu, also one of the highest officials in the court.

Zhao She was originally a common government official whose duty was to collect tax on land. He was very loyal, selfless, and treated everybody equally. Once, he went to collect tax from Zhao Sheng, also known as Lord of Pingyuan, who is the brother of King Huiwen of Zhao State. Zhao Sheng's housekeeper took advantage of his power, teased Zhao She and refused to pay the tax. Zhao She was not afraid of Zhao Sheng's power and influence. He handled this matter justly and killed those trouble-makers in accordance with the law of Zhao State.

After Zhao Sheng heard of this matter, he was hopping mad. In order to demonstrate his power and influence, he was determined to kill Zhao She. After Zhao She knew Zhao Sheng's ideas, he immediately went to see Zhao Sheng and sincerely persuaded, "You are the pillar of this country, a high official with great responsibility. You should show the common citizen that you conduct matters legally. Now your housekeeper relies on your power and influence, violates our national law blatantly. If the common people refuse to pay tax similarly, will our country be peaceful and prosperous? Will you still hold such prominent status? However, if you can be law-abiding, the common people will be accordingly. Thus our country will be stable, powerful and prosperous. How can you ignore your influence?"

Hearing these words, Zhao Sheng was ashamed deeply. Then, his anger turned to joy. He recommended Zhao She to King Huiwen of Zhao State and the King made Zhao She an official who was in charge of all the taxes in the country. When Zhao She took his office, he never bullied the common people on his power and influence. He still handled all the matters selflessly and impartially.

Later, Zhao She was appointed as an important general and established a lot of achievements in different battles.

The idiom "To Be Law-Abiding" indicates that government officials must act in compliance with laws and without irregularity. If there is no law-abiding government officials, there is no stable and harmonious society.

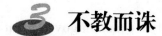

不教而诛

这则成语也可以叫做"不令而诛"。

战国时期赵国著名的思想家和教育家荀况在其著作《荀子》中指出:"事先不教育人,一犯错误就严酷惩处,那么结果是法度繁多而邪恶不能禁止;只是进行教育而不严惩,那么邪恶之人就不能得到处置。"

它的原意是不经警告就将人处死。现在用来指事先不对人进行教育,一犯错误就加以惩罚。

这则典故讲述了治国者的治人之道。若要杜绝邪恶,则应教育在先,严惩在后。

To Punish Without Prior Warning

This idiom is also called "To Punish Without the Issuing of Orders".

During the Warring States Period, Xun Kuang, a famous thinker and educator from Zhao State, mentioned in his works *Xunzi* that, "Hence, if you punish or execute people without prior educating, the law and moral standard will be numerous while the evil can not be prohibited. If you just educate people without harsh punishment, the wicked will not get his just deserts."

The original meaning of the idiom is to execute someone without prior warning. Today, it means punishing people as soon as they made mistakes without prior educating.

This idiom enlightens us on the principles to govern the people. If we would like to prohibit the evil, we should educate the people first and punish the wicked afterwards.

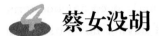
蔡女没胡

这则典故也叫做"蔡女没胡尘"。

董祀的妻子,名字叫蔡琰,字文姬,乃是东汉末年著名的文学家和历史学家蔡邕的女儿。她学问广博而且极有才能,并且对音乐也非常有造诣,她的音乐作品《胡茄十八拍》曾经广为流传,受到人们的称颂。

蔡文姬起初嫁给河东的卫仲道,丈夫死后没有儿子,回到娘家。

兴平年间,天下战乱,蔡文姬被进犯中原的胡骑抓获,嫁给匈奴的左贤王,生二子,在胡地生活达十二年之久。

由于曹操早年与蔡文姬的父亲蔡邕关系非常好,哀痛蔡邕死后没有子嗣,于是派人用重金把文姬从漠北赎回,并改嫁董祀为妻子。

我们通常用"蔡女没胡"比喻战争使人颠沛流离。

这则典故通过蔡文姬的故事反映了人民憎恶战争渴望和平的心声。

Cai Wenji Fell into the Huns

This idiom can also be called as "Cai Wenji Fell into the World of the Huns".

Dong Si's wife, Cai Yan with alias Wenji, was a daughter of the minister Cai Yong who was a famous literateur and historian during the end of Eastern Han Dynasty. She was very learned and talented. Besides, she was quite accomplished in music. Her music composition *Eighteen Songs of a Nomad Flute* was once widely spread and highly praised.

Originally, Cai Wenji was married to Wei Zhongdao who died shortly after without any offspring. Then she returned to her parents' home.

During the Xingping period, the country was filled with chaos caused by wars. The chaos brought the Huns nomads into central China and Cai Wenji was taken as prisoner to the northern lands. During her captivity, she became the wife of King Zuoxian of the Huns, and bore him two sons. She had lived in the northern lands for twelve years.

  Cao Cao, who had formerly been on good terms with Wenji's father, was distressed about his friend having no heirs. Then Cao Cao dispatched his underling to redeem Cai Wenji with a lot of gold and then married her to Dong Si.

  This idiom indicates that war makes people homeless and miserable.

  Through Cai Wenji's story, this idiom reflects pcoplc's hatred for war and their longing for peace

同甘共苦

  战国时期，齐国乘燕国国内混乱，出兵伐燕，把燕国打得大败。战后，燕国太子姬平继承了王位，史称燕昭王。

  燕昭王面对破碎的山河，不知如何才能富国强兵，复仇雪耻。

  一天，他听说有一个叫郭隗的人很有计谋，便把他请来问强国复仇之计。

  郭隗说："只要您广泛选拔有本领的人，并亲自去拜访，那么，天下的贤士就会投奔到燕国来。"

  燕昭王问道："那么我应该去拜访谁呢？"

  郭隗回答说："您就先重用我这个才能平平的人吧，天下的贤士看到我这样的人都能受到重用，定会不顾路途遥远，前来投奔大王。"

  燕昭王立即拜郭隗为师，为他造了一座华丽的住宅。

  消息传开，乐毅、邹衍、剧辛等才能之士纷纷从魏、齐、赵等国来投奔燕昭王。燕昭王一一委以重任，并关怀备至。

  燕昭王与百姓同甘共苦，二十八年后，燕国终于变得国富民强。

  燕昭王看到时机已到，就拜乐毅为上将，联合秦、楚、韩、魏、赵五国军队，攻打齐国。齐国大败，都城临淄被燕国军队攻陷，燕昭王终于报了国耻家仇。

和 谐 篇

"同甘共苦"这则成语的意思是有福同享,有困难一起承担。

该成语告诉我们,治国者应和贤士同甘共苦,以聚拢人才,使得国富民强。

To Share Pleasures and Pains

During the Warring States Period, Qi State attacked Yan State when Yan State was in civil turmoil. Yan was defeated. After the war, Ji Ping, the prince of Yan, succeeded the throne, known as King Zhao of Yan State in history.

Faced with the broken country, King Zhao of Yan didn't know how to make his country rich and build up its military power in order to wipe away its former humiliation.

One day, he heard that a person named Guo Wei was full of stratagems, so he invited him to the imperial house to ask him for some advice.

Guo Wei said, "As long as you choose the intelligent person with great abilities widely and visit them personally, they will seek shelter in State of Yan."

King Zhao of Yan State asked, "Whom should I visit?"

Guo Wei answered, "You can trust me who is without excellent talent with an important position first. If other talented persons see that such a person like me can be trusted as an important position, they will come here to seek shelter one after another in spite of the long distance."

King Zhao of Yan acknowledged Guo Wei as a master immediately, and built a magnificent residence for him.

When the news spread, many talented persons like Yue Yi from Wei State, Zou Yan from Qi State and Ju Xin from Zhao State, etc. all came to King Zhao of Yan to serve him. King Zhao of Yan trusted all of them with important positions and gave thorough consideration to them.

King Zhao of Yan shared bliss and misfortune with common people. Twenty-eight years later, Yan State became rich and powerful.

King Zhao of Yan thought the opportunity ripe, so he offered Yue Yi the position as the general and united the five states of Qin, Chu, Han, Wei and Zhao to attack Qi State. Qi was defeated. Its capital Linzi was broken through by Yan troops. King Zhao of Yan finally got revenge for the national humiliation.

This idiom "To Share Pleasures and Pains" means sharing bliss and misfortune together.

The significance of this idiom lies in the fact that we need talents to build up a harmonious society and the government should share pleasures and pains with them in order to attract the right people and make our country rich as well as powerful.

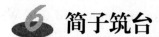

赵简子春天在邯郸命令百姓建筑高台,这时的春雨下个不停。

简子对左右说:"是不是该赶紧播种了?"

尹铎回答说:"因为您的事情太急切,百姓才把播种暂时放下来建筑高台。所以百姓想抓紧播种是不可能的啊。"

简子马上警觉醒悟,于是放下建筑高台的事情,免了百姓的劳役。他说:"我把建筑高台看作急事,不知百姓农事急迫啊。"

我们现在用这个典故来比喻体恤民情。

这则典故告诉我们在社会建设中,民生应被放在第一位。

Jianzi Building a Platform

In spring, Zhao Jianzi had a platform built in Handan, but the spring rain kept falling.

Jianzi asked the attendants around him, "Is it the high time for the common people to hurry to sow seeds?"

Yin Duo answered, "Your business is very urgent, so they have to stop

和 谐 篇

sowing and undertake the platform building. Therefore, it is impossible for them to sow even if they want."

Being aware immediately, Jianzi stopped building the platform and exempted the common people from their service. At the same time, he said, "I think that building the platform is urgent, but I am not aware that the common people's sowing is more urgent. It is because I stop building the platform that the common people will realize that my intention is to love and protect them."

Now we use this idiom to indicate that the ruler shows the solicitude for the common people's life.

This idiom tells us in construction of society, the livelihood of the people should be put in the first place.

7 负荆请罪

战国时期，赵国的蔺相如出使秦国，临危不惧，战胜了骄傲的秦王，立下大功，因而赵王封他为上卿。赵国名将廉颇，屡次战胜齐、魏等国，立下不少战功。他见蔺相如官位比自己还高，很不服气。

廉颇到处扬言，说："我有攻城野战的大功，而蔺相如不过是动动口舌，况且又是一个下等人，我为位居其下感到羞耻！如果碰到蔺相如，一定要当面羞辱他。"

蔺相如听说后，就处处躲开廉颇，避免和他见面。蔺相如手下的人很不痛快，就问他："您的官位比廉颇大，为什么还要怕他呢？"蔺相如反问："你们看，秦王和廉将军谁厉害？"他的部下说："当然是秦王了。"蔺相如笑道："是的，秦王是一个强国的君主，我都不怕他，何况一个廉将军？但是要知道，别的国家所以不敢侵犯我国，就是因为文臣有我，武将有廉将军。如果我们两人不和，不能团结一致，那么敌人就会趁机侵入我国。个人之间的恩怨是小事，不该计较。国家的利益是大事，必须摆在首位。"

蔺相如的这些话传到了廉颇耳里，他知道自己错了，便光着上身，背着荆条，到蔺相如家请罪，向他表示赔礼道歉。从此，两人团结一致，一心为国，别的国家不敢轻易侵犯。

后人用"负荆请罪"比喻完全承认错误，诚心请求对方惩罚。

这则成语教导大家做人处事的道理。为人处事应像蔺相如一样，凡事以国家大局为重，不计较个人恩怨；像廉颇一样，勇于承认错误，改正错误。

To Proffer a Birch and Ask for a Flogging

During the Warring States Period, as an emissary to Qin State from Zhao State, Lin Xiangru, because of his not shrinking in the face of great danger, won over the arrogant King of Qin and returned the jade intact to Zhao, so the King of Zhao made him the Senior Minister of Zhao State. Lian Po, a famous general of Zhao who had ever defeated Qi and Wei and made great contributions to his country in battle, believed that it was unjust that Lin Xiangru should have a higher official rank than he.

So Lian Po spread everywhere that, "I have performed many meritorious deeds in battlefields. I am ashamed to be subordinate to Lin Xiangru, a humble man who just has eloquence. I am going to put Lin Xiangru to shame if I ever meet up with him."

After Lin Xiangru heard about this, he went out of his way to avoid meeting Lian Po. Lin's subordinates felt uncomfortable and unhappy. They asked, "You are senior in rank than he. Why are you afraid of him?" Lin asked a question in reply, "The King of Qin and General Lian Po, who is more powerful?" "The King, of course." Lin's subordinates answered. "Yes. I'm not even afraid of the King of Qin, then why should I be afraid of General Lian Po? It is because of the two of us that other states dare not invade Zhao. If we were to disagree and not on good terms, other states would take advantage of it and attack Zhao. Personal resentment is a meaningless trifle and should always make way for the interests of the State which must be put in the first place."

When Lian Po heard about this, he knew he himself was wrong. He was so ashamed that he took off his shirt, and with a bunch of branches on his back, asked Lin Xiangru to flog him. From then on, these two were on very good terms and devoted themselves to the interests of Zhao, and other states dare not invade Zhao easily.

Today, this idiom "To Proffer a Birch and Ask for a Flogging" describes any situation in which a person knows he has done wrong, and earnestly asks the person whom he has wronged to punish him.

This idiom informs us of the principles to handle affairs. We should be like Lin Xiangru who laid emphasis on the interests of the country over his own，and like Lian Po who did not hesitate to acknowledge and correct his mistake.

8 梅开二度

"梅开二度"来自一出戏剧《二度梅》。其中主人公梅良玉的父亲被奸臣所害，他侥幸被人救出并送到其父的好友陈日升家中寄居。陈日升的女儿陈杏元长得很漂亮，与梅良玉青梅竹马。陈日升视梅良玉如己出，常带他在花园的梅树边拜祭故友。梅良玉不辜负厚爱，发誓要苦苦读书，决心要考取功名，出人头地，将来好为父报仇。

一日，盛开的梅花被夜晚的风雨吹打的凋谢了。陈日升带梅良玉诚恳地再拜，祈求让梅花重开。诚心感动天地，结果真的满园芬芳。

梅开二度，这是个吉兆！梅良玉最终学成进京，中了状元，还和陈日升的女儿结为琴瑟之好。他俩相爱后，好景不长，尚未成婚，北国南侵，唐王难以抵抗，就送陈杏元到北国去和番。那时的邯郸是边陲重镇，凡到番邦去的人，一般都要登临邯郸的丛台，与社稷亲人垂泪相别。于是，陈杏元与梅良玉也来到丛台之上进行告别。如今的丛台仍然有这样八个大字："夫妻南北兄妹沾襟"。

陈杏元泪别梅良玉赴番邦。路经悬崖，痛不欲生时，王昭君的阴魂背起陈杏元直送陈家与梅良玉喜结良缘。此事感动了陈家的梅树，在梅陈完婚之日，梅树二度重开。

"梅开二度"原本表达的意思是好事再现。现今用来形容一个人的状态回勇、事业再次辉煌等。

从这则典故可以看出人若遇到挫折，不应放弃，坚持下去，事情总会有转机。

The Plums Booming Twice

The idiom "The Plums Booming Twice" originated from a drama "Er Du Mei (The Plum Booming Twice)". In the drama, Mei Liangyu's father had been framed by some treacherous court officials. He was saved luckily and sojourned with Chen Risheng, his father's best friend. Chen Risheng's daughter was very beautiful and she was Mei's childhood sweetheart. Chen Risheng treated Mei as his own son. Chen often took Mei to pay their respect and hold a memorial ceremony for Mei's father by the plum tree in their garden. Mei Liangyu was worthy of Chen's kindness and expectation. He promised to study hard and determined to stand out and obtain fame and power to take his revenge for his father.

One day, those fully-bloomed plum flowers withered from the wind and rain at night. Chen Risheng took Mei Liangyu to sincerely show their admiration again and prayed that those blossoms would re-appear. Their sincerity moved Heaven and Earth. Soon the sweet perfume from the plum blossoms overflowed their garden.

The plum flowers bloomed twice! How favorable this auspice was! Then Mei Liangyu finished his study and went up to the capital and came out first at the National Exam. He and Chen Risheng's daughter fell in love with each other and started to date. However, good times did not last long. Before their marriage, the northern country invaded the south. The Emperor of Tang could not fight back their invasion, so he had to send Chen Xingyuan to the northern country to marry to their king. Handan was an important border city at that time. Anyone who had to go to the barbarian countries would climb up to Congtai in Handan to say farewell to his/her families in tears. Chen Xingyuan and Mei Lianyu also went up there…Because of this story, there are still eight large words in Congtai, "The couple will be separated and families are all in tears."

Chen Xingyuan left Mei Liangyu for the barbarian country in tears. When she passed by a cliff and fell in deep sorrow, Wang Zhaojun's ghost carried Chen back to her home to marry Mei. This deeply touched Chen's plum trees. On their wedding day, the plums blossomed again.

The idiom "The Plums Booming Twice" expresses good things reappearing. Nowadays, people use this idiom to describe that somebody returns to a wonderful state or one's career has been brilliant again. Sometimes, people use it to refer to a woman who is remarried.

From this idiom, we can conclude that if one suffers setbacks, as long as one does not give up and carries on, he/she will encounter a favorable turn.

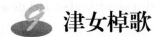 津女棹歌

战国时，赵简子率军渡河南击楚。负责管理渡口的官吏醉卧失职，即将被依法处死。

这名官员的女儿对赵简子巧妙陈词："我的父亲听说君王要渡河，怕有大风，所以祈祷各路水神，以求风平浪静。但是喝多了巫祝的残杯剩炙，所以醉酒误事，我愿意代替父亲受罪。"

人马马上要渡河了，正好少一个摇船的人，于是这名女子拿上船楫，一起划船渡河。到中流时，女子唱起船歌，鼓舞了大军的士气。

赵简子很高兴，把她娶为夫人。

这个典故通常用来指孝女救父。也可以比喻女子智勇双全，有胆识。

我们可以从中学到两点：第一，为人子女，孝字第一；第二，现代女性应注重内在智慧的培养，力争做一名智勇双全，有胆有识的人。

Ferry Girl's Oaring Songs

During the Warring States Period, Zhao Jianzi led an army to cross the river in order to attack Chu State. After arriving at the ferry, he found that the official in charge had been drunk and fallen asleep, which was a breach of duty and he should be punished to death according to the law.

Then this official' daughter tactfully defended for her father, "Before your coming, my father heard that you were going to cross the river. In case of the heavy wind, my father prayed all kinds of water gods for calm and tranquil water. Nevertheless, to our surprise, he ate and drank too much of the sorcerer's leftovers and became drunk, which delayed your plan. I was so sorry and I would rather you kill me instead of my father."

At that important instance, the army was going to cross the river, but a rower was wanted. This girl took the oar, got on the ship, and rowed the ship together with the other people. When they arrived at the midstream, this girl sang some oaring songs, which greatly inspired the army's morale.

Seeing that, Zhao Jianzi was very glad and determined to marry this girl as his wife.

This idiom often means that the filial daughter saving her father; we also use it to indicate that a girl is both brave and intelligent, with a great courage and insight.

We can learn two points from this idiom. First, as a son or daughter, one should show filial obedience to the parents. Second, modern women should emphasize the cultivation of wisdom and take efforts to be a girl with courage and insight.

改革篇

河伯娶妻

　　战国时期，西门豹任魏国邺县令。上任后，他问当地老人有关老百姓的苦处。这些人说："苦于给河伯娶妻，使本地民穷财尽。邺县的三老、廷掾每年都向百姓搜刮钱财。他们只用其中极少数为河伯娶妻，而和巫祝一同分那剩余的钱。一到时候，女巫若看中小户人家的漂亮女子，便马上下聘礼娶去。十几天后，女巫让这个女子坐在床铺枕席上面，浮到河中，几十里后便沉没了。有漂亮女子的人家，担心女儿被河伯娶去，大多带着女儿远逃，因此城里越来越空荡，以致更加贫困。老百姓的俗语有'不给河伯娶妻，就会大水泛滥，把百姓都淹死'的说法。"西门豹说："到时候，希望三老、巫祝、父老都到河边去送新娘，我也要去送送这个女子。"

　　到了为河伯娶媳妇的日子，西门豹到河边与众人相会。三老、官员、有钱人、地方父老都会集在此，看热闹的百姓也有二三千人。巫祝是个老婆子，已经七十岁。跟来的女弟子有十余人，都站在后面。

　　西门豹说："叫新娘过来，我看看是否漂亮。"西门豹看了看，回头对三老、巫祝、父老们说："这个女子不漂亮，麻烦大巫婆为我去禀报河伯，需要重找一个漂亮的，迟几天送去。"叫差役们一齐抬起大巫婆，把她抛到河中。

　　过了一会儿，西门豹说："巫婆为什么去这么久？叫人去催催她！"西门豹便以派人催问为借口，把巫婆的三名弟子和三老相继抛到河中。这样一来，那些干坏事的家伙都吓得跪地饶命。邺县的官吏和老百姓都非常惊恐，从此不敢再提起为河伯娶妻之事。

　　西门豹接着就征发老百姓开挖了十二条渠道，把黄河水引来灌溉农田，还消除了水患。老百姓从此家给户足，生活富裕。

　　这则成语的意义在于告诫政府应废除不合理的制度，惩处恶吏，以保证老百姓生活富足，民心归一。

Hebo Getting Married

During the Warring States Period, Ximen Bao was appointed magistrate of Ye county of Wei State. He asked the old people about the sufferings of the local people.

They said, "People suffer from poverty because Hebo (the river god) gets married. Each year the Three Aged and the county officials extort money from the people, but they use a tiny amount of it on Hebo's marriage and share the rest with the witch. When the day is getting near, the witch will choose a pretty girl of a poor family as the bride of Hebo. More than ten days later, the girl will be seated on the well-decorated bed and pushed into the river. After many miles, the bed sinks with the poor girl. Therefore, most of the families with pretty girls fled from the county for the fear of losing her, and consequently the town becomes emptier and poorer. There is an old saying going like this 'He Bo will flood the place and drown all the people if they don't find him a bride.'"

Ximen Bao said, "I will see the girl off, and I hope the Three Aged, the witch and all the people will come."

On the wedding day, Ximen Bao met those people on the riverbank. The Three Aged, officials, the rich, and the local young and old people all gathered there. The witch was about seventy years old, with over ten women followers standing behind her.

Ximen Bao had the bride brought here to see if she was beautiful. Ximen looked at her and said, "She is not beautiful enough, I have to ask the witch to tell Hebo that we will send a more beautiful one a few days later." Then, he ordered the officers to throw the witch into the river.

After a while, he said, "Why hasn't the witch come back? I'd like someone to find out what happens." Then, in a short time, he had three of the witch's followers and the Three Aged successively thrown into the river. On seeing this, those evil persons were frightened and kowtowed down to beg for mercy. After that, the officials and the citizens were so scared that they never dared to mention Hebo's marriage again.

Thereafter, Ximen Bao led the local people to dig twelve channels to draw the water of Yellow River to irrigate the farmland and eliminated the floods. Accordingly, every household became rich, and people started to live a happy life.

The significance of this idiom lies in that the government should abolish unreasonable systems, punish the wicked officials to guarantee common people's abundant lives and finally win their support.

胡服骑射

战国时期的赵国，北方大多是胡人部落。他们和赵国虽然没有发生大的战争，但常有小的掠夺战斗。胡人都是身穿短衣、长裤，作战时骑在马上，动作十分灵活方便，开弓射箭运用自如，往来奔跑，迅速敏捷，而赵国军队虽然武器比胡人精良，但多为步兵和兵车混合编制，加上官兵都是身穿长袍骑马很不方便，在交战中常处于不利地位。因此赵武灵王想向胡人学习。首先，必须改革服装。可他的做法遭到了一些人的反对。

他做了大量的思想工作，但仍有一些王族公子和大臣极力反对，他们说："衣服习俗，古之礼法，变更古法是一种罪过。"武灵王批驳："古今不同俗，有什么古法？帝王都不是承袭的，有什么礼可循？"后来武灵王力排众议，下令在全国改革穿胡服，因为胡服给人带来方便，得到了百姓的拥护。武灵王在改革穿胡服的措施成功后，接着训练骑兵队伍，改变了原来的军事装备，赵国的国力也逐渐强大起来，不但打败了过去经常侵扰赵国的中山国，而且还向北方开辟了上千里的疆土，成为当时的"战国七雄"之一。

这则典故告诉我们在改革中，应排除传统旧势力、旧观念对人的影响。

The Policy of Adopting Hu Tribe's Clothing and Learning Their Cavalry Archery

During the Warring States Period, the northern neighbours of Zhao State were mostly Hu tribes. There were no major wars, but constant minor predatory fighting between them. The Hu all wore short jackets and long pants and fought on the back of the horse, so that they could move flexibly and conveniently, handle the archery skillfully and run swiftly. Although Zhao State owned more sophisticated weapons, they often established their infantry together with the chariots. In addition, the officers and the soldiers all wore long robes which made it inconvenient to ride a horse. Because of these, Zhao State was often in an inferior position in a battle. King Wuling of Zhao (Wuling) wanted to learn from the Hu tribes. First of all, the clothing of Zhao State must be changed. But many people were in opposition with him on this reform.

He tried to change their ideology, but there were still some royals and ministers who were strongly against the reform. They said, "We must follow ancient etiquette in clothing and customs. Changing old etiquette is a kind of crime." King Wuling refuted, "People have different traditions and customs today from those in the past. What ancient etiquette must we follow? Emperors are not inherited. What rituals must we be adhered to?" Later, King Wuling prevailed over all dissenting views and ordered all the citizens to wear Hu-styled clothes. Since Hu-styled clothes brought convenience to the common people, this reform was widely supported. After this successful reform, King Wuling endeavored to train cavalry troops and improved their military equipments. Gradually, Zhao State became stronger and stronger. It defeated Zhongshan State which had often invaded Zhao State in the past, and expanded thousands of miles of its territory to the north. In the end, Zhao State became one of the strongest seven countries at that time.

This idiom tells us, that in our reform, we should eliminate the affections from the out-of-date traditions and old institutions.

3 腹心之患

这个成语也可以叫做"腹心之疾"或"心腹之疾"。

战国时期，武灵王继承赵国的王位后，锐意改革创新，号召大家穿胡服学骑射，发愤图强。

他请大臣楼缓帮助他分析局势，说："我先王根据世事的变化，来做属地的君长，南面利用滏阳河和漳河之险，北边建起长城，夺取了蔺和郭狼，在荏打败了林人，也未能建全功。如今中山国是我的腹心之患，北边有燕国，东边有胡人，西边有林胡、楼烦、秦国和韩国与我们接壤，我们却没有强大的兵力自救，这是要亡国的。该怎么办呢？"

我们通常用"腹心之患"来形容隐藏在内部的祸患，亦比喻要害之病。

这则成语教育我们若要真正解决问题，必须正确分析形势，找出问题的要害所在。

Diseases in One's Vital Organs

This idiom can also be called as "Sickness in One's Vital Organs" or "Sickness in One's Important Organs".

During the Warring States Period, after King Wuling inherited the throne of Zhao State, he made a lot of efforts to carry out the reform and innovation, summoned every citizen to wear Hu tribe's clothing and learn their cavalry archery, and went all out to make the nation strong.

He asked Minister Lou Huan to help him analyze the situation. He said, "My ancestors, according to the change of the world, became the king of this appanage. They took advantage of the danger from Fuyang River and Zhang River in the south, built the Great Wall in the north, conquered Lin and Guolang, and defeated Lin's army at Ren. However, they still failed to achieve the entire success. Now Zhongshan State is just like a disease in our vital organs. We also have Yan State in the north and Hu in the east. Lin Hu, Lou Fan, Qin State and Han State border on us in the west. However, we do not possess formidable military strength to protect us. Someday, we might perish. How can we survive?"

We often use this idiom to describe the threat from within, or serious disease in vital organs.

This idiom enlightens us that on the way to solve a problem, one must analyze the situation accurately and discover the strategic point to the problem in order to deal with it.

主父入秦

赵主父就是历史上大名鼎鼎的赵武灵王。

赵武灵王经过胡服骑射的重大军事变革，使赵国的国力空前强盛。赵国新建的骑兵部队所向无敌，赵武灵王率领这支军队击败了楼烦、林胡等少数民族，又灭掉了北边的心腹大患中山国，拓地千里，使赵国北边的国土直达今天的内蒙古河套地区。

为了能够一心放在军事上，赵武灵王把王位传给了儿子赵何（即赵惠文王），自己称赵主父，只负责带兵作战。

他想从云中、九原等地直接向南袭击秦国，于是化装成赵国的使者潜入秦国，不但了解了秦国的虚实，并且和秦昭王进行了交谈。

秦昭王开始不知道实情，后来对他的伟岸的相貌产生了怀疑，因为他的言谈举止不像是臣子的气度。秦王赶紧派人追赶，可是赵武灵王已经离开秦国的国界。后来经过仔细了解，才知道他就是赵主父。秦国人都大吃一惊。

我们现在通常用这个典故来比喻领导者亲自冒险深入敌营去了解情况。

这则典故告诉我们做大事者应智勇过人，不畏艰险。

Zhu Fu Visiting Qin State

Zhao Zhufu was the famous King Wuling of Zhao State in the history.

After King Wuling's military revolution of adopting Hu tribe's clothing and learning their cavalry archery, Zhao State became unprecedentedly rich and powerful and the new cavalry troops therefore became undefeatable. King Wuling led this army, not only defeated the minorities Lou Fan and Lin Hu, but also eliminated his serious hidden danger —Zhongshan State in the northern area. From then on, an area of a thousands li was occupied by Zhao State, and the territory of Zhao State had been extended to the area of today's Hetao District of Inner Mongolia.

Later in order to concentrate on the military actions, King Wuling passed his throne to his son Zhao He, and called himself Zhao Zhufu (the father of King Huiwen of Zhao State), only in charge of leading troops and fighting.

After military preparations, he wanted to attack Qin State directly from the area of Yunzhong and Jiuyuan. So in order to understand the situation of Qin State, he disguised himself as an emissary of Zhao State, entered Xianyang, the capital of Qin, and even had a talk with King Zhao of Qin State.

At the beginning, King Zhao of Qin did not know the truth, but later he began to doubt on the emissary's identity because he had a strapping appearance and his speech and deportment were not like an official. Then the King of Qin immediately sent the people to catch him, but King Wuling had left the boundary of Qin at that moment. After a careful investigation, the people of Qin were surprised to find that the emissary was the very Zhao Zhufu.

Now we usually use this idiom to indicate that the leader personally takes risk to go deep into the enemy's camp to investigate the situation.

This idiom tells us a man of great achievements should be wise and brave, fearless of danger and difficulty.

哲学篇

得心应手

相传在春秋时期的齐国，一天，齐桓公正在堂上琅琅读书，堂下忙于制造车轮的工匠扁轮却听得烦心，于是放下工具上前问道："请问您读的是什么书？"

齐桓公对他的冒失颇为不悦，但仍回答道："我读的都是圣人的书。"

"那圣人还在吗？"

"不，他已经死了。"

"既然人已经死了，您读的就是古人遗留下的糟粕了。"

齐桓公见他如此唐突自己，不禁勃然变色，说道："寡人在这里读书，你一个工匠怎敢随便议论？你说为什么古人遗留下来的都是糟粕？说不出道理来，就把你处死。"

扁轮摸了摸胡子，不慌不忙地答道："大王息怒。我不过是根据自己的手艺得出的想法。我做工匠的技术，得心应手，口中说不出来，但其中自有奥妙。我无法用话语传授给儿子，儿子也无法继承，所以我七十多岁还得做车轮混饭吃。古代圣人的学问中那些精妙独到的东西是无法用话语传授给别人的，必然随着他们的死亡而消失。所以您现在读的不是古人无用的糟粕又是什么呢？"

齐桓公无法辩驳，就没有治他的唐突之罪。

这则成语的意思是心里怎么想，手里就怎么做，形容技艺纯熟，运用自如。

我们在日常生活和工作中只有从小事做起，从基层中学习并积攒经验，才能在今后的工作中得心应手，运用自如。

The Hands Respond to the Heart

During the Spring and Autumn Period, one day, Qi Huangong, the ruler of Qi State, was reading a book out loud. The noise irritated Bian Lun, an old craftsman who was making wheels nearby. So Bian Lun put down his tools, went to the king and asked, "What are you reading, Your Majesty?"

The king was unhappy for being interrupted. But still he answered, "I'm reading a book by a wise man."

"Is that wise man still alive?"

"No, he is dead." answered the ruler.

Bian Lun said, "If the writer is dead, what you are reading now is the dregs he left."

The king was angry with the craftsman. He said, "I'm reading my book here. You, as a craftsman, are standing here commenting on this. You have to tell me why things left by ancient people are dregs. If you don't have a good explanation, I'll have you executed."

Stroking his beard, Bian Lun replied with ease, "Your Majesty, don't be angry. I made the conclusion based on my own career experience. When doing my homework, I have ideas in my heart, and my hands will respond to it. It cannot be expressed in words. So I cannot pass this kind of intuition and skill on to my son, and my son cannot get it from me. That's why, at the age of 70, I still have to make wheels to support myself. The essence of ancient wise men's thoughts must be something that can't be put into words. Their profound and inexpressible ideas died together. Therefore, if what you are reading now is not dregs, what are they, Your Majesty?"

The ruler thought what the craftsman said made some sense and had no words to refute. So he didn't punish him for his abruptness.

This idiom means that the hands respond to the heart and it describes skilled marksmanship to act in an expert way.

In our daily life and work we should begin with the minor matters and learn from the grass roots to accumulate experience. Only in that way can we become experts.

2 利害唯己，谁贵谁贱

弟子问庄子："先生说，从道的角度观察世间万物。无贵无贱，无大无小。那么有没有一定的是非标准呢？也就是说，先生您知道万物有一个共同认可的真理吗？"

庄子说:"我怎么知道?"

弟子问:"那您知道您所不知道的原因吗?"

庄子说:"我怎么知道?"

弟子问:"那么万物就不可知了吗?"

庄子说:"我怎么知道?即使如此,我不妨尝试着说说。怎么知道我所谓知不是不知呢?又怎么知道我所说的不知不是知呢?我且试着问你几个问题:人睡在湿地上则会腰痛,泥鳅会这样吗?人在树上则心惊胆战,猿猴会这样吗?这三者谁知道真正的处所?人喜欢吃蔬菜肉食,麋鹿喜欢吃草,蜈蚣喜欢吃蛇,猫头鹰喜欢吃老鼠,人、兽、虫、鸟这四者谁知道真正的美味?毛嫱和丽姬,人人都认为她们是绝色美人,可鱼儿一见到她们就躲避于深水之中,鸟儿一见到她们就飞得更高,麋鹿一见她们就逃得更远,这四者谁知道真正的美色?在我看来,仁义的准则,是非的选择,或对我有利,或对别人有害,利害各有其标准,我怎能搞清其中的区别?"

这个典故告诫我们,不要用一己之见去衡量天下万物,利害是非各有其标准。同时,我们在处理问题的过程中要遵循趋利避害的原则。

What Is Advantageous and What Is Hurtful, Who Is Noble and Who Is Humble, All Depend on Yourself

A disciple asked Zhuangzi, "Sir, since you said to treat everything with Tao, no noble or no humble, no great or no small. Is there a common standard? Do you know, Sir, a common truth that all creatures can accept?"

Zhuangzi replied, "How should I know it?"

"Do you know the reason why you do not know?"

Zhuangzi replied, "How should I know it?"

The disciple continued, "Then are all creatures thus not understandable?"

Zhuangzi said, "How should I know it? Even so, I will try to explain my meaning. How do you know that when I say 'I know it', I am really indicating I do not know it, and that when I say 'I do not know it', I am really indicating that I do know it?

哲 学 篇

And let me ask you some questions: If a man sleeps in a damp place, he will have a pain in his loin; but will it be so with an eel? If he stays on a tree, he will be frightened and all in a tremble; but will it be so with a monkey? And does any one of the three know his right place? Men eat meat and vegetables; deer feed on the thickset grass; centipedes enjoy small snakes; owls delight in mice; but does any one of the four know the right taste? Mao Qiang and Li Ji were accounted by men to be most beautiful, but when fishes saw them, they dived deep in the water from them; when birds saw them, they flew from them aloft; and when deer saw them, they separated and fled away. But did any of these four know in the world which is the right female attraction? As I look at the matter, the first principles of benevolence and righteousness and the paths of approval and disapproval are inextricably mixed and confused. They are either beneficial to one or harmful to another. Benefit or harm, they have different standards. So how is it possible that I should know the differences among them?"

This idiom warns us that we should not just use our own standards to decide what is good or what is bad, because that depends. And in dealing with problems we shoud try to seek advantages and avoid disadvantages.

3 穷通自乐

庄子将死。弟子站立床前哭泣着说："伟大啊，造物者！他将把您变成什么，把您送到何方？把您变化成老鼠的肝脏吗？把您变化成虫蚁的臂膀吗？"

庄子道："对于子女来说，父母无论让他们去东西南北，他们都只能听从吩咐调遣。自然的变化对于人，则不啻于父母；它使我靠拢死亡而我却不听从，那么我就太蛮横了，而它有什么过错呢！大地把我的形体托载，用生存来劳苦我，用衰老来闲适我，用死亡来安息我。所以把我的存在看作是好事，也因此可以把我的死亡看作是好事。弟子该为我高兴才是啊！"

弟子听了，竟呜咽有声，情不自禁。

庄子笑道："你不是不明白：死是生的开始，生是死的结束。人的生死，只

不过是气的聚散。气聚则为生,气散则为死。死生为伴,都是天地之气,你又何必悲伤?"

弟子道:"生死之理,我何尚不明。只是我跟随您至今,受益匪浅,弟子却无以为报。想先生贫困一世,死后竟没什么东西陪葬。弟子也是因为这个才悲伤的!"

庄子坦然微笑,说道:"我把天地当作棺木,把日月当作连城之璧,把星辰当作陪葬珠宝,世间万物都可以成为我的陪葬。我的葬具岂不很完备吗?还有比这更好更多的陪葬品吗?"

弟子道:"没有棺木,我担忧乌鸦和老鹰啄食先生的遗体。"

庄子平静笑道:"把尸体放在地面上会被乌鸦和老鹰吃掉,把尸体深埋地下会被蚂蚁吃掉,二者有什么区别呢?夺过乌鸦、老鹰的食物再交给蚂蚁、老鼠,何必这样偏心呢?"

在现实生活中我们应当学习庄子,在困境中依然保持积极、乐观的生活态度。

Enjoyment Outside the Dust and Dirt

Zhuangzi was dying; his disciple stood in front of the bed, wept and said, "Great indeed is the Creator! What will He now make you become? Where will He take you to? Will He make you the liver of a rat, or the arm of an insect?

Zhuangzi said, "Wherever a parent tells a son to go east, west, south or north, he simply obeys. The Yin and Yang are more to a man than his parents are. If they are hastening my death, and I do not quietly submit to them, I shall be obstinate and rebellious. Where is it to blame? The great nature bears of my body; toils my life; entertains my old age; and relieves me at death: which has made my life a good will make my death also a good. You should feel happy for me.

After hearing it, the disciple choked with sob, and couldn't refrain from tears.

Zhuangzi smiled and said, "You are not unaware, life is the result of death, and death is the start of life. Life is the gathering of breath and the dispersing of breath is death. Death and life are accompanied with each other and they are ordained. No use to be so sad.

The disciple said, "I am not unclear about the principle of life and death. I have benefited greatly since becoming your student, but I am unable to repay your kindness. I feel sorrowful in thinking that you do not have anything to be buried with after spending a poor life."

Zhuangzi smiled at ease and said, "Heaven and earth are my coffin. The sun and the moon are my jades, the stars my pearls and gems, and the whole world escorts me. Aren't the things buried with me completed? Is there anything better than these?

The disciple said, "Without a coffin, I worry that the crows and eagles will eat your flesh."

Zhuangzi smiled calmly and said, "Be eaten by the crows and eagles on the ground, by ants and mice under ground. What's the difference between them? Why to be so partial to seize the food of crows and eagles to give ants and mice.

In reality we should learn from Zhuangzi to face difficult position with active and optimistic attitude.

死亦可乐

庄子骑着一匹瘦马,慢慢行走在通向楚国的古道上。凛冽的西风扑打着庄子瘦削的面孔,掀起他萧瑟的鬓发。庄子顾目四野,但见哀鸿遍野,骷髅遍地,一片兵荒马乱后的悲惨景象。

夕阳西下,暮野四合。庄子走到一颗枯藤缠绕的老树下,惊起树上几只昏鸦盘旋而起,聒噪不休。庄子把马系好后,想找块石头坐下休息,忽见树下草丛中露出一个骷髅来。

庄子走近去,用马鞭敲了敲,问它道:"先生是患病而落到此地步的吗?还是国破家亡、刀斧所诛而落到此地步的呢?先生是因有不善之行、愧对父母妻子

而自杀才到这地步的吗?还是因冻馁之患而落到此地步的呢?亦或是寿终正寝所致?"

说完,拿过骷髅,枕之而卧。不一会儿,便呼呼入睡。

半夜时,骷髅出现在庄子梦中,说道:"先生,刚才所问,好像辩士的口气。你所谈的那些情况,皆是生人之累,死后则无此烦累了。您想听听死之乐趣吗?"庄子答:"当然。"

骷髅说:"人一旦死了,在上没有国君的统治,在下没有官吏的管辖,也没有四季的更替。从容安逸地把天地的长久看作是时光的流逝。即使是南面称王的快乐,也不可能超过这个。"

庄子不信,问:"如果让阎王爷使你复生,还你骨肉肌肤,还你父母、妻子、乡亲、朋友,您愿意吗?"

骷髅现出愁苦的样子,道:"我怎么能抛弃南面称王的快乐而再次经历人世的劳苦呢!"

Even Death Can Be Happy

Zhuangzi was walking slowly on a horseback on the ancient road to Chu State. His haggard face was beaten by the chilling west wind and his grey hair waved. Zhuangzi looked around, seeing the famished refugees moaning everywhere and skeletons lying all over the land. It was a miserable scene after the chaos of wars.

The sun went west, and the night fell. Zhuangzi came under a rugged tree twined round by dried vines and some crows were startled to hover over the tree with harsh cries. He tethered his horse to the tree and tried to find a stone to rest on. Then he glimpsed a skull in the grass.

He approached and tapped it with his horse lash, asking, "Did you end up like this because of illness? Or was it because your country was destroyed and you were beheaded? Or was it because you were involved in some unsavory conduct and committed suicide due to the shame to face your parents, wife, and children? Or was it because of your suffering from starvation and cold? Or was it because your time was up and died in the bed?"

哲 学 篇

Then he picked up the skull and made a pillow of it when he went to sleep. Soon he was in a sound sleep.

At midnight, the skull appeared in his dream and said, "You seem to be a sophist by the tone of your questions just now. What you mentioned was all the burdens in life. None of them exists after death. Would you like to know the happiness of death?" "Yes", said Zhuangzi.

The skull said, "When you are dead, there is no ruler above you and no subjects below you; there are no toils of the four seasons. Time passes peacefully as it does for heaven and earth. No king in his court has greater happiness than that."

Zhuangzi didn't believe it and said, "Would you like it if I could make Hades (the King of Hell) restore your life, give back your bones and flesh and shin, and return your parents, wife, children, and acquaintances?"

The skull said with an air of sorrow, "How should I cast away the happiness of my royal court and undertake again the toils of living?"

5 乐极生悲

战国时期，齐威王经常饮酒作乐，不问朝政，弄得百官荒乱，国家危机。楚国乘机发兵讨伐，幸亏淳于髡请求赵国出兵援救，楚国才将兵马撤回。因为淳于髡保国有功，齐威王在后宫摆设酒宴，请他喝酒。

在酒宴上，齐威王问淳于髡："先生喝多少酒才会醉啊？"

淳于髡回答说："我喝一斗也醉，喝一石也醉。"

齐威王觉得奇怪，又问："先生既然喝一斗就醉，怎么又能喝一石呢？这是什么道理啊？"

淳于髡是一个能言善辩的人，他想趁这个时候规劝齐威王，以后不要再通宵饮酒了，所以他委婉地说："原因是这样的：如果您赏给我酒喝，您坐在我的面前，执法官站在旁边，御史官站在后面，我感到恐惧，所以喝酒不过一斗就会醉的；若是遇见久不相见的朋友，在一起高高兴兴地交谈，可以喝五六斗才能醉；若是在民间百姓聚会，不分男女坐在一起，一边饮酒一边游戏，喝上八斗也不会醉；假如到了夜里，主人把我留下，无拘无束地坐在一起，这时候我最欢喜，能饮一石。"说到这里，他瞧着齐威王的眼睛，缓缓地说："所以古人说，酒喝到了极点，就不能遵守礼节；人快乐到了极点，就会发生悲哀的事情！"

齐威王这才明白，淳于髡是在讽谏自己，他叹了口气："唉！你说的好啊！"从此以后他再也不通宵饮酒了。

后人多用"乐极生悲"形容欢乐过度而招致悲伤的事情。

这则成语告诫我们做事情要遵循适度的原则。

Extreme Joy Begets Sorrow

In the Warring States Period, King Wei of Qi State always indulged in wine and pleasure, so he never cared about the state affairs. As a result, all the officials were neglectful of their duties, and the state was faced with various crises. At this moment, Chu State invaded Qi. Due to Chun Yukun's asking for help from Zhao State, Chu troops withdrew from Qi. To cite Chun Yukun's contribution, King Wei of Qi repasted for him in the palace.

During the dinner, King Wei asked Chun Yukun, "How much wine can make you drunk?"

Chun Yukun replied, "I will be drunk with either a dou (about 1 decalitre) of wine or a dan (about 1 hectolitre) of wine."

King Wei was amazed, so he asked, "Since you will be drunk with a dou of wine, how can you drink a dan of wine? Can you tell me the reason?"

Chun Yukun was an eloquent man. He wanted to persuade King Wei not to drink overnight any longer, so he said, "If you send me some wine to drink, but you are sitting in front of me, the executive official is standing by my side and another official is standing behind me, I will feel scared, so I will be drunk with a dou of wine; if I meet some friends whom I have not seen for a long time, and we will talk and drink happily, so I can drink five or six dous of wine; if I attend a party with common people, we will sit together and play games while we are drinking, I can drink eight dous of wine; if the host asks me to stay the whole night, I will be very happy without any constraints, so at this time, I can drink a dan of wine." Then he looked at King Wei's in the eyes, and said slowly, "It is said that if a person drinks to the extreme, he will not follow the etiquette; if a person joys to the extreme, he will meet something sorrowful."

At this time, King Wei understood that Chun Yukun was admonishing him politely. He sighed, "Eh, you are right!" Then he never drank too much wine throughout the night.

People use this idiom to express that if a person overexcites himself, he will meet something woeful.

This idiom tells us to keep moderate in doing any daily activities.

6 一枕黄粱

传说唐朝时候，有个名叫卢生的青年书生，到京城参加考试。当他来到邯郸时，住在一家旅店里，在店中遇见了一个名叫吕翁的道士。卢生向他诉说了自己的穷困处境，希望能够得到功名利禄和荣华富贵，恳求道士指点实现美好愿望的良方妙法。

吕翁答应了他的要求，借给他一个青瓷枕头，告诉他说："你只要枕着它睡上一觉，就会感到称心如意。"卢生高兴地接过枕头，枕着它很快就进入了梦乡。这时店主人刚刚煮上一锅小米饭。

卢生在梦乡考上了进士，当了大官，娶了一个贤惠、美丽的妻子，有了五个儿子、十个孙子，儿孙个个功成名就，飞黄腾达……他尽享了人间的荣华富贵，一直活到八十多岁。可是一觉醒来，方才的一切就成了泡影，他仍旧睡在邯郸的旅店里，只有吕翁坐在他的身旁。这时，店主人那一锅小米饭还没有煮熟呢！

"一枕黄粱"、"黄粱一梦"或"黄粱美梦"后来被人们用来比喻根本不能实现的企图和愿望，或是那些虚幻、一场空的事物。这则成语提醒我们做事情要脚踏实地，不要抱任何幻想。

A Golden Millet Dream

It is said that in the Tang Dynasty, there was a young scholar named Lu Sheng who was going to the capital to attend the imperial examination. When he arrived in Handan, he met a Taoist named Lu Weng at an inn. Lu Sheng told the Taoist about his own poor living conditions and his wish to obtain great wealth and a high position. He pleaded to the Taoist for a good and effective way to realize his wishes.

Lu Weng accepted his request and lent him a celadon pillow, and then told him, "So long as you rest your head on it for a sleep, your wishes will be satisfied." Lu Sheng took over the pillow happily, and soon he fell asleep with his head on it. At this moment, the innkeeper just put a pot of millet on the stove.

Lu Sheng dreamed that he became a successful candidate in the highest imperial examinations, and then he was promoted to a high position in the royal government. He married a virtuous and beautiful wife and gave birth to five sons, and later he obtained ten grandsons. All of his descendants gained fame and success and rose in the world. He enjoyed wealth and glory on earth until he died in his eighties. But when he woke up, what he had experienced disappeared. He was still lying at the inn in Handan and only Lu Weng sat by his side. And the pot of millet on the stove hadn't got prepared yet.

People use "A Golden Millet Dream" or "A Brief Dream of Grandeur" to mean the attempt or wish which cannot be realized, or the unreal things. This idiom reminds us to work in a down-to-earth way and not to have illusions on the unexisting things.

7 兼听则明

唐朝唐太宗时候，有一位著名的政治家，名叫魏征。他出身于贫苦家庭，因为生活困难，从小就到庙里当了道士，后来当了兵，做了官吏，并且一直升到朝廷的谏议大夫。

魏征极聪明，又善于从历史上总结经验，因此他给皇帝出了许多有利于朝廷的主意，深得皇帝的器重。一次唐太宗问他："作为国家的君主，如何才能断事正确、明白而不糊涂呢？相反，办错了事情又往往是因为什么原因呢？"

魏征回答说："各方面的意见你都听一听，自然会得出正确的结论；如果你只听信一面之辞，那就会因为片面而把事情办错。"接着魏征又列举了历史上的教训，说明作为君主，如果偏听偏信，那将造成多么严重的后果。

他说："秦二世偏信赵高，而招来望夷之祸；梁武帝偏信朱异，而自取台城之辱；隋炀帝偏信虞世基，而导致了彭城阁之变。相反，如果多了解一些情况，多听取一些意见，就可以避免或防止一些祸害。比如说尧帝经常访问百姓，有苗这个人的坏事他就掌握了；舜帝由于耳聪目明，共、鲧的罪行就逃不脱。因此说，聪明的君主不能堵塞了言路，应让下面的情况能够反映到上面来，你才会做出正确的决定啊！"

唐太宗听了魏征的话，满意地说："太好了，太好了。"

这句成语的意思是说：听取多方面的意见，才能明辨是非；只听信一方面的话，就会容易做出错误的判断。

Listening to All Sides

In Taizong Period of Tang Dynasty, there was a famous statesman named Wei Zheng who was born in a poor family. When he was a child, he once lived in the temple as a Taoist. Then he joined the army, and became a government official. At the end he was promoted to the royal government and became the imperial censor.

Wei Zheng was very clever and skilled in summarizing experience from history, so he could offer the Emperor a lot of advice beneficial to the state. The Emperor also regarded him highly. Once the Emperor asked him, "As the monarch of the state, how can I judge things correctly and wisely? On the contrary, why do I sometimes make mistakes?"

Wei Zheng replied, "If you listen to opinions of all sides, you can draw the right conclusion; if you trust only one-side statements, you will be benighted and make mistakes." Then he listed to the Emperor some instructive lessons in the history to show that if the monarch trusted only one-side statements, it would bring about very serious consequences.

He said, "The Second Emperor of the Qin Dynasty only trusted Zhao Gao, as a result, it led to the disaster of his being killed by Zhao Gao in Wangyi Palace; Emperor Wu of the Liang Dynasty only listened to Zhu Yi, as a result, he brought himself insult in Taicheng; Emperor Yang of the Sui Dynasty only trusted Yu Shiji, as a result, this led to Pengchengge mutiny. On the contrary, if one can try to understand more details and listen to different opinions, he can avoid and prevent some troubles or disasters. For example, Emperor Yao always paid visits to common people, so he could know the bad deeds made by You Miao; Emperor Shun was sensible and well informed, so he could see the guilt of Gong's and Gun's. Thus we can see that a sensible monarch would not cut off various ways of opinions. He should encourage everyone to express different ideas. Only in this way can you make a correct decision."

The Emperor was very satisfied with this and said, "Quite good! Quite good!"

This idiom tells us that one should listen to different opinions so as to judge from right and wrong; if he trusts only one-side statements, he will make mistakes easily.

8 南辕北辙

　　战国时期，魏王想发兵攻打赵国的都城邯郸。魏国大夫季梁听说后，立刻从半路上返回来，衣服顾不上换，脸也顾不上洗，匆忙来见魏王。魏王看他这样风尘仆仆、慌慌忙忙赶来，觉得很奇怪，便问："你怎么走到半路就回来了？难道有什么特别紧要的事吗？"

　　季梁说："是啊，这次我从外地回来，在太行山下看到这样一个人，他驾着一辆马车，朝北驶去，但却告诉我说：'我打算到楚国去。'我对他说：'您到楚国去，为什么不朝南走反而朝北走呢？难道您不知道楚国在南面吗？'他回答说：'没关系，我的马好，跑得快！'我说：'您的马虽然好，可是这不是去楚国的路啊！'他又说：'不怕，我带的路费多。'我说：'您的路费多又有什么用呢，这确实不是去楚国的路呀！'他还坚持说：'我的车夫赶车的本领高。'他的这些条件再好，如果朝北走去，离楚国只能是越来越远呀！"

　　魏王听了觉得好笑，就说："天下哪有这么糊涂的人！"

　　季梁接着说："现在，您的志愿是要建立霸业，想当诸侯的首领，一举一动都要慎重考虑。可是您却倚仗国家强大、军队精锐，用攻打赵国的办法，来扩大地盘，抬高威望。您这样攻打别国的次数越多，离您的愿望就会越来越远。这正像那个人要去楚国而朝北走一样啊！"

　　我们用这句成语来比喻做事背道而驰，行动和目的相反。在现实生活中我们应当按照既定的目标行事，不可南辕北辙。

Diametrically Opposed to Each Other

　　During the Warring States Period, the King of Wei State intended to invade Handan, the capital of Zhao State. Ji Liang, the Grand Minister of Wei, returned halfway on hearing of this news. He rushed to visit the king without washing face and changing his clothes. The king felt so surprised at his great rush and asked, "Why do you come back halfway? Is there anything urgent?"

　　Ji Liang said, "I come back because I met a man at the foot of Taihang

Mountain. The man drove a cart north, but told me he would go to Chu State. I asked him, 'Why not go south since you will go to Chu State? Don't you know Chu is in the south?' He answered, 'It doesn't matter. My horse runs very fast.' I said, 'Although your horse runs fast, this is not the road to Chu state! ' He continued, 'I don't fear of it, for I have carried a lot of money with me.' I said, 'What's the use of carrying a lot of money, this is indeed not the way to Chu! ' He insisted, "My carter is skillful.' No matter how good these conditions are, he will get farther and farther away from Chu State if he travels north continually."

The king felt funny after listening to this, and said, "How can there be such a stupid person in the world?"

Ji Liang continued to say, "Since your aspiration now is to build up the hegemony and become chief of all the states, your every action should be weighed carefully. However, if you rely on your powerful country and crack troops to invade Zhao, hoping to expand the territory and raise your prestige, you will get farther away from your aspiration as you attack other states more. This is just like the man who intends to go to Chu moves north.

We use this idiom to mean that the action and the purpose are running in the opposite directions. When doing anything in daily pratice, we should stick to the set objective and should not run in the opposite directions.

智者千虑，必有一失

秦朝灭亡以后，刘邦与项羽争霸天下。有一次刘邦派韩信去攻打赵国，韩信用计杀退了赵兵，杀死了成安君陈余，活捉了广武君李左车。

韩信知道广武君是一个很有才能的人，便亲自为他解下绑绳，并且十分客气地向他请教说："我打算向北边攻打燕国，向东边讨伐齐国，用什么办法才会成功呢？"

广武君感到很羞愧，说："打了败仗的将军，不能与他讨论勇敢；亡国的大臣，不能保全生命。我是一个吃了败仗的俘虏，哪有资格谈论这样的事情呢？"

韩信急忙安慰他说:"成安君的失败,是因为他没听你的计谋。如果他按你的意见作战,我也要被你们俘虏了。今天我诚心想听听你的高见,请别推辞了。"

广武君见韩信是诚心实意地请他出主意,便客气地讲出了自己的看法,他说:"我听说聪明的人考虑一千次,可能有一次还会是错的;愚蠢的人考虑一千次,也许有一次想对了。所以我的意见未必可用,只算是表示我的心意吧。我看燕国和齐国不宜用武力征服,最好派一位外交官,带上你的信,说服他们归顺。"

韩信按照广武君的意见去执行,果然获得成功。这则成语告诉我们在日常的生活和工作中要多听取别人的意见,三思而后行。

Even the Wise Are Not Always Free from Error

After the downfall of Qin Dynasty, Liu Bang and Xiang Yu contended for the hegemony. Once Liu Bang sent Han Xin to attack Zhao State, Han Xin used tricks to put Zhao troops into flight, and killed Chen Yu, Lord of Cheng'an and captured Li Zuoche, Lord of Guangwu.

Han Xin knew that Lord Guangwu was a very talented man, so he untied Lord Guangwu in person, and asked politely for advice, "I intend to attack Yan State in the north and Qi State in the east, how can I succeed in this?"

Lord Guang Wu felt very ashamed and said, "The defeated general shouldn't show off bravery, a grand minister of a conquered nation shouldn't intend to survive. I am a captive being defeated, what right do I have to talk about such matters?"

Han Xin hastily consoled him and said, "The failure of Lord of Cheng'an is caused by his failure to adopt your strategies. If he acted after your advices, I would have been your captive. Today, I sincerely want to hear your opinions, please do not refuse it."

Lord Guangwu knew Han Xin was sincerely asking his advice, he then told about his idea politely. He said, "It is said that even the wisest man makes an error in his thousand schemes, while even a fool occasionally comes up with a good idea if he thinks hard. So my idea may not be applicable, I just use this to express my state of mind. In my view, it is inadvisable to conquer Yan State and Qi State by force. You'd better send a diplomat carrying your letter to persuade them to offer their submission.

Han Xin followed Lord Guangwu's advice, and surely enough he won the success. In daily life we should listen to others' advices with an open mind and think thrice before taking action.

 豚蹄穰田

战国时期，齐国有个叫淳于髡的人，因为身材矮小，貌不出众，被看成是齐国的无用之人。但是淳于髡很有学识，多才善辩，说起话来非常幽默。

齐威王在位八年的时候，楚国派兵侵入齐国边境，齐威王没办法抵抗，就派淳于髡到赵国去求救兵。临行之前，齐威王交给他一百斤黄金、十辆马车，作为送给赵国国王的礼物。淳于髡一看这些礼物，仰起脖子哈哈大笑，把系帽子的绳都笑断了。

齐威王觉得奇怪，便问他："你是嫌拿的东西太少吗？"他回答："那我怎么敢呢？"齐威王又问："那么你笑的是什么？"淳于髡这才告诉齐威王说："今天我从东方来，看到有一个人，在向神祈祷田地丰收。他拿着一只猪蹄子，一碗酒，向神祷告说：'神啊！让我在山地上种的粮食得到满垄的收获，让我在洼地种的谷物得到满车的收获。保佑我种的庄稼都丰收，让粮食装满我家的房屋！'我看他祭神的东西很少，而向神要的东西却极多，所以我才这样笑。"

齐威王听了这番话，明白了他的意思，便增加黄金一千斤、白璧十双、马车一百辆。淳于髡这才高高兴兴地出使赵国去了。

赵国的国王见到这么多的珍贵礼物，立刻答应派出十万精兵、一千辆战车去救援齐国。楚国得到了赵国派援兵救齐的消息，当夜就悄悄把兵撤回去了。

人们后来用"豚蹄穰田"这则典故来比喻给予人的很少，向别人要求的极多。

To Expect Tremendous Return from Meager Investment

During the Warring States Period, there was a man named Chun Yukun in Qi State. He was short and ordinary-looking, so he was considered to be useless in the state. In fact, Chun Yukun was knowledgeable and eloquent full of humor.

During the eighth year of King Wei's throne in Qi State, Chu State began to invade Qi. The king of Qi was not able to resist the invasion, so he ordered Chun Yukun to go to Zhao state to ask for reinforcements. Before he left, King Wei offered him one hundred jin of gold and ten carriages as the gifts giving to the King of Zhao State. At the sight of the gifts, Chun Yukun bursted into laughter to such a degree that the lace of his hat broke.

King Wei was surprised and asked, "Don't you think the gifts enough?"

Chun Yukun replied, "I don't mean that."

Then King Wei asked, "Then why do you laugh?"

Chun told him, "Today I came from the east. I saw a man was praying for a plenteous harvest next year. He put a pig's trotter and a bowl of wine to pray to the Heaven, 'My Heaven! Please let me have a plenteous harvest of grain in the hilly fields, and a bountiful harvest of cereals in the valleys. Please bless me with a harvest of all my crops and let the grains fill my house.' I saw that his oblation was so little, but he expected a tremendous return from the Heaven. So I can't help laughing."

King Wei understood his meaning. He added his gifts up to a thousand jin of gold, ten pairs of white round jade and one hundred carriages. Chun Yukun went to Zhao State with these gifts cheerfully.

The king of Zhao State was content with so many precious gifts. He immediately agreed to send a hundred thousand soldiers and a thousand chariots to help Qi State. When Chu State heard of the news, they withdrew their soldiers at the same night.

Now, people use this idiom to express that people expect a tremendous return from meager investment.

鹬蚌相争

战国时代,赵国打算进攻燕国,著名的说客苏代就去赵国劝阻,替燕国说情。

苏代给赵惠文王讲了一个故事:

有一天,一只河蚌张开蚌壳,在河滩上晒太阳。这时有一只鹬鸟,正从河蚌身边走过,就伸嘴去啄蚌肉。河蚌急忙把两片蚌壳闭合,把鹬嘴紧紧夹住。

鹬鸟用尽力气,怎么也拔不出嘴来。蚌也脱不了身,没法回到河里去。

鹬鸟和河蚌相持不下,争吵起来。

鹬鸟威胁说:"如果你不张开壳子,今天不下雨,明天不下雨,就会晒死你!"

河蚌也不示弱,它对鹬鸟说:"我把你狠狠钳住,今天不放你,明天不放你,就会憋死你!"

它们两个谁也不肯放开谁,死死地纠缠在一起。这时,恰巧有一个渔夫走过来,没费一点力气,就把它们两个一起捉住,拿回家去。

苏代讲完故事,就对赵惠文王说:"现在赵国准备进攻燕国,如果真的打起来,燕、赵两国将会长期相持不下,弄得疲惫不堪。我担心强大的秦国会象渔翁那样,趁机把燕、赵两国一起吞并掉。希望大王慎重考虑。"

赵惠文王听了,点点头说:"你说的对。"于是就取消了进攻燕国的计划。

现在用"鹬蚌相争"这则成语来形容双方争执不下,第三者因而得利。这则成语告诉我们在处理事情时要注意外部情况,权衡得失,不要只想着对自己有利的一面,要相互谦让。否则,只顾与对手争强好胜,只会两败俱伤,使第三者得利。

When the Snipe and the Clam Grapple, the Fisherman Profits

In the Warring States Period, Zhao State planned to attack Yan State. A famous persuasive talker named Su Dài went to Zhao State to try to prevent the attack against Yan State.

Su Dai told a story to King Huiwen of Zhao State.

One day, a clam opened its shell to enjoy sunbathing on the bank of the river. At this time, a snipe passed by. When the snipe saw the clam, he tried to peck its meat. The clam closed its shell hurriedly, and the snipe's beak was squeezed tightly.

The snipe exerted himself, but he still could not push his beak out. Yet the clam also couldn't get free from the snipe to go back to the river.

Neither of them would yield, so they began to quarrel with each other.

The snipe said, "If you don't open your shell, you will be parched to death by the sun without rain for two days."

The clam didn't give way and refute, "I will squeeze you tightly. If I don't open my shell for two days, you will be suffocated to death!"

Neither of them would like to give way to the other, so they tangled together firmly. Just at the moment, a fisherman came near; he seized both of them without any effort and took them home.

Having finished the story, Su Dai told King Huiwen of Zhao State, "Now, Zhao State is gong to attack Yan State. If the battle breaks out, both of you will be stalemated and dog-tired. I am afraid that at that time, the powerful Qin State who is just like the fisherman, will annex both of you. I hope Your Majesty can think it over cautiously."

King Huiwen of Zhao State nodded and said, "You are right." Then he cancelled the plan of attacking Yan State.

Now, we use this idiom to express that if both sides stick to their guns and are stalemated, the third one will gain the benefit. This idiom tells us that when resolving a dispute, we should pay attention to the external situation, weigh the pros and cons, accommodate each other and not just be concerned with our own advantages. Otherwise, both sides will suffer, only a third party will benefit.

12 舍本逐末

战国时期，诸侯各霸一方。

一天，齐王派出了一个使者，要他到赵国去问候赵威后。

这位使者没到过赵国，但他早已听说，赵威后是一位贤德的王后。他想去向赵威后问安，赵威后一欢喜，说不定会回赐一件贵重的礼品。因此，他觉得此次出使赵国，是一件难得的美差。

邯郸，在齐王使者的想象中十分美丽。因此，他一路上盘算，待办完了公事，一定要饱饱眼福。

到了赵国的都城邯郸，他直奔赵王城，去问候赵威后。

礼仪过后，齐王使者把随身带来的齐王问候赵威后的亲笔信，递给了赵威后。

但赵威后竟然没有先去拆阅齐王的信，却躬身问齐王使者道："你们齐国今年的收成好吗？"

"好。"齐王使者答。

赵威后又问："黎民百姓好吗？"

"好。"齐王使者答。

赵威后再问："齐王也很好吗？"

"也很好。"齐王使者答。

使者回答过了问候，可心里却很不是滋味。于是问道："尊贵的威后，吾奉吾王旨意，专程向你来问安。你若回问的话，也该先问候我们的大王。可你先问的，却是年景和百姓。你怎么把低贱的摆在了前头，而把尊贵的摆在了后头呢？"

赵威后微微地笑了，说："话可不能这么说。我所以先问年景和百姓，后问候你的大王，自有我的道理。"

齐王使者问："什么道理？"

赵威后说："你想想看，假如没有好年景，那黎民百姓靠什么活下去呢？同样，假如没有黎民百姓，又哪里有大王呢？所以说，我这样问才合乎情理；不这样问，便是舍本逐末。你说是不是这样呢？"

齐王的使者顿时哑口无言。

现在人们用"舍本逐末"来比喻做事不注意根本，而只抓细微末节。这则成语告诉我们做事要抓主要矛盾，不要丢了西瓜捡了芝麻。

To Neglect the Root and Attend to the Tip

During the Warring States Period, China was torn by vassal principalities, with each principality dominating a region.

One day, King of Qi sent an envoy to compliment Empress Wei of Zhao State.

Although the envoy had never been to Zhao State, he had heard, for long time, that Empress Wei was a virtuous woman. He thought that after he complimented her, Empress Wei might be so happy that she would bestow him some precious gift. Therefore, in his opinion, this diplomatic mission would be a cushy job.

Handan, the capital of Zhao, was a beautiful city in his imagination. So he planed to feast his eyes on its beautiful view after he finished his mission.

Arriving in Handan, he went directly to the palace to compliment Empress Wei.

After the salutation, the envoy submitted a greeting letter written by King of Qi to Empress Wei.

Before the letter had even been opened, Empress Wei bowed and asked the envoy "Is the harvest in your state good?"

"Yes." was the answer.

"How are the people?"

"Fine."

"Is the king well?"

"Yes, he is well, too."

Having answered her questions, the envoy was displeased and said, "Your servant has been sent on a mission to compliment you with my King's decree, noble Empress Wei. Instead of complimenting my King, you enquired first about the harvest and the people. Could it be that you are concerned more with the lowly than with the noble?"

Empress Wei smiled and replied, "Not so. I felt justified to say so."

"Why?"

Empress Wei said, "If there were no good harvest, how could the people live? And if there were no people, how could a king exist? Therefore when one makes enquiries, should one neglect the root and attend to the tip?"

The envoy became tongue-tied.

Today, the idiom "To Neglect the Root and Attend to the Tip" means attending to trifles and neglect the essentials.

This idiom reminds us that we should pay more attention to the essentials and grasp the principal contradiction in doning anything, avoiding sacrificing the substance for the shadow.

13 掩耳盗铃

春秋末年，晋国的智伯联合魏桓子、赵襄子和韩康子打败了范吉射，范逃离晋国。

一天，有一个人走进了范家，发现了一口钟，便心生歹意，想把它偷走。但是，这口钟太重了，他背不动。

他思索了一会儿，终于想出了一个办法，决定把钟敲碎，然后一块一块地取走。于是，他找了一个铁锤，竭尽全力向钟敲去。

然而，铜铸的钟发出了洪亮的响声，震耳欲聋，却没有碎裂。他再砸一次，钟照样发出响声，还是没有碎。

钟声使他猛然醒悟，别人一旦听到，他就偷不成了。

他自以为聪明地认为，捂住自己的耳朵，自己听不见，别人一定也听不见，就可以把钟偷走了。

结果是：别人听到钟声，把他抓住了。

古时候，钟和铃都是乐器，所以"掩耳盗钟"也叫"掩耳盗铃"。

这则成语的意思是捂住耳朵偷铃，形容自己欺骗自己。这则成语告诫我们做事要实事求是，不要欺骗自己和他人。

To Plug One's Ears While Stealing a Bell

During the last years of the Spring and Autumn Period, Zhi Bo in Jin State united Wei Huanzi, Zhao Xiangzi and Han Kangzi together to defeat Fan Jishe, who escaped from Jin State.

One day, a person came into Fan's family. He saw a bell and wanted to steal it. But the bell was too heavy; he couldn't carry it away on his back.

He thought for a while and a good idea hit him. He could slam the bell into small pieces, and then he could take them away one by one. Therefore, he found a hammer and slammed the bell with all his strength.

However, the bronze bell just gave off a sonorous and ear-splitting sound, and it didn't break into pieces at all. Then he tried once more, and the case was same.

Hearing the sound, he came to his senses suddenly. He realized that once the other people heard the sound, he couldn't steal the bell.

He thought himself to be wise in his own conceit that if he plugged his own ears, he wouldn't hear the sound, so other people would not hear it, either. In this way, he could steal the bell away.

The result was that other people heard the sound and caught him on the spot.

In the ancient times, "zhong" and bell was both a kind of musical instrument. So, "To Plug One's Ears While Stealing a 'Zhong'" can also be used as "To Plug One's Ears While Stealing a Bell".

This idiom means that somebody plugs his ears while he steals a bell. It means self-deception. It reminds us to be practical and realistic in whatever we do and never intend to deceive others and ourselves.

14 惊弓之鸟

战国末期，诸侯各国联合起来对付秦国。赵国派魏加到楚国去拜见春申君。见面后，魏加问他道："您有领兵的将军吗？"春申君回答："有呀，我打算让临武君作将军。"

魏加想了一下，说："我小时候喜欢射箭，我想用射箭说明一个道理，可以吗？"

春申君说："当然可以。"于是魏加就讲了一个故事：魏国有一个叫更羸的人，有一次，他正和魏王一起谈话，忽然抬头看见一只飞鸟。更羸望了望，就对魏王说："大王您看，我拉开弓，不必搭上箭，只要空拉一下弓，就能把天上这只雁给您射下来。"

魏王说："您射箭的技术难道能高到这种程度吗？您是在开玩笑吧？"

更羸回答："这不是开玩笑，我可以做到。"

正说着，那只雁已经飞了过来。更羸马上拉开弓，装作射箭的样子，只拉弦不发箭，那只雁果然随着弓弦的响声掉了下来。

魏王惊叹地说："先生真有这样的本事呀！"

更羸指着地上的雁，说道："其实，这是一只受过伤的雁呀！"

魏王更加奇怪，忙问到："先生怎么知道它是一只受了伤的雁？"

更羸回答："这只雁飞得很慢，叫得很凄惨。飞得很慢，说明它受过伤，伤口疼；叫的凄惨，说明它和雁群失散很久。旧伤没长好，心惊胆战，因此听到弓弦声，就以为又有人用箭射它，于是拼命高飞。结果伤口破裂，疼痛难忍，支持不住，自然掉落下来。"

魏加讲完这段故事，又对春申君说："临武君曾经被秦国打败过，心中一定害怕秦军，我看他不能作为抵抗秦国的将军。"

后来，人们用"惊弓之鸟"这个成语比喻受过惊吓的人，遇到类似的情况，就惶恐不安，也可以说成"伤弓之鸟"。在现实生活中我遇事要保持镇定，不要被曾经碰到过的困难吓倒，要针对具体问题进行具体分析。

A Bird Startled by the Mere Twang of a Bow-String

During the late Warring States Period, the other states united to fight against Qin. Zhao State sent Wei Jia to Chu State to pay a formal visit to Lord Chunshen. After meeting, Wei Jia asked Lord Chunshen, "Do you have a leading general in your troops?" Lord Chunshen answered, "Yes, I have. I would like to make Lord Linwu the general of my troops."

Wei Jia thought about it and said, "Since I liked archery when I was a child, please allow me to explain a principle through archery".

Lord Chunshen answered, "Of course, go ahead." Then Wei Jia told a story.

There was a man called Geng Ying in Wei State. Once while talking with the King, he suddenly glimpsed a flying wild goose in the sky. He watched the goose and told the king, "Your Majesty, my mere twang of the bow-string can shoot down the wild goose as long as I pull the bow without hanging on the arrow."

The King of Wei said, "Is your archery skill so perfect? Are you kidding?"

Geng Ying answered, "I am not kidding. I can do it."

At this time, that goose flied over. Geng Ying pulled the string immediately and pretended to shoot, but he didn't really carry out the shooting. As expected that goose fell down on hearing the sound of the bow-string.

The King of Wei said surprisingly, "Sir, you really have such a skill!"

Geng Ying pointed at the goose on the ground and said, "In fact, it is a goose that has been hurt."

The King of Wei was more surprised, he asked, "Sir, how do you know this is a wounded goose?"

Geng Ying answered that, "this goose flied slowly and shouted sadly. Flying slowly means that it has been hurt, the wound is hurting. Shouting sadly means that it has been separated from the group for a long time. The old wound hasn't healed up. As hearing the twang of the bow-string the goose was so frightened that it believed someone was shooting. So the goose flied higher desperately. As a result, the old wound had broken, the goose could not bear the pain and fell down on the ground.

After telling this story, Wei Jia said to Lord Chunshen, "Since Lord Linwu has been defeated by the Qin troops, he must have fears in heart. So I think he is not fitful to be assigned as the general to resist the Qin troops.

Later, we use this idiom to compare those people who have been frightened and felt anxious in encountering similar situations. It can also be put as "A Bird Hurt by a Bow". In our daily life, we should stay composed in crisis and not be scared easily by the previous difficulty. What's more, we should make a concrete analysis of a concrete problem.

15 望洋兴叹

相传很久很久以前，黄河里有一位河神，人们叫他河伯。河伯站在黄河岸上，望着滚滚的浪涛由西而来，又奔腾跳跃向东流去，兴奋地说："黄河真大呀，世上没有哪条河能和它相比。我就是最大的水神啊！"

有人告诉他："你的话不对，在黄河的东面有个地方叫北海，那才真叫大呢。"

河伯说："我不信，北海再大，能大得过黄河吗？"

那人说："别说一条黄河，就是几条黄河的水，也装不满北海啊！"

河伯固执地说："我没见过北海，我不信。"

那人无可奈何，告诉他："有机会你去看看北海，就明白我的话了。"

秋天到了，连日的暴雨使大大小小的河流都注入黄河，黄河的河面更加宽阔了，隔河望去，对岸的牛马都分不清。这一下，河伯更得意了，以为天下最壮观的景色都在自己这里，他在自得之余，想起了有人跟他提起的北海，于是决定去那里看看。

河伯顺流来到黄河的入海口，突然眼前一亮，海神北海若正笑容满面地欢迎

哲 学 篇

他的到来。河伯放眼望去，只见北海汪洋一片，无边无涯，一眼望不到边，他呆呆地看了一会儿，深有感触地对北海若说："俗话说，只懂得一些道理就以为谁都比不上自己，这话说的就是我呀。今天要不是我亲眼见到这浩瀚无边的北海，我还会以为黄河是天下第一！那样，我必定会贻笑大方了。"

这个成语告诉我们看问题要全面，不能用孤立的眼光来看问题，只看见局部，看不见整体和全部。

To Lament One's Littleness Before the Vast Ocean

It is said that long, long ago in the Yellow River there lived a god known as Hebo (river god). One day, Hebo stood on the riverbank and watched the turbulent waves from the west surging forward to the east. He said excitedly and conceitedly, "The Yellow River is so big that no other rivers in the world can match it. And therefore I am the greatest river god in the world."

Someone told him, "You are wrong. There is a place to the east of the Yellow River called the North Sea, which is large indeed."

Hebo said, "I don't believe it. Big as the North Sea is, can it be bigger than Yellow River?"

The man said, "Should the water of several Yellow Rivers flow into the North Sea, it could not be filled up, let alone one Yellow River."

Hebo said obstinately, "I don't believe it, for I have never seen the North Sea."

Having no alternative, the man told him, "You will not be able to understand what I mean until you have a chance to see the North Sea yourself."

Autumn was coming. The continuous rain had been falling for days. Big and small rivers poured their water into the Yellow River. The Yellow River became even broader. Standing on one side of the river, people could hardly distinguish an ox from a horse. Thus Hebo felt more proud of himself. He believed that all the magnificent sights in the world were accumulated here. Then, remembering the North Sea which had been mentioned to him, he decided to go there and have a look.

Hebo went downstream and arrived at the river mouth to the sea. Suddenly something caught his eyes. The sea god, named Beihairuo was smiling to welcome his arrival. Hebo looked ahead and found that the North Sea, with its vast expanse of water, was boundless. With a dull look in his eyes, He Bo stood there for a while. Finally he said to Beihairuo with deep feeling, "As the proverb goes, some people go so far as to think that they are more knowledgeable than anybody else when they have obtained some knowledge. Actually I am one of them. Today if I haven't seen the boundless North Sea, I will still hold that the Yellow River is matchless in the world. If I remained like that, I would be laughed at for ever by sensible people."

The idiom tells us to view a problem in its entirety. We should not consider the problem in isolation and only see the partial, but not see the whole.

16 三人成虎

战国时期，魏国和赵国签订了友好盟约，魏王要把儿子送到赵国的都城邯郸去作人质抵押，派大臣庞葱陪同前往。

庞葱担心魏王不信任自己，临走之时就对魏王说："大王，如果有一个人对您说，大街上来了一只老虎，您相不相信？"

魏王回答："我不相信。老虎怎么会跑到大街上来呢？"

庞葱接着问："如果有两个人对您说，大街上来了一只老虎，您相不相信？"

魏王回答："如果两个人都这么说，我就有些半信半疑了。"

庞葱又问："如果有三个人都对您说，大街上来了一只老虎，您相不相信？"

魏王回答："如果大家都这么说，我只好相信了。"

哲 学 篇

庞葱说:"您想,老虎不会跑到大街上来,这是人人皆知的事情。只是因为三个人都这么说,大街上有老虎便成为真的了。邯郸离我们魏国的都城大梁,比王宫离大街远得多,而且背后议论我的人可能还不止三个,请大王到时候仔细思考啊。"

魏王点头说:"我知道了,你放心去吧。"

庞葱陪同魏王的儿子到了邯郸。不久,果然有很多人对魏王说庞葱的坏话,魏王确实相信了,就不让庞葱再去见他。

现在人们用"三人成虎"这个成语比喻一句谣言,或一件虚假事物,说的人一多,就能使人认假为真。我们在日常的工作和生活中要坚持眼见为实,耳听为虚的原则,不要轻易相信传言。

A Repeated Slander Makes Others Believe

During the Warring States Period, Wei State and Zhao State signed a treaty of alliance. The King of Wei assigned Pang Cong to send his son as the hostage to Handan, the capital of Zhao State.

For fearing that the king would not trust him, Pang Cong asked the king before leaving, "Your Majesty, will you believe in it if someone tells you there is a tiger on the street?"

The king answered, "I wouldn't believe. How could the tiger run on the street?"

Pang Cong continued to ask, "If two persons tell you there is a tiger on the street, will you believe?"

The king answered, "If both of them say as that, I will be half-believing."

Pang Cong asked again, "If three persons all tell you there is a tiger, will you believe?"

The king answered, "If all the persons say like this, I have to believe it."

Pang Cong said, "Even if it is known to all that the tiger will not come on the street, it becomes true that the tiger is on the street only because three

persons say like this. The distance from Handan to our capital, Daliang, is much farther than the distance from the street to our palace. And there are more than three persons who will speak ill of me behind my back. Your Majesty, I advise you to consider it over and over again."

The king nodded and said, "I know it; you can set your mind as ease."

Accompanying the son of the king, Pang Cong arrived in Handan. Soon, it is true that there are many persons who speak ill of Pang Cong behind him to the king. The king of Wei believed the ill remarks indeed and refused Pang Cong to visit him.

Now we often use this idiom to mean a rumor or a false thing, once spread by many, will be made a truth. In daily life and work, we should obey the rule that things seen are mightier than things heard and never believe the hearsay.

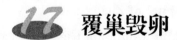

17 覆巢毁卵

谅毅受赵王命赴秦国，秦昭王要求赵国杀掉赵豹和赵胜，否则将率诸侯军队攻打赵国都城邯郸。

谅毅说："赵豹、赵胜是我们君王的亲兄弟，就像大王有叶阳君、泾阳君两个弟弟一样。我听说鸟巢倾覆毁坏了鸟蛋，凤凰就不再飞到这里；剖开兽胎焚烧小兽，麒麟就不会再来。赵国因为害怕不敢不执行大王的命令，不过恐怕会伤害叶阳君、泾阳君的心吧？"

我们通常用"覆巢毁卵"来比喻灭门之灾，无一幸免，也比喻整体覆灭，个人不能幸存。

这个成语也叫做"覆巢破卵"或"覆巢无完卵"。作为存在于集体中的我们，应当时刻注意维护国家和集体的利益，不能只顾私利，集体没有了，个人的利益也就不复存在了。

The Nest Being Overturned, No Eggs Staying Undestroyed

Under the order of the King of Zhao State, Liang Yi went to Qin State. King Zhao of Qin State requested the King of Zhao to kill Zhao Bao and Zhao Sheng, otherwise he would lead the army to attack Handan, the capital of Zhao.

Liang Yi said, "Zhao Bao and Zhao Sheng are our King's blood brothers, just like Your Majesty has Lord of Yeyang and Lord of Jingyang as your blood brothers. I heard when the bird nest had been overturned and the bird eggs had been destroyed, the phoenix would never fly here; when the womb of the beast had been dissectioned and the baby beast had been burned, the kirin would not come. Out of fear, Zhao State will carry out Your Majesty's order, but I am afraid this will hurt Lord of Yeyang and Lord of Jingyang's feelings?"

We often use this idiom to mean the extermination of a whole family, which no one can escape from; or during an overall destruction, no individual can fortunately survive.

This idiom is also known as "The Nest Being Overturned, No Eggs Being Unbroken" or "The Nest Being Overturned, No Eggs Staying Whole". As members in the collective, we should always safeguard our country and the collective interests. Not to be only concern with our own private interest. Without the collective, private interest cannot exist.

赵王之爵

战国时期，赵王得到一块产自于阗的美玉，命高手工匠把它做成了一只酒爵，说："我要用它给有功之人喝酒。"

后来邯郸被秦军包围，平原君赵胜到魏国向魏国公子信陵君求救。

信陵君使人盗得魏王的兵符，率领兵马发起进攻并大败秦军。

邯郸的包围解除后，赵王很恭敬地拿这个酒爵向魏公子无忌进酒，为他祝福，魏公子行礼后受酒。这是一件多么美好而荣耀的事情啊！

所以鄗南的一次战役胜利后，赵王没有东西来赏赐将士，就用这只爵来让将士们饮酒，大家都很高兴。因此赵国人把能用这只爵饮酒，看得比十辆车马的俸禄还重要。

后来，赵王让受宠信献媚、溜须拍马的人也用此爵饮酒。

秦国军队再次攻打赵国，大将李牧率领赵军英勇奋战，击败了秦军。

赵王又拿这只爵来赐酒，将士都不喝，并且很生气。

我们通常用这个典故比喻神圣的东西遭到玷污便一文不值。这个成语故事从另一个角度提醒管理者要注意做到知人善任，赏罚分明。

The King of Zhao State's Wine Vessel

During the Warring States Period, the King of Zhao State gained a piece of precious and beautiful gem found in Yutian, and ordered his proficient craftsmen to make it into a wine vessel and claimed that, "It will be used for the meritorious people."

Later the Qin troops surrounded Handan; Zhao Sheng, Lord of Pingyuan went to Wei State and asked Wei Wuji, Lord of Xinling, for help.

Then Lord of Xinling had the tally of the King of Wei stolen, and led the army of Wei to attack and defeated the Qin troops seriously.

After Handan was rescued, the King of Zhao State used that wine vessel to propose a toast to Prince Wuji and blessed for him. Wuji saluted to him and drank the wine. How nice and honorable the vessel was!

Later, after the victory in the Battle of Haonan, the King of Zhao State had nothing to reward his generals and soldiers but use that vessel for them to drink, which made all of them very happy. From then on, the people of Zhao State thought that using the vessel to drink more valuable than the salary of ten carriages and horses.

However, later, the King of Zhao State also let those flatterers whom he specially trusted drink with the vessel.

Later, the Qin troops attacked Zhao State again. General Li Mu led the army, fought bravely, and defeated the invaders.

This time the King of Zhao again used the vessel to reward the officers and soldiers, but they all became infuriated and refused to drink.

Now we usually use this idiom to indicate that the holy thing will turn out to be worthless after it is stained. From another point of view, this idiom indicates as a leader one should know one's men well enough to assign their work according to their abilities and be strict and fair in meting out rewards and punishments.

交浅言深

冯忌求见赵王，怕说话得罪他，而讲了以下这个小故事：

我有一个朋友，介绍一个人去拜见服子，过后服子要求治这个人的罪。

朋友问那个人有什么罪。

服子说："您的客人有三条罪过：望我而笑，是轻视我；谈话而不称老师，这是背叛我；交情浅而言语深，这是迷惑我。"

客人说："不是这个样子。看见客人笑，这是和蔼；言谈不称呼老师，因为老师是庸俗的称呼；交情浅而言语深，这是忠诚。"

"交浅言深"这个成语的意思是两人交情虽浅，规劝的话语却很深切。指对交情不深的人能加以恳切的规劝。这则成语告诉我们日常生活和工作中待人处事要诚恳亲切。

To Have a Hearty Talk with a Slight Acquaintance

During the Warring States Period, there was a man named Feng Ji. One day he went to see the King of Zhao State, and in case of offending the King, he told the King the following story first.

One day, a friend of mine introduced a guest to see Fuzi. But later Fuzi wanted to have the guest punished.

The friend asked for the reason.

Fuzi said, "Your guest has three offences. The first one is that he smiled when he watched me, which indicates despising me; the second one is that he didn't call me teacher when we were talking, which indicates betraying me; the third one is that he had a hearty talk but with a slight acquaintance, which indicates confusing me.

The friend retorted, "It is not the case. The guest's smiling indicates his clemency; he didn't call you teacher because this address is too common; and having a hearty talk but with a slight acquaintance indicates his loyalty.

This idiom means that although two people have a slight acquaintance, their suggestions are very sincere. It often indicates giving those slight acquaintances the sincere advice. This idiom tells ue to be kind and sincere to others in daily life and work.

 一言兴邦

战国时代，赵国的赵惠文王特别喜欢剑术。剑士们纷纷前来献技，达三千人之多。他们日夜在文王面前相互拚杀，每年为此而死伤的人数以百计，但赵王仍喜好击剑从来就不曾得到满足。于是，民间喜欢击剑的风气盛行，耕田之人日益减少。

太子赵悝为此忧虑不已，召集左右大臣商量道："谁既能让大王满意，又能说服大王停止比试剑术，我将赠予他千两黄金。"左右异口同声说："庄子可担此任。"于是，太子便派使者带上千金去请庄子。

庄子听明使者来意，说道："此事何难，竟值千金之赏？"坚辞不受金而偕使者去见太子，问道："太子赐给我千金的厚礼所为何事？"

太子道："闻先生神明，特奉上千金作为您一路上的开销。先生不收，我还敢说什么呢？"

三天后，太子带他去见赵惠文王。赵惠文王长剑出鞘，白刃相待。道："太

子介绍您来，欲以什么教给寡人？"

庄子道："臣闻大王好剑，故特以剑术拜见大王。"

王说："您的剑术有何特长？"

庄子说："十步之内可杀一人，行走千里谁也挡不住我。"

赵惠文王听了，大为欣赏，赞道："天下无敌矣！"

于是，赵惠文王以比剑选择高手，连赛七天，死伤者六十余人，得五六位佼佼者。便让他们恭候庄子来一决雌雄。

庄子欣然前来，赵惠文王问道："不知先生要持什么样的剑？"

庄子答："臣持什么剑都可以。不过臣有三剑，专为大王所用。请允许我先言后试。"

赵惠文王点头，道："愿闻三剑究竟何样？"

庄子道："此三剑分别是：天子剑、诸侯剑、百姓剑。"

赵惠文王好奇相问："天子之剑何样？"

庄子道："天子之剑，用以匡正诸侯，威加四海，德服天下。"

赵惠文王又问："诸侯之剑何如？"

庄子道："诸侯之剑，就好像雷霆震撼四境之内，没有不归服而听从国君号令的。"

赵惠文王点头，接着问："百姓之剑又如何？"

庄子道："百姓之剑，相击于大王之前，上斩脖颈，下刺肝肺。百姓比剑，跟斗鸡没有什么不同，一旦命尽气绝，对于国事就什么用处也没啦。如今大王坐拥天子之位却喜好百姓之剑，我私下替大王深感遗憾。"文王坐下，沉思良久。从此，赵惠文王戒掉喜欢看击剑的毛病，一心治理国家。

这个故事告诉我们，作为国家的管理者其一言一行可以使一个国家灭亡，也可以使一个国家强盛，因此国家的管理者要时刻注意自己的一言一行。

A Timely Warning May Avert a National Crisis

In the Warring States Period, King Huiwen of Zhao State was particularly fond of fencing. More than three thousand swordsmen came to perform their skills. They fought each other day and night in front of the king.

Hundreds of them were killed or injured for this every year, but the king was still keen on it. So fencing became more and more popular, at the same time less and less people cultivated in the field.

Prince Zhao Kui worried about this; he called the ministers together and consulted with them, "If someone can stop the fighting of the swordsmen and please the king at the same time, I will reward him a thousand pieces of gold." The ministers expressed with one voice, "Only Zhuangzi can take on this responsibility." Thereupon, the prince dispatched a messenger carrying a thousand pieces of gold to invite Zhuangzi.

Understanding the intention of the messenger, Zhuangzi said, "It is not a difficult task, how can it be worth a reward of a thousand pieces of gold." He refused to accept the reward and went to see the prince with the messenger.

Zhuangzi asked the prince, "Your Highness, why will you give me so high a reward?"

The prince said, "It is said that you are a sage, so I offer the gold as the expenses on your road here. Since you have refused, what dare I say?"

Three days later, the prince led Zhuangzi to see the king. King Huiwen drew his sword out of the sheath and asked, "The prince recommended you here, what will you teach me?"

Zhuangzi answered, "Your Majesty, I hear that you are fond of fencing, so I come to visit you with the art of fencing."

The king asked, "What is special in your art of fencing?"

Zhuangzi said, "If I have to kill a person within ten steps, I can walk one thousand li and no one can stop me."

King Huiwen appreciated and praised, "you are invincible throughout the world！"

Hence, the king chose the best swordsmen through competition. It lasted seven days. As a result, more than 60 died or injured and only 5 or 6 became the outstanding ones. Then they were ordered to wait for a fight with Zhuangzi.

Zhuangzi came with pleasure. The king asked, "Sir, I want to know what kind of sword you would like to use?"

Zhuangzi answered, "I can use any kind of sword. But I have three kinds of swords specially prepared for Your Majesty. Please allow me to explain before practicing."

The king nodded and said, "I would like to know what the three kinds of swords are."

Zhuangzi said, "The three kinds of swords are the king's sword, the vassal's and the commoner's."

The king was surprised and asked, "What is the king's sword?"

Zhuangzi answered, "The king's sword is used to rectify the vassal's mistakes, to show power in the world and to make people submit to your virtue."

The king asked again, "Then what about the vassal's sword?"

Zhuangzi answered, "The vassal's sword is like thunder—like power. Everyone in the world has to obey your order."

The king nodded and continued to ask, "Then what is the commoner's sword?"

Zhuangzi said, "The commoner's swords hit each other before Your Majesty, they chop the necks or thrust the livers and lungs. Their fencing is the same as cockfighting. Once being careless, the fighters will lose their life. And it is not beneficial to the country. Today Your Majesty is on the king's position; but fond of the commoner's sword. I feel regret over this!"

King Huiwen sat down and meditated upon it for a long period. From then on the king gave up his interest on fencing and devoted himself in running the state.

This idiom idicates that as the manger of a country, his words and deeds can make a country destroyed and can also make a country strong. So the manger of a country should always pay attention to his words and deeds.

21 前功尽弃

战国后期，秦昭王为了统一天下，重新启用大将白起。白起领兵先后打败了魏国和韩国，斩杀两军首级达 24 万颗，后来又夺取两国许多城池。公元前 281 年，白起又领兵攻打魏国的都城大梁。苏秦的弟弟苏厉立即去劝说白起。

"您大破韩国和魏国的军队，杀了魏国的大将师武，又在北方夺取了赵国的蔺和离石等地，为秦国立下了汗马功劳。现在您又要经过韩国去进攻魏国，这样会有危险。一旦攻打大梁失利，您就会前功尽弃，所以劝您还是称病不出为好。"

白起听了，果然放弃了进攻魏国的军事行动。

但是白起最后的命运很可悲，他因为与秦王和相国范雎的意见不合，反对攻打赵国的都城邯郸，而被逼自杀。

这则成语的意思是以前的辛劳和努力全部白费。如今这则成语给我们带来的启示是做事情要持之以恒，坚持不懈，不能半途而废，否则将会前功尽弃。

All One's Previous Efforts Wasted

In the later part of the Warring States Period, in order to unify the whole country, King Zhao of the Qin State restored General Bai Qi. Bai Qi led the Qin troops to defeat Wei State and Han State successively and cut off more than 240,000 enemy soldiers' heads. Later he conquered many towns of the two states. In 281 B.C., Bai Qi led his troops to attack Daliang, the city of Wei State. Su Li, the younger brother of Su Qin, went to persuade Bai Qi immediately.

"You have defeated the army of Wei and Han seriously and killed General Shi Wu of Wei. At the same time, you have occupied the towns of Lin and Lishi from Zhao State in the north. You have made great contributions in battles for Qin State. Now you will go to attack Wei by passing Han state. That will be dangerous. Once you suffer a military failure in attacking Daliang, you will turn all of your previous labor and hardship to

哲 学 篇

nothing. So you'd better plead illness and give up the attack."

Hearing his advice, Bai Qi really gave up his military action to Wei State.

But Bai Qi's final destiny was very pitiful. He was compelled to commit suicide, because he disapproved to attack Handan, the capital of Zhao State, which was the King's and the prime minister Fan Sui's opinion.

This idiom means turning all the previous labor and hardship to nothing. It inspires that whatever we do, we need make unremitting efforts and cannot give up halfway. Otherwise, all that has been achieved will be spoiled.

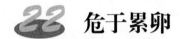 危于累卵

战国时期，说客苏秦曾经对赵国的奉阳君李兑说：

"我今天来晚了一些。昨天我曾经寄宿在别人家的地里，旁边有一片树林。睡到半夜时，我听见了土偶和木偶的争辩：加入土偶会遭受大风和连阴雨的侵袭，但是身体坏了还可以再回到土中去。而加入木偶一方，一旦受到大风和连阴雨的侵袭，就会漂入大海，没有停止的地方。"

"我认为是土偶胜利了。如今你杀死武灵王，灭了他的族人，您立于天下人面前，就像迭起来的鸡蛋那样危险，您听我的计策就生存，不然就会灭亡。"

我们现在用"危于累卵"这个典故来比喻情况非常危险。生活中我们应当注意在危难面前保持冷静，仔细分析别人的意见，理智地作出选择。

Hazardous Like a Pile of Eggs

During the Warring States Period, there was a persuasive talker named Su Qin. One day he said to Li Dui, the Lord of Fengyang of Zhao State, "Today I came a little late, because yesterday I lodged in someone's field beside a blanket of trees. At midnight, I heard a debate between a clay idol and a wooden idol: Being a clay idol will suffer from the attack of heavy wind and continuous rain, if broken, it can go back to the earth. But being a wooden idol, if attacked by heavy wind and continuous rain, ill float into the sea and have no stopping place."

"I think the clay idol has won. Right now, you have killed the King Wuling and his entire family. Now your situation is very dangerous, just like a pile of accumulated eggs. If you adopt my strategies, you can survive; otherwise, you will become extinct."

Now we use this idiom to indicate that the situation is very dangerous. In our daily life, we should remain calm in face of danger, listen to other's advice carefully and make a choice with senses.

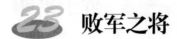 败军之将

楚汉战争期间，韩信被汉王刘邦拜为大将，奉刘邦之命率三万人马伐赵。他领精兵在井陉口背水列阵，吸引敌军主力，却派轻骑以拔旗易帜的策略大破赵军二十余万，杀了赵国领兵大将陈余，俘获了赵王，平定了赵国。

韩信非常欣赏赵国的谋士广武君李左车的才能，知道是由于陈余不听广武君的计谋才使自己取得了胜利。于是他恭敬地向李左车问计："我想从北面攻击燕国，东面攻击齐国，怎样才能取得成功呢？"

李左车辞谢说："我听说打了败仗的将军，不能与他讨论勇敢，亡国的大臣，不能保全国家。今天我战败作了你的俘虏，怎么能够胜任权谋大事呢！"

"败军之将"这个成语是指打了败仗的将领，现在多用于指失败的人。我们应当学习韩信虚心的态度，他能够注意听取败军之将的意见，善于运用他人的长处，知人善用。这是作为领袖任务所应有的气度。

A Defeated General Cannot Claim to Be Brave

During the period of the War between Chu State and Han State, Han Xin was given a general post by Liu Bang who ordered him to suppress Zhao

State with thirty thousand military forces. He commanded the picked troops to fight with their back to the river at Jingxingkou in order to attract the main force of the enemy. At the same time, he sent the light cavalry to defeat the two hundred thousand soldiers of Zhao with the strategy of replacing their flags with the flags of Han. Han Xin killed Chen Yu, the general of Zhao and captured the King of Zhao State. State of Zhao was conquered.

Han Xin appreciated the talents of Lord Guangwu, who was an adviser of Zhao State named Li Zuoche. He knew that he could defeat Chen Yu just because Chen Yu didn't follow Lord Guangwu's strategy. Therefore, he asked Li Zuoche with great respect, "I want to attack Yan State from north and attack Qi State from east. How can I be successful?"

Li Zuoche declined him politely, "People said you couldn't talk with a defeated general about bravery; a minister whose nation was conquered doesn't have the ability to protect his motherland. Now, I am defeated and become your captive, how can I be competent to plan matters as making strategies?"

A defeated general refers to a military officer who loses a battle. Nowadays, people often use this idiom to indicate a loser. This idiom inspires us to learn from Han Xin's modesty. He can pay attention to a defeated general's views and knows how to adopt other people's strengths. This is a good quality that every leader should have.

24 强而后可

从前，赵简子派王良陪自己宠幸的小臣奚驾车去打猎，不料一整天都没有打到一只鸟兽。

奚回来报告说："王良是天下最笨的驾车人。"

有人把这句话告诉了王良。

王良说："请让我再驾一次。"

经强求后奚才同意,结果一个早晨就猎获了十只鸟兽。

奚回来报告说:"王良是天下最能干的驾车人。"

简子说:"我就叫他专门给你驾车。"他把这话也对王良说了。

王良不肯,说:"我为他按规矩驾车,一整天打不到一只;不按规矩驾车,一个早上就打到了十只。《诗经》上说,不违反驾车规矩,箭一出手就能射中。我不习惯给小人驾车,请同意我辞掉这差事。"

我们通常用这个典故来表示经过强求后才答应。这则成语中王良的行动告诉我们做事情要循规蹈矩,坚持原则。

Promising after Importuning

Once upon a time, Zhao Jianzi dispatched Wang Liang to drive carriage for one of his minion Xi to hunt. However, for the whole day, they got no game.

Xi came back and reported to Zhao Jianzi, "Wang Liang is the most stupid driver in the world."

Later those words were told to Wang Liang.

Then Wang Liang asked Xi the second time, "Let me drive for you for the second time."

Xi was unwilling, but agreed after the importuning of Wang. To their surprise, they had gained ten games in only a morning.

Then Xi came back and reported to Zhao Jianzi, "Wang Liang was the best driver in the world."

Jian Zi replied, "Since that, I will ask him only to drive for you." Then he told the same words to Wang Liang.

Hearing the decision, Wang Liang refused and said, "I drove for him according to the rules, nothing was gained for a whole day; but if I drove without the rules, ten games were gained only in a morning. The Book of Odes said, 'If we do not violate the rules, the arrows will hit the target after they are shot, I am not used to driving for the flunky, so please allow me to quit this job."

Now we usually use this idiom to mean promising after importuning. Wang Liang's action in this idiom tells us that one should do everything by rules and stick to principles.

 罚不当罪

战国时期,赵国有一位著名的思想家,名叫荀况,人们称他的著作为《荀子》。书中提出一个看法:国君要在百姓面前做出好的榜样。残暴的国君被推翻,如夏桀被商汤打倒,商纣被周武王消灭,这些都是好事而不是坏事。

荀况主张赏罚要分明,要根据犯罪人罪行的大小,给与相应的惩处。如果杀人的不偿命,伤人的不判刑,那就会纵容犯罪,扰乱社会。有人说:"古代没有肉刑,只是象征性地用刑。如不使用鲸刑而以墨画脸来替代,不用割鼻之刑而用戴上草做的帽子来替代,在现在这个乱世是行不通的。如果让犯罪的人得不到惩罚,犯罪行为就会越来越多。"

荀子自己的主张是:一个人的地位要和品德相称,官职要和才能相称,赏赐要和功劳相称,处罚要和罪行相称。否则,就会带来极大的不幸和严重的后果。

这则典故表示处罚过宽或过严,与所犯的罪行不想称。这个典故告诉我们作为领导者应该注意做到处事公正,赏罚分明。

Punishment Does Not Fit the Crime

During the Warring States Period, there is a famous thinker named Xun Kuang from Zhao State, whose works was called Xunzi. An idea mentioned in this book is that the monarch should set a good example to his citizens. It's a good deed that the cruel kings were overthrown, such as King Jie of Xia Dynasty annihilated by King Tang of Shang Dynasty, King Zhou of Shang Dynasty by King Wu of Zhou Dynasty.

Xun Kuang claims that rewards should be fair and punishments should fit the crimes accordingly. It would indulge the crimes and disrupt the society if the murderer needn't pay his life and one who hurts others hasn't got sentenced. Some say that in ancient times there were only symbolic punishments instead of corporal ones, such as paintingink on a criminal's face instead of tattooing characters on his face, and wearing a straw hat on a criminal's head instead of cutting his nose. But such punishments are not suitable in troubled times. There will be more crimes if the criminals have not received the deserved punishments.

Xunzi believes that one's status should match his moral character, one's official rank should match his ability, the rewards should match his contributions, and punishments should match the crimes. Otherwise, it would bring terrible misfortunes and serious consequences.

This idiom means that punishment is too excessive or relented to fit the crime. From another point of view, this idiom indicates that as a leader one should deal justly with matters and be strict and fair in meting out rewards and punishment.